YOUR

NEIGHBOR

AS YOURSELF

"Race, Religion and Region:
North America Into The
Twenty-First Century"

by

BRIAN A. BROWN

With an introduction by

MICHAEL MCLUHAN

And a foreword by

JOHN KENNETH GALBRAITH

Cross Cultural Publications, Inc.

CrossRoads Books

Published by **CROSS CULTURAL PUBLICATIONS, INC.**
Cross Roads Books
Post Office Box 506
Notre Dame, Indiana, 46556, U.S.A.
Phone: (219) 273-6526, 1-800-561-6526
FAX: (219) 273-5973

YOUR NEIGHBOR AS YOURSELF

"RACE, RELIGION & REGION:

NORTH AMERICA INTO THE

TWENTY-FIRST CENTURY"

by

Brian A. Brown

DEDICATION

TO THESE "BRONCO-BUSTING" RIDERS
OF THE FOUR HORSES OF THE APOCALYPSE

PROFESSOR ANGELA DAVIS
I had the privilege of monitoring the 1972 trial of Ms. Davis at San Rafael, California, when she was acquitted of murder by an all white jury. Her calm deportment inspired in me a vision of the strength inherent in human dignity.

PREMIER RENE LEVESQUE
This friend was prepared to put principle ahead of personal or political advantage and had a vision of "Sovereignty - Association" which may finally serve as a model for the relationship between Canada and the USA.

DOCTOR RUTH STAFFORD PEALE
This conservative evangelical Christian convinced me that the "religious right", which has been temporarily panicked into negative reactions by the collapse of liberal ethics, can still contribute to a new ethical consensus for the future.

CHIEF JOHN SNOW
My colleague in ministry shared a vision of how every people has its own "older testament" that it can bring to the new consensus among neighbours we all need to put the racism and bigotry of the twentieth century behind us at last.

INTRODUCTION

TABLE OF CONTENTS

ACKNOWLEDGMENTS

"Rich man, poor man, beggar man, thief: doctor, lawyer and Indian chief," each could bring a unique perspective to these questions. My particular editorial "sounding board" included a nurse and her patient, a horse fancier and the president of an advertising company, French and English, a druggist and a veterinarian, Black and White, Hindu and Christian, fundamentalist and agnostic, a teacher and a student, young and old, married and single, Canadian and American. I offer sincere gratitude to these people and others who gave this book their critical consideration from a variety of perspectives:

RATNA ARYA	JENNY BROWN
ARTHUR GOSINE-BROWN	LEELA GOSINE-BROWN
INDIRA SINTON-BROWN	HELEN CHALIFOUX
LEO CHALIFOUX	TONY KEELING
VELMA KEELING	MARY MARTIN
RON MARTIN	JOHN MATTHEW
JACKIE MERSICH	LANCE McCLUSKIE
LORNA McCLUSKIE	GARRY McEACHERN
WILLIAM McKENZIE	JOHN MILNE
CAROL MULDER	ARSINOEE QUAMMIE
JEANNETTE SCHIECK	BETH SCHILDS
EVA SCHWARTZENTRUBER	JOHN SIEBERT
JENNIFER SUTHERLAND	ROBERT WHETSTONE

A special word of thanks to Michael McLuhan for his preface and for editing the following introductory section, which also contains the foreword generously contributed by John Kenneth Galbraith who is acknowledged elsewhere. Michael is the youngest of Marshall McLuhan's six children. He holds the Master of Photographic Arts from the Professional Photographers of Canada and the Master of Photography degree from the Professional Photographers of America. His work has been exhibited at the Epcot Center at Walt Disney World and is included in the collection of the Public Archives of Canada. Because they are both Canadians whose work has been influential in Canada and the USA, which is the dual setting for this book, I am especially delighted and honored to have the names of McLuhan and Galbraith associated with this modest contribution to our sense of neighborhood, and what we are to do together in North America in the twenty-first century.

Thank you all,
Brian

ILLUSTRATIONS

INTRODUCTION

INTRODUCTION

MICHAEL MCLUHAN : EDITOR

PREFACE by Michael McLuhan
FOREWORD by John Kenneth Galbraith
PROLOGUE by Brian A. Brown

A Neighborhood in the Global Village

PREFACE

"A NEIGHBORHOOD AS OUR PLACE IN THE GLOBAL VILLAGE"

by

Michael McLuhan

In the sixties Marshall McLuhan was designated the "Guru of the Electronic Age." To me he was just "Dad." Having been brought up on a steady diet of McLuhanisms since preschool days, much of what Brian Brown has written has had a feeling for me of "coming home."

This book expands upon my father's initial concept of the Global Village and sees the evolution of our first steps into the coming millennium as the development of the international region or neighbourhood. Written in a lucid "magazine" style or format, at first you have the impression of reading a series of articles. When finished, you understand the coherence and cogency of the work. If Americans find this to be a Canadian perspective on our merging cultures, they are wrong. As my father was fond of pointing out, Canadians have no perspective, or rather, we could expand on that and say that the Canadian perspective is a North American perspective.

John Kenneth Galbraith, internationally respected economist, and policy advisor to four American presidents, is the author of the foreword to this book. He gives us the economic blueprint which will have to be implemented if we are to successfully make the transition first to regional, then to global community. We will need an economics and a politics of compassion, not expediency.

When my father first spoke of the Global Village in the early sixties, he saw the effects of the electronic media, as extensions of the human nervous system, eliminating the distances between us. In this abrogation of human space, he saw the world transforming into a village community "where everyone meddles in everyone else's business." This signals the death of the individual, the demise of privacy. With this loss of individual identity there would be a reversion to tribalism, the group eclipsing the individual in importance, with a concomitant rise in racial, linguistic or religious communal identities.

The old order of visual, literate culture is supplanted by a new order, an acoustic, post-literate culture. With the collapse of individualism and literacy, we would see a rise in violence as one group asserted itself against another. This is not the vision of the Age of Aquarius! One need look no further than the former Yugoslavia, Northern Ireland or Chechnya to see the veracity in these statements and to wonder about the divisions in North American society. Are Red Power, Black Power, White Power and French Canadian Nationalism temporary phenomena or preludes to the realities of the twenty-first century?

15

INTRODUCTION

Brian Brown writes of Race, Religion and Region. Indeed we can consider these the three R's of the post-literate age. The phenomenon of international regionalism, as experienced in economic/cultural unions such as the European Community and NAFTA, can be seen as the next step in an ever shortening journey toward a global community. But there are things we must learn before we can go on to that stage of human development.

My father could not have presaged the existence of the World Wide Web or else his view would have been less pessimistic. To be sure, the computer itself, like television, was like an acoustic, more tribal, less literate medium. However, the WWW is a new, exciting, unifying development. Yes, it strengthens our "global village-ness" but in allowing more immediate and intimate communications between far flung "neighbours," it transcends tribalism and even regionalism as it accelerates our march toward global community.

A step into a new millennium is always bound to involve visions of an impending "apocalypse". Brown's use of the imagery of the four horses is brilliant. These four diverging cultural and racial impetuses must converge if we are to see an harmonious growth into neighbourhood in North America. Including the voices of the (White) religious right along with Black, French and Aboriginal North Americans in the appendices is illuminating, to say the least.

To paraphrase Dickens, "we live in the best of times; we live in the worst of times." We may be sure that "uncertainty" will be the byword in the twenty-first century. Many remain blind to the revolutionary changes ahead of us and now in our midst. Yet if we open ourselves to the inevitable which is ahead, we have the opportunity to form a more caring, compassionate and just society. For the first time in human history we can give shape and form to the ideals and morals which have been the basis of our social and religious beliefs, as diverse as they may be, for centuries. The new era is a spiritual opportunity.

Brian Brown's vision is a positive one. Yes, there are many obstacles which could impede us, but ultimately, we shall triumph. I like this vision of a North American Neighbourhood. It is a place we must strive together to build.

Michael McLuhan

INTRODUCTION

FOREWORD

Neighbor
"THE GOOD ^ SOCIETY"

by
JOHN KENNETH GALBRAITH

Professor John Kenneth Galbraith has combined a broad range of interests as president of both the American Academy of Arts and Letters and the American Economics Association. From books like The Affluent Society in the fifties to The Good Society in the nineties, he has influenced both political leaders and common folk in understanding of how economic policies are to be servants of our visions rather than masters of our lives. Dr. Galbraith is the Paul M. Warburg Professor of Economics Emeritus at Harvard University. He offers this foreword to "set the economic stage for the future" and as "illustrating the parallels between our concerns" lest the visions in this book be seen as pie-in-the-sky idealism when in fact they represent the very best principles of business.

M. McLuhan

These thoughts, originally penned for inclusion in my book, The Good Society, are offered here in support of the thesis that a fully participatory economic system, which is inclusive of all elements of society, is simply good business.

Such an economic foundation for the vision that follows in the book, Your Neighbor as Yourself, by Dr. Brian A. Brown, may help thwart the frequent but unwarranted assumption that this is pie-in-the-sky idealism, only suited for discussion by Church groups and study by Sunday School children.

Full participation in every facet of life in the North American "neighborhood" is perhaps the most important item on the agenda of the business community and the most essential element on the curricula of our universities.

If put in sufficiently general terms, the essence of the good society can be easily stated. It is that every member, regardless of gender, race or ethnic origin, should have access to a rewarding life.

Allowance there must be for undoubted differences in aspiration and qualification. Individuals differ in physical and mental facility, commitment and purpose, and from these differences come differences in achievement and in economic reward. This is accepted.

In the good society, however, achievement may not be limited by factors that are remediable. There must be economic opportunity for all ... And in preparation for life, the young must have the physical care, the discipline, let no one doubt, and especially the education that will allow them to seize and exploit that opportunity.

No one, from accident of birth or economic circumstance, may be denied these things. If they are not available from parent or family, society must provide effective forms of care and guidance.

While the economy must provide everyone a chance both to participate and to advance according to ability and ambition, there are two further requirements that must be met.

There must be a reasonable stability in economic performance; the economic system cannot recurrently deny employment and aspiration because of recession and depression.

Moreover, the system may not frustrate the efforts of those who plan diligently and intelligently for old age and retirement, or for illness or unanticipated need. The threat in this case is, of course, inflation - the diminished purchasing power of money - and with it the loss of provision for the future.

Finally, the good society must have a strong international dimension. The state must live in peaceful and mutually rewarding association with its trading partners on the planet. It must be a force for world peace; it must work cooperatively with other nation-states to this end.

War is the most unforgiving of human tragedies, and is comprehensively so in an age of nuclear weaponry. There must also be recognition of, and effective support for, the needs and hopes of the less fortunate members of the world community.

As a Canadian-born American citizen these days, I am sure Canadians and Americans will strive to attain the goals of a "good society" together in this North American neighborhood.

Yours faithfully,

John Kenneth Galbraith

Harvard University,

Cambridge, Massachusetts

Best wishes to our Canadian neighbors,

PROLOGUE

"NEIGHBORS"

by

Brian A. Brown

Brian Brown is one of Canada's more prolific writers. Born in Nova Scotia in 1942, his university studies included a bachelor's degree in Classics from Dalhousie University in Halifax, a master's in Pastoral Psychology at McGill in Montreal and a doctorate in Organizational Behaviour from a University of California affiliate in San Francisco. He is a minister of the United Church of Canada who also has extensive experience in educational administration, business and media. In previous books Brian Brown has worked in cooperation with Rene Levesque, Premier of Quebec while that province was exploring its "place." He has collaborated with W.A.C. Bennett of British Columbia, the former premier of Canada's fastest growing province. Her Royal Highness, Princess Anne contributed a foreword to his book on peacekeeping and he has also collaborated with Perrin Beatty, now president of the Canadian Broadcasting Corporation. The author of ten previous books, none except "in house" publications in the last decade while this major work was in preparation and other priorities took precedence. Your Neighbor as Yourself is Brown's first foray into the American scene except as student, consultant and speaker. With his wife, Jenny, Brian lives in a retreat environment surrounded by friends and family on Georgian Bay, north of Toronto.

M. McLuhan

Is it possible for a White Anglo-Saxon Protestant Male to love a Black Islamic French Female neighbor in Peoria, Illinois? This is a book about "pluralism," specifically neighbors - how to get along with them, how to do business with them, even how to love them.

The neighborhood is North America and the neighbors under consideration are Canadians and Americans of all stripes. As a new millennium begins, there is a popular idea that a world culture is upon us. This book is not about establishing a world culture; such a thing is beginning to exist as a powerful influence but it is spotty and it is experienced at different levels in various places. At best, we may have outgrown nationalism but the world is not entirely ready for complete integration. Before Canadians and Americans are ready for the world, we have some significant unfinished business of our own.

Mexico, now economically linked to Canada and the United States, remains part of the Central American neighborhood, in spite of the popularity of ice hockey among 10,000 Mexican Little League players and the growing influence of ten million Hispanic citizens of the US and Canada. Even in the global village, there are still a variety of different neighbourhoods. Trade replaces aid *en route* to a world economy, and this may produce a world culture when people are ready. Regional neighborhoods are intermediate steps, but in most neighborhoods there are still unresolved problems. North America is no exception. In the neighborhoods the greatest problems are still racism, nationalism and religious bigotry. In the twenty-first century, North Americans at least may tear down these "walls that divide" and, at the same time, establish appropriate new ethical standards for their society in the Information Age.

Not everyone likes it, but the fact is that Canada and the United States are moving into a "regional culture." Europe has embraced regionalism and it begins to emerge elsewhere as the fundamental unit of the twenty first century - as compared with the "empires" of the nineteenth century, "nation states" in the twentieth and possibly a "world culture" by the twenty second century.

This book is also a sincere plea for North Americans to insist on establishing better human relationships than some of those that too often brought the twentieth century to the brink of the apocalypse. Even in this favored culture the "Bosnia Syndrome" still lurks between Black and White, French and English, Native and newcomer. A new era may be possible but nothing is certain yet. Choices remain to be made and some of them are hard choices.

There are also practical matters in establishing the new regionalism on this continent. Canadians are almost invisible to Americans, in spite of the fact that they have an influence on America out of all proportion to their numbers. For example, each day the American networks telecast the figures comparing the US dollar to the pound, the franc, the mark and the yen without reference to the Canadian dollar which accounts for trade almost equal to all the others combined. The effects of this invisibility, pro and con, will be examined.

INTRODUCTION

Moreover, in spite of this gigantic trade, to send for tickets from Buffalo for a Toronto Blue Jays baseball game, or from Windsor to request tickets to watch the Detroit Red Wings hockey team, a self- addressed, stamped envelope is normally required. This usually necessitates a drive over the border to obtain stamps valid in the other country, since a pre-stamped envelope must have a stamp from the country where the return mail will originate. This procedure between neighbors is laughably ludicrous in the age of the Information Superhighway. Many such quirks, which have been ironed out between neighbors elsewhere in the world, will also be considered.

With the advent of digital cameras, the old family photo album is being replaced in many homes by the family CD-ROM collection, which stores snap shots, wedding pictures, portraits, landscape scenes, home movies, videos and any other electronic images. These can be brought up to view on the monitor or printed out. This book is designed as just such a kaleidoscope of images.

Many books are based on "chapters" of somewhat equal length, through which the plot unfolds or the argument is advanced in an orderly fashion. This examination of an emerging cultural/ economic/technological empire is "post-modern" in style, in that each small section stands on its own. The book offers "insights" through "windows" of information. These windows may be of various sizes but they all open to reveal images resembling snapshots, portraits and landscapes, old movies and modern video clips plus a few "virtual reality" glimpses into the future. This cyber-culture photo album is part of the "bigger picture" of a phenomenon now taking place in North America.

University seminars and church discussion groups alike will find it convenient for members to read the whole, and then to consider any of the various parts together in a study they may easily design themselves. No "Study Guide" should be required if members of the class or study group would volunteer to review for discussion the sections in which they have an interest or expertise.

Brian A. Brown

PART ONE

WINDOWS ON THE PAST

(From the United Empire to the Rush for Gold)

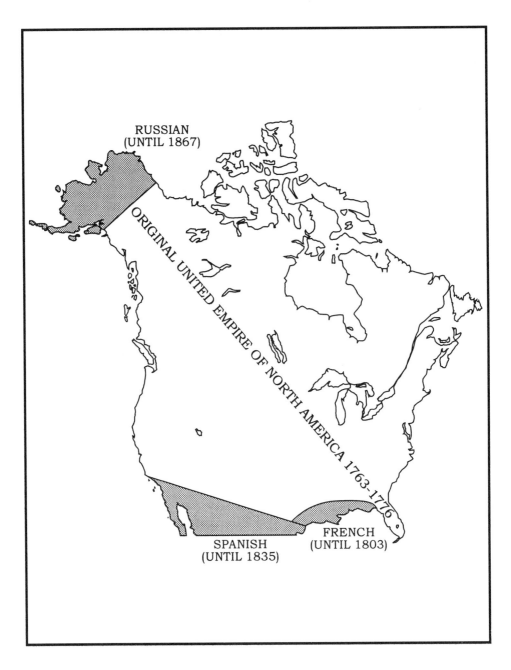

RUSSIAN
(UNTIL 1867)

ORIGINAL UNITED EMPIRE OF NORTH AMERICA 1763-1776

SPANISH
(UNTIL 1835)

FRENCH
(UNTIL 1803)

The United Empire 1763-1776

1.

THE NORTH AMERICAN EMPIRE

Once upon a time America was part of Canada. Put that way, it sounds like a fairy tale but it is true, of course, that from 1763 until 1776 the two were part of one North American Empire. The British already administered an African Empire, an East Indian Empire and a South Pacific Empire. Then in 1759 Britain captured Quebec City and by the Treaty of Paris in 1763 France turned all its North American possessions over to Britain, to go with Newfoundland, Nova Scotia, New England and various other territories in this hemisphere.

This was a North American Empire that stretched from the North Pole to the Gulf of Mexico. Nobody actually called the whole thing Canada but that is what it became, minus the New England colonies and some other territories they eventually acquired by various means. Canada was the largest part of this Empire which remained united for thirteen years until the thirteen New England colonies separated from the thirteen provinces and territories of Canada, as they are at the end of the twentieth century.

So now the Canadian bias of this book is revealed. With all those thirteens, the North American Empire was probably doomed from the beginning anyway. However, the entity known as the United States of America, which separated itself out of that earlier union, began with the thirteen New England states and is being reclaimed these days by the thirteen Canadian provinces and territories. No shots will be fired and Canadians do intend to leave America with its precious political independence, even while they cherish their own. In every other respect these two clusters of former British colonies are being united for life together again in the twenty-first century.

The relationship goes far beyond the 1990 free trade deal between these partners, which so rapidly grew to include Mexico in NAFTA and others in what might be called "AFTA." Political distinctions will remain, and they must remain; neither Canada nor America is ready to give them up. Though they are less important than they used to be, the political distinctions will safeguard the unique contributions that Canada, in particular, can make to the larger whole, as the smaller in population and political power of the two partners.

"Manifest Destiny" was a slogan used by American politicians of the nineteenth century who favored union with Canada in a political context. A type of Manifest Destiny is now being fulfilled through economic union in an age when political union is becoming increasingly irrelevant. The economic union may encompass North, Central and South America as a major fact of life defining this part of the world of the twenty-first century. At the same time, another broader unity between Canada and the United States is already taking shape through irresistible forces in practically all areas of life except politics.

The concept of manifest destiny implies that it was bound to happen sooner or later. The basis for this is the natural north-south flow of trade and other activities. Originally the dominant European cultures were organized in a north-south configuration anyway. The English maintained control from Baffin Island and Newfoundland through Nova Scotia and New England to the Gulf of Mexico, once they pushed the French out of Acadia, the Dutch from New Amsterdam and the Spanish from Florida. New France then included all of Quebec, Ontario, and the Mississippi region through Detroit, St. Louis, Baton Rouge to Louisiana and New Orleans, also on the Gulf. The west was mainly "Indian Territory" except for the coast which was Spanish to a point north of Vancouver and Russian beyond that.

Then the French lost their North American empire and the spoils were soon divided between newly independent America and the remnants of the British Empire which became Canada. The desire to accommodate a major French element in Canada required a political structure uniting east and west in a deliberate determination to overcome the natural north-south flow of goods and people. This national dream was facilitated by monumental railroad construction, the "iron bands" that held the nation together. Cut off north and south by the British and Spanish, American expansion also pushed west in spite of mountain ranges and river systems which might have dictated a natural north - south development of North American nations.

Today cross-border satellite communication replaces the east-west shunting of trains. The natural affinities of English speaking majorities for each other, the ambivalence of Quebec toward the rest of Canada, racial tensions in America, plus a myriad of other factors point to a virtual erasure of artificial borders. This is the fulfillment of a north-south manifest destiny on this continent which includes an economic realignment and many other elements with the exception of politics.

There may always be classes, races, religions, languages and other distinctions, and these can play a creative role in human society except when people are restricted to what they can embrace, or when the characteristics of a dominant culture are forced on unwilling individuals and minority groups. The ideal is freedom-in-community, and in the North American setting America has fostered freedom while Canada has nurtured community. The two will come together in the twenty-first century through a convergence of historical trends from the past and the advent of a future internet "cyber-culture." If Marshall McLuhan's vision of a "Global Village" is yet to come, North Americans may at least look forward to a "continental village" in the very near future.

That Canada is better positioned to take the lead in bringing this to pass was well put many years ago by wise old Andrew Carnegie when he compared Canada and the United States to Scotland and England, in a 1910 speech to the Canadian Club in Ottawa. "Canada, the Scotland of America, is to play the part of Scotland and annex her southern neighbor as Scotland did, and boss it for its good both in 'church and state', as Scotland did."

Both Canadians and Americans despise petty nationalism when they observe it elsewhere in the world. However, they each think of their own case as different, Americans in their myopic isolation from their best friends and Canadians in their insecurity and prejudice toward their closest neighbor. These particular nationalisms will evidently be one of the first casualties of the neighborhood regionalism of the twenty-first century.

Through the nineteen nineties, Canadians were concentrating on Quebec and the national unity question. At the same time Americans were more aware of their growing interface with Mexico and the other Americas where borders are still valid for a variety of reasons. These distractions, important as they were, have diverted the attention of almost everyone from the bigger picture of a virtual "sea change" in the already close relationship between the United States and Canada. An old, short lived United Empire, which once embraced the United States and Canada, is rising again as artificial impediments of history are swept away by modern technology, plus economic, cultural and other trends.

Great empires are built on realities like military force or economic power but they are facilitated or brought into being by new inventions or ideas. Religion was the facade which bestowed legitimacy and unity on the Holy Roman Empire, The Ottoman Empire and other old style political empires. Economic unions like the North American Free Trade Association, The European

Community and others are based on technology and a culture of information.

Both the U.S.A. and Canada are world traders and active participants in various aspects of the life of the whole planet. Yet if they have a special and growing relationship with each other, Canadians are often shocked that Americans not only take them for granted but seem genuinely uninformed about this important dimension of their own national life. Japan is not even close to being America's main trade partner, for example, since the US trades twice as much with Canada as with Japan. The US trades three times as much with Canada as with Germany and twenty times as much as with Russia. This is not just a difference of degree, but a difference in the kind of relationship.

Likewise British, Italian and French actors appear in American screen and stage productions with some regularity. However, like the trade figures, Canadians are invisibly present many times as frequently in American productions, but largely unrecognized as such. The same point can be made and illustrated in the fields of sport, invention, technology, spirituality, media, higher education and health care.

This is a relationship like no other on earth, but it is in discovering where the relationship is headed that the story of greatest interest is to be found. Like a "live-in" partner who realizes that she is too much taken for granted, it is now time for Canada to insist that her partner acknowledge the relationship and not only "make an honest woman" of her, as people used to say, but also make the marriage work for greater fulfillment for everyone in the home.

The diminishing significance of the national borders between the United States and Canada is a powerful parable for other borders in North America which may also diminish in the next century. Race, language, and religion are always factors to be reckoned with, but Black power, French Canadian nationalism, Native Land Claims and the "religious right" (white, homophobic, English-speaking, protectionist) may be but muted examples of emotions that have led to "ethnic cleansing" and wars elsewhere. Their power in recent years may be regarded as the last gasp of a pre-cyberculture society in the twentieth century which was based on divisions that could disappear in North America at least in the twenty-first century.

The special relationship between Canada and the United States, which is now neither British nor political in character, is more like a modern marriage. Each partner loves the other but each maintains a sense of self which the other must respect even while uniting their fortunes, sharing their dreams and living together with an intimacy that is not extended to other business partners or friends. For over a hundred years, from the end of the United Empire until the dawn of the twentieth century Canadians and Americans eyed each other warily. There were flash points of open conflict, wars and rumors of war, refugees, displaced peoples and many other things to be sorted out before the next era of co-operation and harmony which lasted through the twentieth century, as a prelude to the re-integration now foreseen in the century to come.

2.

NORTH AMERICAN *REFUGEES*

This is the forest primeval. The murmuring pines and the hemlocks,
Bearded with moss, and in garments green, indistinct in the twilight,
Stand like Druids of eld, with voices sad and prophetic,
Stand like harpers hoar, with beards that rest on their bosoms.
Loud from its rocky caverns, the deep-voiced neighboring ocean
Speaks, and in accents disconsolate, answers the wail of the forest.

Canadians and Americans have penetrated each others borders in the past, frequently and for a variety of reasons. In the eras of British conquest and following the American War of Independence, for example, there were two significant exchanges of population. Today both groups would be called refugees. One such group was forcibly moved due to an "ethnic cleansing" program on the part of the British. The other group was kicked out by their American neighbors who regarded them as politically undesirable.

As the world powers of the day battled for supremacy in empire, in 1713 the Treaty of Utrecht awarded the Maritime Provinces, known as Acadia, to Britain from France. The British were beginning to consolidate their North American Empire and all went well with the two thousand or more Acadians in that Atlantic area for some years, despite the intense religious and linguistic prejudices that separated English speaking Protestants from French speaking Roman Catholics everywhere else.

Forty years later, however, like the Israelites in Egypt, this colony within had multiplied by over four fold at a time when the political situation regarding the continuation of a New France in Quebec was coming to a head. Both the British government back in England and the Government of Massachusetts began to exert intense pressure on the colonial administration in Halifax to get rid of the peaceful Acadians. Nobody abroad trusted in their profession of neutrality in the event that push came to shove in what was left of New France in nearby Quebec, as it eventually did.

Ten thousand French speaking Acadians were suddenly rounded up and assembled for deportation in 1755. They were loaded on board ship and forcibly removed from the colony of Nova Scotia by the nervous British for "security reasons" even though there had been no untoward incident on their part. Their farms were expropriated and awarded to "trustworthy" colonists (English speaking Protestants) from the rapidly expanding New England area. The Acadians were then resettled in southern colonies of what would become the United States where these "Cajuns" make up a significant part of the population today. The American poet, Henry Wadsworth Longfellow, laments this ancient act of "ethnic cleansing" in his immortal poem, "Evangeline."[1]

In the same era, or just shortly thereafter, forty thousand American refugees who had sided with the losing British cause in the War of Independence were forced to flee to what became Canada. There this group of professional and entrepreneurial refugees identified themselves by the more lofty distinction as "United Empire Loyalists."

Becoming the majority in the two colony/provinces of Ontario and New Brunswick, their impact on Canada was even more significant than that of the Cajuns in the United States. Their American homes and business properties too were expropriated by neighbors who appear to have done well ever since. In this case, because they had ingratiated themselves with a powerful ally, these refugees were compensated by the British and given land grants, especially from lands expropriated earlier from the French and Native Indians.

Today, nearly half a century after the Cuban Revolution of 1959, descendants of Cuban refugees and displaced American business interests are still looking for compensation. None was offered the Natives, the Acadians or the Blacks, and following America's own bloody revolution, no compensation was paid to United Empire Loyalist refugees. A Canadian minister who was recently a guest preacher in New York's Riverside Church, pointed to a lighthouse under the George Washington Bridge that once belonged to his family. America's friends want to say it may be time for the United States to move on to a new phase in its relationship with Cuba.

Acadians and Loyalists integrated themselves loyally into their new political environments. Despite Cajun preference for their own ghettos at first, and brief "Loyalist" dalliances with revolutionary ideas of their own in Canada, neither group caused any real trouble. Yet amazingly, both still remain somewhat distinct more than two hundred years later, and each maintains a measure of wistful affection for the earlier homeland.

Meanwhile, an even more disastrous displacement of people was taking place in the marginalizing of Native Indian "first nations" both north and south of the border. Of those who were not decimated by European diseases, some were moved to virtual "concentration camps" (called "Reservations" in America and "Reserves" in Canada) where they were unable to maintain traditional economic pursuits.

The majority of Natives were simply moved time and again further west into a diminishing "Indian Territory" until goaded into wars they could never win against the technological superiority of the newcomers. Their lands too were basically expropriated under the guise of treaties and legal agreements. Most of these are before the courts again in modern times, on the presumption that by now the rule of law really does hold sway in North America. Time will tell.

The major migration to Canada by Black former slaves comes just slightly later in the historical sequence, but without question, the frontier was every bit as brutal. The French, disgruntled Whites, Native Indians, and Black communities still bear the scars deep within the modern communal psyche. In addition to dysfunctional individuals who have not managed to surmount these impediments, there are ancient communal ghosts which must be exorcised in North America before the neighborhood can fulfill its potential.

Modern divisions in North American society, relating to gender, more recent immigrations and other cleavages which lead to violence and social problems, are perhaps incapable of resolution in isolation from these unresolved neighborhood feuds, if such a euphemistic term can be used to describe the extremes of racism and bigotry that once held sway through this whole region. Resolution of a myriad of modern ills depends on a final acceptance of the principles required to overcome these lingering alienations and ancient wrongs.

This is the forest primeval; but where are the hearts that beneath it
Leaped like the roe, when he hears in the woodland the voice of the huntsman?
Where is the thatch-roofed village, the home of Acadian farmers,-
Men whose lives glided on, like rivers that water the woodlands,
Darkened by shadows of earth, but reflecting an image of heaven?
Waste are those pleasant farms, and the farmers forever departed!
Scattered like dust and leaves, when the mighty blasts of October
Seize them, and whirl them aloft, and sprinkle them far o'er the ocean.
Naught but tradition remains of the beautiful village of Grand Pre.

3.

THE FIRST AMERICAN WAR

Popularly called "The Longest Undefended Border in the World"2 these days, during the first hundred years the US-Canada border was the scene of hostilities during three separate conflicts. In each case there was an unsuccessful American invasion of Canada, not unlike certain American adventures in South and Central America. There were two differences in the case of Canada. Firstly, the Americans did not merely wish to overthrow the government but to annex the country, and, secondly moreover, the invasions were successfully repulsed each time.

The first instance took place during the War of Independence. Aside from the battle of Bunker Hill, near Boston, the main event of the first year of the American Revolution was the attempted invasion of Canada. In a theme that was to recur in future erstwhile invasions, the invaders expected the incursion to be a walk-over since surely the Canadians wanted to be liberated from British tyranny. Such has never been the case and the Americans were soon routed.

Two U.S. armies under General Benedict Arnold and General Richard Montgomery actually succeeded occupying parts of Canada from September 1775 until May of 1776. After seizing the villages of Ticonderoga and Crown Point, Montgomery captured the military fortresses at Fort Chambly and Fort St. John, just outside Montreal.   At this, the Canadian Governor, Sir Guy Carleton (Lord Dorchester) abandoned Montreal. He sent the troops of the British Garrison to Quebec City and the Americans took over in Montreal where they had some support, particularly in the English speaking business community.

Meanwhile, despite considerable hardships and many desertions, Arnold managed to bring about seven hundred soldiers up the Kennebec and Chaudiere river systems to the outskirts of the capital, Quebec City by mid November.   The (French) Canadian Militia, the British troops, the influential Roman Catholic clergy, rural seigneurs and city business leaders formed a strategic united front to resist the invasion.   Montgomery led three hundred American soldiers from Montreal to join Arnold by December, rightly guessing that if they could take Quebec, Canada was theirs.

They attacked Quebec City, on December 31, New Year's Eve. The Regimental Ball had to be postponed, which was no small matter but the Americans were soundly beaten with many casualties and fatalities in the midst of a Canadian winter blizzard. The Americans did actually penetrate the walled city's defenses but surrendered under counter attack when Montgomery and most of his officers were killed in hand to hand combat.   The others retreated and spent the rest of the winter huddled in camps in the countryside with Benedict Arnold awaiting reinforcements that never came.

In the spring they were driven from the country, making their retreat through Montreal and taking the soldiers there with them to protect the flanks of the more dispirited from Quebec. But before long the redoubtable American negotiator, Benjamin Franklin was back in Canada at the head of a commission dispatched by the "Continental Congress." That title of the US Congress at that time is revealing ....   Their purpose was to try to persuade Canadians, especially business leaders in Montreal, to join the revolution but, again, to no avail. Canadians as a whole still resisted the proposed political reunion.

The influx of loyalist refugees from the United States after 1776 contributed to Canada's determination to develop its own democratic institutions along parliamentary lines, rather than following the route to republicanism through bloody revolution.   Whether or not it can be supported by observations elsewhere in the world, many Canadians hold an opinion that a nation born in violence will itself be violent, at home and abroad.

The questions about the reunification of the old "empire" remain. Can Canada derive a new vigor from America and can America ever be at peace with itself through the healing of a traumatic birth wound to its collective psyche? Can these goals be accomplished without political union? These questions are the subject of negotiations at various levels today.

After the revolution, a number of American colonial militias reorganized in Canada, such as the Queen's Loyal Virginians and veterans from the famous Rogers' Rangers of New Hampshire who served together in Virginia as the Queen's Rangers. They came together again in Canada at York (Toronto) to become the Queen's York Rangers.

This distinguished Canadian Regiment has served well in every war since then and as one of five officially designated "American Regiments" reorganized in Canada, the Rangers were given the honor by the Crown of being referred to as the "First American Regiment," an honor previously bestowed upon their predecessor regiment in Virginia. This history is acknowledged by nearly identical plaques on the parade squares today in Yorktown, Virginia and North York, Ontario (where the regiment's original colors still hang).[3]

The only organized military groups to join the loyalist exodus *en masse* from America at this time were native warrior bands under Joseph Brant. They had become disillusioned in the attempt to hold significant lands for native economic survival against American expansion and so allied themselves with the British throughout the War of Independence. After the final cessation of hostilities, Brant brought several thousand families of the warriors to Canada in 1784. The British rewarded their loyalty with a large tract of land in Ontario in compensation for lands lost in America. The shameful reality is that these lands in Canada were eventually illegally compromised also, through connivance between Loyalist white settlers and British colonial administrators who frequently combined incompetence with corruptibility.

Because a Canadian infrastructure was already in place, few other American institutions relocated in Canada holus-bolus but, for example, a prominent New York clergyman became the first Anglican Bishop outside Britain anywhere in the world, in Nova Scotia as of 1787. Early Canadian hospitals and institutions of higher learning likewise benefitted from what many considered to be a mass exodus of the American intelligentsia to Canada following the War of Independence. No particular Canadian contribution to American life seems to have resulted from this conflict but that might come in later times.

4.

THE SECOND AMERICAN WAR

Another native leader played an even more prominent role in the next outbreak of war involving the United States and Canada. This conflict, the War of 1812, involving Britain, France, Germany, Russia and others, was so widespread that it might well have been called a World War. In June of that year the United States declared war on Britain and attacked the Canadas, as certain of these colonies were then called.

Because there were so many loyalists north of the border, former Americans with family and business connections in the United States, the prevailing view south of the border was that Upper Canada (Ontario) at least was "a compleat American colony." Then former President Thomas Jefferson declared that conquering Canada would be a "mere matter of marching" since by now even the Canadians must be ready to throw off the British yoke. Wrong again!

By this time there were only about two thousand British regulars in the Canadian garrison. This battle would be fought by the Canadian Militia and their native allies, who had only recently lost their last effort to hold on to significant "Indian Territory" in the eastern half of the United States at the Battle of Tippecanoe. ("Regulars" are professional soldiers whereas "Militia" is a term used in Canada to refer to citizen soldiers trained by the government as official supplement to the armed forces, similar to the "Reserves" or the "National Guard" in the United States.)

As in the War of Independence, this would also rank as a major test of the loyalty of French Canada which could just as easily have used the occasion to gain its own independence, - an "on again, off again" proposition that is frequently proposed but may never happen permanently, if the aftermath of the latest Quebec "referendum" is any indication.

On the face of it, one can easily understand the American anticipation of an easy victory with a "fifth column" of American loyalists, natives in disarray, restless French Canadians and other colonials who must be chafing against the British. However the British regulars, under the Canadian General and Governor Sir Isaac Brock, managed an early victory at an outpost on Lake Huron and then took Detroit and held it. These victories encouraged their native allies to believe that the Americans could be beaten again. This lucky strike by the remaining British also influenced French Canadian thinking as to the likely outcome and prepared the Canadian Militia for its first test.

That first skirmish with the Canadians took place on October thirteenth when thirteen hundred American troops crossed the Niagara River in thirteen boats. It seems that unlucky number has never worked for American plans in Canada. Their intention was to take the area known as Queenston Heights but the brilliant tactics of General Isaac Brock thwarted them. Brock himself was actually killed on the battle field in a charge against the invaders, but the Americans were repulsed in bayonet combat and driven out of the country.

As soon as he arrived with warriors from Ohio, Tecumseh, the Shawnee chief whose people had been beaten at Tippecanoe, successfully engaged the American forces on the western side of the Niagara peninsula when they next attempted to invade from that side. He was given the rank of General in his new country and won one battle after another in 1812 and 1813 until he too was killed on the field of battle at Moraviantown. British and Canadian forces have never fought a war against natives in Canada and have frequently found them to be important allies at moments crucial to the country's survival. This is possibly a notable difference between Canadian and American nation building experiences, though for the natives it has all turned out about the same, since Canada later ignored many of the provisions in the treaties it made with its allies until recent court challenges.

Meanwhile the conflict spread all along the border. Luck was still with the Canadians, as when the famous heroine Laura Secord overheard plans being made by American officers who were eating at her house and slipped away to report in detail to the nearest militia garrison. Or there was the American Commander who was too fat to ride a horse so that his forces had to move at a walk, reportedly a General Brown. Such foibles matched a similar amount of Canadian ineptitude, except that the Canadian militia was on its own turf.

The Americans had some success in moving up Lake Champlain to enter Quebec along the St. Lawrence, though they failed in their objective to take either Montreal or Quebec City. Back in Ontario in 1813 they succeeded in attacking Toronto (still called York), occupying the city, burning down the public buildings and looting all manner of supplies. The Niagara peninsula also continued as a center of conflict at many locations. The Americans took Fort George but lost battles at Stoney Creek and Beaver Dam before taking Newark (now known as Niagara-on-the-Lake) and burning it to the ground. This latter action so incensed the Canadian forces that they marched on Buffalo and while not attempting to hold the city, they exacted severe reprisals there. American naval power controlled most of the Great Lakes throughout the war.

It was a different matter on the Atlantic coast. The remnants of the British fleet and Canadian privateer sailors were a potent force to be reckoned with. One of the more colorful naval engagements of all time, for example, occurred on June 1 of 1813 between the American frigate *Chesapeake* and HMS *Shannon*. This aging British warship had been left in Halifax, Nova Scotia with British officers and a pickup crew of Canadian fishers, merchant marines and sailor trainees - mostly thugs from the Halifax docks.

The *Chesapeake* had been marauding Canadian shipping and fishing vessels along the Maritime coast and into the gulf of St. Lawrence and was known to be in nearby Boston to take on supplies and munitions. Early in the morning of June first, the citizens of Boston were surprised to see the *Shannon* strutting the British flag around their harbour, a daring taunt to the *Chesapeake* which was getting ready to sail.

Before long the docksides and piers were lined with people expecting to see a fight. They were not kept waiting for long as the *Chesapeake* slowly moved out into position in the middle of the harbour, the *Shannon* circling all the while. Their opening salvos were fired almost simultaneously and the battle was well and truly joined. They fought all day with first one and then the other seeming to gain the upper hand. The crowd would cheer whenever the *Shannon* sustained visible damage, as when part of a mast and a whole sail was blown off. They would groan when the *Chesapeake* was hit: indeed people shrieked and fainted when a well placed shot from the *Shannon* blew up a store of munitions on the *Chesapeake*.

At the end of the day, and to the amazement of many, there was little for the crowd to cheer about. The American frigate was disabled and forced to lower her flag in surrender or be sunk before the heartsick audience. Boarding proved unnecessary at that point and there may have been some fight left in the American sailors had they been given that chance. The crew of the

41

Shannon attached a line to the *Chesapeake* and towed the crippled American vessel back to Halifax as a trophy. The American crew was imprisoned in the dungeon of the Halifax Citadel.

Emboldened by victory, and led personally by Sir John Sherbrooke, then Lieutenant-Governor of Nova Scotia, himself an experienced military commander, forces from Halifax next invaded the state of Maine. They captured the city of Castine and made it their provisional capital. Indeed, they managed to hold most of Maine for the duration of the war. Rather than return their bounty afterwards, these "Haligonians", as the citizens of Halifax are called, looted the treasury of taxes collected during the occupation and used the money to establish Dalhousie University, a leading institution of higher learning in the province. A large cairn stands in the quadrangle of the university in Halifax still today with an inscription of gratitude to the taxpaying citizens of the United States.

As a final action before the end of the war, these sailors and soldiers from Halifax attacked the city of Washington and destroyed most of the American capital. Indeed, they burned down the White House itself, forcing President Madison and the government to flee. The burning of Washington and the White House was seen by many Canadians as a fitting reprisal for the burning of Niagara-on-the-Lake and the public buildings of Toronto.

American history prefers to regard this as an act by the British, rather than to believe a disgruntled neighbor could get that angry. Even historians have had difficulty distinguishing between British and Canadians at that point, but the myth that the dirty deed was done by 4,000 British Regulars should be corrected to 2,000 "good old boys" from Halifax and possibly a similar number of professional soldiers who may have been on board the British Fleet.

It was these British soldiers in uniform who posed for the famous picture with the city of Washington smoldering in the background. However, the couple of thousand British still left at Canadian outposts of the empire were mostly officers, stretched across thousands of miles, married to Canadians in many cases or at least preparing to accept a land grant in lieu of pension so they could retire in Canada.

Soon thereafter the war was settled by the superpowers of the day and hostilities between Americans and Canadians ceased, to the intense relief of everyone. Amazingly enough, but typical of the growing mutual respect between them, the Canadians and the Americans agreed to simply return to all their 1811 borders and forget the whole thing. A few Canadians still feel badly about burning down the White House but, in the present climate of much improved relations, they can practically promise that they will never do it again.

5.

THE REVOLUTION THAT NEVER HAPPENED

Having twice misjudged the Canadian temperament, it is understandable that the United States was hesitant to intervene in Canada again. This was highly ironic since in 1837 popular revolutions broke out in both Upper Canada (Ontario) and Lower Canada (Quebec) based on grievances which had developed within a decade of the War of 1812. For once, American invaders would have had Canadian allies. This was the only time in Canadian history that a republican political ideology had any significant following.

The common folk still had a secure attachment to the crown, which has been regarded as the people's protector against rapacious business or other powerful private interests since the signing of the Magna Carta in 1215. Originally a pact between the knights and the monarch, designed to ensure that neither could attain absolute power, the result of this charter was an effective guarantee of freedom to all the people, since the crown then rested on their forbearance for its balance of power against influential rivals.

43

However, Britain was in the process of withdrawing the last vestiges of its expensive colonial administration and military presence in North America. Autocratic Canadian regimes, known as the "Family Compact" in Ontario and "The Chateau Clique" in Quebec had succeeded the British with little evidence of true democracy. Business interests seemed able to buy power. The "knights" were taking over, the very thing people feared in unchecked republican systems. Only Nova Scotia was developing "responsible government" and these northern colonies had not yet entered into anything like a permanent political union as had their American cousins.

The leaders of the rebellions, William Lyon Mackenzie in Ontario and Louis-Joseph Papineau in Quebec, were both republicans, and each favored union with the United States. They each had fairly widespread political support and successful electoral experience. When frustrated in their proposals for reform of inbred Canadian institutions, they had resorted to appeal before the British courts and the Parliament in London. They always seemed to win their case but to little avail at home in Canada, where the judgments were ignored by the bureaucracy which was controlled by a governing elite.

In the winter of 1837 Papineau led an armed revolt in Quebec and Mackenzie took up arms in Ontario but both rebellions were quickly quashed. After controlling a bit of countryside for a few weeks, the French "Patriotes" were put down at St.-Eustasche, just north of Montreal, with particular brutality by the remaining British regiment in Quebec. Several hundred Quebecers were killed and five hundred were imprisoned somewhat indiscriminately. Of these, a dozen were executed and fifty-eight sent off to hard labor in the British penal colony of Australia.

In Ontario the matter was handled by the Canadian Militia, which was loyal to anti-republican sentiment that was still dominant in many quarters. However, of the eight hundred rebels in the field, just sixty were ever taken into custody, resulting in two of their officers being executed as an example to anyone else getting revolutionary ideas. Everyone else was given parole.

Amazingly enough, the "would-be" revolutions were totally uncoordinated. Since both leaders were more interested in union with America than with each other, there was no communication between these equally aggrieved parties - a remarkable symbol of the "two solitudes" that still exist between French and English speaking Canadians of nationalist aspiration nearly two centuries later.

Papineau had received no support whatsoever from America, and all Mackenzie got was the supply ship *Caroline* based in Fort Schlosser, New York. After being routed in the one Toronto skirmish, "The Battle of Montgomery's Tavern," Mackenzie had withdrawn to an island in the Niagara River held by a few hundred of his troops in expectation of American reinforcements via the *Caroline*.

A force of Canadian Militia entered the United States and slipped into Fort

Schlosser where the *Caroline* was preparing to embark. A brief encounter ensued in which one American was killed and others wounded and tied up. The *Caroline* was set ablaze and then adrift. She foundered above the falls and sank before she went over, taking Canadian aspirations of revolution and republican life crashing down forever. This was the entire extent of American involvement in either rebellion.

Had like-minded Americans given the Canadian revolutionaries aid with anything approximating the efficiency demonstrated by the loyal Canadian Militia, or even if Papineau and Mackenzie had coordinated their efforts, the political history and destiny of North America might have been very different. As it was, the revolutionary leaders were all either killed in battle or jailed except for Papineau and Mackenzie who were somehow permitted to flee to the United States. There they were given refuge and protection, waiting for another day which never came.

6.

THE UNDERGROUND RAILROAD

Immigration to both the United States and Canada was phenomenal through the nineteenth century. The flood of Scots pushed out by the English landlords making room for sheep during the "highland clearances," and the Irish starved out of their homes through deliberate famine meant that over seventy five percent of the newcomers had some sort of British ethnic identity. Most of the rest came from Scandinavia or depressed areas of eastern Europe, so that while they tended to cluster in ethnic pockets, they too were soon able to blend in with white, English speaking majorities in both countries.

Meanwhile another significant movement of population between the United States and Canada was taking place. The first Canadian anti-slavery law had been passed in the Legislative Assembly of Upper Canada in 1793 at the instigation of Lieutenant-Governor John Graves Simcoe. Enforcement difficulties remained in respect to international trade until slavery was abolished throughout the whole British Empire in 1833. By then the Underground Railroad was in full operation, bringing fugitive slaves to freedom in Canada from America. As a country, the United States was not the leader of the column of human progress in this regard and has paid a heavy price ever since for its reticence.

47

A sizable number of free blacks had come to Nova Scotia earlier from New England as United Empire Loyalist refugees. This new underground network established by free blacks in the northern states, and white abolitionists - both American and Canadian - was part of a worldwide campaign. Like the Civil Rights Movement a century later, or Alcoholics Annonymous and Amnesty International today, there was no official religious connection, but the Underground Railroad was largely supported by people with spiritual convictions. It was facilitated and coordinated by churches on both sides of the border.

This so-called Underground Railroad was so effective that indeed many of its proponents as well as its opponents believed at times that there was actually a system of underground tunnels leading into Canada. In truth, in the great age of railway building, it was a secret code employing phrases like "station", "track", "switch" and "terminal" that used railway language and imagery.

After the American government passed the <u>Second Fugitive Law</u> in 1850, providing for the forced return of slaves who had escaped in one state and taken refuge in another, the Underground Railroad to Canada really "picked up steam". The largest number of slaves came into Canada by way of the Detroit River at its narrowest point, into Amherstburg, Ontario, the largest "terminal" in Canada, near the city of Windsor.

The typical winter crossing on the frozen river by scantily clad southern slaves, most of whom had never seen ice or snow before, was no doubt difficult but exhilarating. In the summer, many swam across the river with their Canadian guides, with their few possessions tied to their backs. Uncle Tom's Cabin, the classic tale by Harriet Beecher Stowe, tells the story of characters who continue to live on in the American vocabulary: the cruel Simon Legree, Topsy who "just grew," Jim Crow and Uncle Tom. This book permanently fixed an image of Canada as a place of refuge and safety almost akin to the Promised Land in American mythology.

In all, between the years 1800 and 1860, approximately 50,000 slaves escaped to Canada via the Underground Railway.[4] The conspiracy was never cracked by either the American government or the organized pro-slavery forces. Sadly, like the Native Indians who fled north before them, the sizable black population in Canada has not entirely escaped prejudice nor overcome the effects of generations of terror under slavery. However, if Franco-American Cajuns still stay in touch with Canadian cousins, and United Empire Loyalist descendants still maintain an affection for America, neither holds a candle to the close connections Canadian Blacks maintain with the Afro-American community in the USA.

The Afro-community has contributed to every aspect of Canadian life, in war and peace, in sports and entertainment, in business, politics and the professions. The second wife of Canada's first Prime Minister, Sir John A. Macdonald, was herself a Black immigrant from Jamaica and many other Blacks have held their own positions of political and social prominence throughout Canadian history. In modern times the Black community is growing again through immigration, mainly from the Caribbean, as another wave of population diversity struggles at first to make its way in the new Canadian environment.

Indeed, the English speaking islands of the Caribbean, as former outposts of the old United Empire of North America, seem to almost have an entree into the emerging North American neighborhood. Aside from the growing Hispanic population already in North America, it would appear that the Hispanic world of Central and South America remains a region or neighborhood of its own for the time being, while Blacks and East Indians from Jamaica, Trinidad and other islands appear to have ready access to North America.

Certain assumptions of racism and religious bigotry are challenged by some of the barriers to Hispanic and Asian immigration at the same time that jet black Maroons from Jamaica and Hindus from Trinidad go to the head of the cue at Canada Customs and Immigration, fitting right in from the day they arrive. Fair skinned Hispanics, Blacks from French islands and Buddhists from Asia (except the wealthy or professionals) often have no such welcome. Perhaps the underground railway set the precedent.

Again, where a welcome exists, it is offered by churches who sponsor refugees, provide language classes, emergency financial aid and opportunities for new community. These days non-Christian religions are also active in these ways, though more typically limiting their assistance to members of their own faith communities.

Circumpolar View of Canadian Pacific Operations One Hundred Years Ago

(One hundred years later Canadian Pacific operations in the US also became so huge that the corporation adopted a two-flag logo. It was dropped in 1997 after paranoid Canadian protests against this seeming "American takeover" when, in reality, it was just another dramatic part of the Canadianization of America!)

50

7.

THE OVERLAND RAILROAD

By 1867 the Canadian provinces had begun to enter Confederation and another railway was under construction as an enticement for colonies as far west as the Pacific Ocean to join in this vast and somewhat unnatural political alignment. The building of the Canadian Pacific Railway, the largest railway system in the world, has been described by popular national historian, Pierre Berton, as "The National Dream."

Built almost entirely by indentured Chinese laborers (none of whom appear in the grand oil paintings of this epic undertaking), this racist system of organized exploitation has "benefitted" all Canada ever since. It also now gives the substantial and growing Oriental population an historical identity in having helped build the country.

The practice of importing huge Chinese gangs of cheap but effective indentured laborers had become established a decade earlier in the western United States. In both countries this source of labor came almost exclusively from South China, giving a Cantonese flavor to the North American Chinese presence ever since, despite the preponderance of the Mandarin language and culture in China as a whole.

American railroads and steamship lines had interesting histories also, but on a local, as opposed to a global scale. However, the Canadian project, which came close to bankrupting the nation even while building and extending it, also has several American connections itself, in addition to eventually acquiring a thousand miles of track through that neighbor's land.

In the first place, a major impetus to build the railway was to link up with British Columbia on the west coast and then to fill the prairies with Canadian settlers and loyal immigrants. This was seen as necessary for national security, before the Americans arrived in a *de facto* occupation of formerly British territory as had already happened in places like Oregon.

Another American note of interest is that the main builder of this wonder of global engineering, economic, and political significance, was himself an American. Cornelius Van Horne was already General Manager of the Canadian Pacific Railway at age forty and president six years later. A few years after completing the railroad, he launched the famous Empress Line of Canadian Pacific Steamships, initially to improve mail, freight and tourist services between Canada and the Orient. It eventually linked London to Hong Kong via Canada in competition with another Canadian company, the Cunard Line with its massive Queen ships, owned and operated by Sir Samuel Cunard of Halifax.

No Canadians are known to have contributed so much to America's own era of the railway, but Canadian and American railway history would not be complete without acknowledgment of the work of another engineer and inventor, Sanford Fleming, a Canadian. He was the inventor of Standard Time as a concept most helpful for the Canadian Pacific Railway which, with its Empress Line, stretched approximately three quarters of the way around the globe. Fleming convened the International Prime Meridian Conference in Washington in 1884 at which he persuaded America and Britain, among others, to also adopt Standard Time.

This Canadian time system is today in universal use, much like a range of more recent Canadian contributions to computer and internet technology. In the nineteenth century Americans were the first to mass produce wood screws, while a little later, a Canadian invented the world's most efficient screw driver, the Robertson squarehead. Typically, Canadians relied on Chinese immigrants and American bosses to build their railway and then adopted an invisible role in making such things work, not only in Canada but in America and elsewhere in the world.

This Canadian-American relationship, a partnership between entrepreneurial drive and supportive infrastructure, is found in so many dimensions of North American life. It is nowhere better demonstrated than in the relationship between Van Horne, the American railway boss, Fleming, the Canadian railway operator and the Chinese laborers, the latest wave of immigrants who always keep the economy moving forward.

The American was knighted by Queen Victoria for his service to Canada, so in an era when Americans were still legally permitted to accept foreign titles he became Sir William Cornelius Van Horne. The Canadian was also knighted to become Sir Sanford Fleming, both of them on the recommendation of the Prime Minister of Canada, Sir John A. Macdonald, in spite of the latter's Tory political connections with Sir Samuel Cunard. If ever there was a privileged clique of White Anglo-Saxon Protestant males, this was it.

The 15,000 Chinese laborers, more than two hundred of whom died in blasting, other construction accidents and disease, remain unrecognized and unnamed. They had worked in appalling conditions, for "slave wages" on indentured contracts, and lived in male gangs without family or female companionship. Many hoped to save a meager stash of cash and return to Canton but most never did in spite of inhospitable immigration laws such as the British Columbia Chinese regulation Act of 1884.

In its preamble it stated that the Chinese "are not disposed to be governed by our laws; are dissimilar in habits and occupation from our people; evade the payment of taxes justly due to the Government; are governed by pestilential habits; are useless in instances of emergency; habitually desecrate graveyards by the removal of bodies therefrom and are inclined to habits subversive of the comfort and well being of the community."[5]

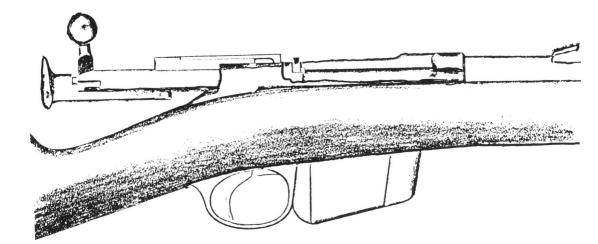

The Lee Enfield
(A Canadian rifle had its field trials by American mercinaries invading Canada)

8.

THE THIRD AMERICAN WAR

These developments were taking place at the same time as the final hostile actions by Americans in Canada in yet another attempt to overthrow the Canadian government. The Fenian Brotherhood was an organization of Irish Americans, some of whom fought against each other during the Civil War but who were united in their interest and commitment to the nationalist cause back in the Irish homeland.

At the conclusion of that sad internal conflict in the United States, there were about a million men demobilized from the various American armies, some of which actually had Irish units. Many of these men could not find work and congregated in military clubs which were the forerunners of organized independent militias sometimes referred to as "patriots", surviving on the radical fringe of American society even still today.

These were well trained and experienced soldiers who were permitted to retain their weapons upon retirement. The Civil War had especially high casualty rates since it was the first conflict in which soldiers were equipped with modern rifles. Most of them had rifles which were forerunners of the "Lee Enfield" invented by a Canadian clockmaker, James Lee of Owen Sound, Ontario. He moved temporarily to Enfield, Massachusetts where he produced his best known weapon which was used by Americans around the world. Gunsmithing and clockmaking were cross-border technologies even back then.

Lee's bolt action, magazine fed .303 calibre rifle was chosen by the American Secretary of War to replace the Springfield as standard issue for the U.S. Army. Lee's Enfield won out in competition over Hotchkiss and Remington among others. Lee eventually returned to Owen Sound in retirement. By then his rifles were also standard issue for Canadian and British forces as well.

Some of the "patriots" found work with their rifles as mercenaries in various American adventures around the globe. On orders from the Irish underground, the Irish-American Fenians sent column after column into Canada in an attempt to force Britain to return large numbers of troops to its former colonies. This strategy was intended to deplete the British forces stationed in Ireland in the years prior to the outbreaks of rebellion which eventually resulted in the successful establishment of the Republic of Ireland.

The British never did rise to the bait and the Canadian Militia was on its own, except for a few British instructors at the Canadian military schools and a few symbolic British garrisons. These "Brits" often took commanding roles or served as advisors, but there was little glory for anybody during the five years of skirmishes along the US-Canada border from the Atlantic to the Prairies.

The United States government stayed out of this conflict officially but had its own grudge against Britain because of British meddling in the Civil War on the side of the southern Confederate States. The American government was therefore inclined to look the other way as the well-financed Fenian Brotherhood acquired war surplus munitions, war *materiel* and even ships to use in the attempted invasions of Canada.

The whole Fenian business might look almost silly in history were it not for the fact that other similar American armed groups were overturning governments almost at will in this hemisphere and elsewhere. A glance at typical battles and skirmishes in New Brunswick, Quebec, Ontario and Manitoba would be of interest in this connection.

On April 9,1866 Fenian General O'Mahony placed 1,000 men in staging areas on the border with New Brunswick in the State of Maine at Eastport and Calais. Their swashbuckling behaviour removed any sense of a surprise element. It was easily realized that their target would be Campobello Island which would give them control of a tiny piece of the British Empire, as they saw it, and possibly force the British hand.

True enough, the British warship *H.M.S. Pleaides* arrived to observe, but actually did nothing except watch as a small advance party of Fenians raided the Canadian customs house on nearby Indian Island. Next came the larger eighty one gun *H.M.S. Duncan* which happened to have a force of seven hundred British regular troops on board, who quietly slipped ashore to join the Canadians.

On April 17 the *U.S.S. Winooski* arrived to observe on behalf of the American government. With it came a surprise in the form of a far more sinister ship. That was the former *U.S.S. Ocean Spray*, acquired by the Fenians as "war surplus" in subterfuge surpassing even the Iran-Contra arms deals of more recent times. The *Ocean Spray* was bristling with heavy artillery and brought one hundred thousand rounds of ammunition along with fifteen hundred stand of arms, mostly the latest rifles. Needless to say, the Canadian Militia was out- gunned, still being equipped with old fashioned muskets!

There were more Canadian and American newspaper reporters assembled for this confrontation than had ever covered any international event prior to this time. There is a decidedly modern coloring to this picture of a media encampment, mostly assembled at Eastport, Maine. The maneuvering also took place under the watchful eyes of the American General, George C. Meade, the victor of Gettysburg in the Civil War. Present also were two British Generals and the Vice-Admiral of the Fleet. Quite an audience for a gang of Irish hooligans and the local farmers and fishers of the Canadian Militia!

Four hundred of the Fenians took positions at Eastport, four hundred at Calais and two hundred were placed strategically in raiding parties at Lubec, Pembroke and Robinson. The Irish-Americans were the better equipped but with all the publicity, they now realized that they were facing a thousand British regulars and twice that number of Canadian Militia.

The well armed Fenians would have dearly loved to engage the British but the presence of so many Canadians was unnerving. They had miscalculated, as Americans had done twice before, believing that as likely as not, the Canadians would join them or at least not resist. The American government by now knew better, but these enthusiastic patriots did not.

Wisely deciding that discretion was indeed the better part of valor in this case, the Fenians turned over their ship and their main supply of weapons and ammunition to General Meade for safe keeping. They then dispersed with the intention of re-grouping another day in another place. Next time they would attempt to use the element of surprise and to find an area that might have a greater predisposition toward Americans or to republicanism. In fact the main upshot of this incursion was to put a little steel into the spine of the wavering Confederation movement in what would become the Maritime provinces of Canada just one year later.

That next action was planned as a three pronged attack along the borders with Quebec and Ontario. This time five thousand Fenians were put into position to give them the kind of numbers that had faced them so unexpectedly in the Maritimes. This force was under the command of Fenian General Sweeny who had just been given one hundred thousand dollars in cash from a convention at Pittsburgh. This represented the purchasing power of several million dollars in modern currency, more than enough for him to establish large caches of arms and ammunition within easy supply range of the border.

One contingent of Fenians was positioned under Brigadier General Speer in Vermont. A second concentration was placed near Buffalo under Brigadier Lynch. A third group, under the direction of Sweeny's Adjutant-General, Charles Tevis was based in Chicago.

From Chicago a strike force would move up through Lake Michigan and Lake Huron to attack the cities of London and Stratford in Ontario. Twenty-four hours later three units would cross Lake Erie to attack the additional Ontario centers of Paris, Guelph and Hamilton. These actions were expected to force the Canadian defence to concentrate on Toronto and cause the only British Garrison of consequence to move in that direction by train from Montreal.

The plan was to prevent the British from returning by blowing up the railway bridge at Ste. Anne de Bellevue after them, leaving Montreal, Canada's largest city of that time, exposed to the attack from Vermont. French Canadian ambivalence toward British rule was more appropriately taken for granted. The Fenians had done their strategic studies carefully this time. The Canadian Militia was weakest in Quebec and they contrived to draw the British force away. If Montreal, by far Canada's largest city, could be taken, the whole thing could be over in a short period of time. This strategy was more worthy of these experienced officers of the Civil War.

However many of the Fenians were named Murphy and according to "Murphy's Law", everything that could go wrong did go wrong. A charter ship refused to leave Chicago at the last moment. A Canadian group of Irish sympathizers switched sides. The central group moved into Canada from Buffalo only to have their horses stolen at night by Canadian farm children. The American government got nervous about other delicate negotiations with the British on matters half-way around the world, and sent the *U.S.S. Michigan* to a position off Fort Erie to prevent reinforcements joining those already in Canada.

If these Fenians seemed more like keystone cops than soldiers, they nevertheless stumbled into a series of victories due to even greater blunders and stupidity on the part of the Canadian Militia. Ill equipped and poorly trained, they marched from place to place without ever really discovering who was on first base. The few British regulars around were infuriated at the Canadians when they chased the Americans toward them in an ambush, only to have the Canadians retreat when they mistook a tiny mounted Fenian scouting party for the American Cavalry.

Then by accident the Fenians took the town of Ridgeway and secured a line of retreat to Fort Erie and Buffalo. The Canadians stumbled into the line of retreat and suffered some casualties before realizing they were "driving the Americans out," a cause of great victory celebrations later.

General Ulysses Grant himself came up to Buffalo to consult with General Meade who was once again on the scene to monitor the situation on behalf of the American government. These old soldiers knew a lost cause when they saw it. On June 6, President Johnson of the United States dashed the hopes of the Fenian Patriots who expected some form of government support from behind the scenes. He condemned them for "high misdemeanours forbidden by the laws of the United States." That night Sweeny was arrested and Meade confiscated the remaining arms and ammunition at the Buffalo base.

Unfortunately the last communication received by the force assembled in Vermont was that the Fenian Force from Buffalo had successfully invaded Canada and was engaged on several fronts. Accordingly, they moved forward rather successfully, entering Canada on June 7,1866, with a thousand advance troops. By the morning of June 8 they had successfully occupied four small Canadian communities at Pigeon Hill, Frelighsburg, St. Armand and East Standbridge, all in Quebec.

General Speer then moved himself and his staff confidently forward into Canada with a further contingent. However, the Montreal newspaper *Le Pays* reported on June 9 that the Fenians were being harassed on every side by the Canadian Militia. The report noted that Speer was having trouble disciplining his troops and was finding it impossible to even buy food from the locals who had been expected to offer support.

By the end of the day the Fenians had retreated across the border and Speer surrendered himself to the American authorities who had caught up with the action once again. Canadian Militia insignia are emblazoned to this day with the names of the great victories at Pigeon Hill, Frelighsburg, St. Armand and East Standbridge. Indeed the American authorities declined to take notice of a brief armed Canadian intrusion into American territory in hot pursuit, resulting in the taking of a number of prisoners back to Canada. Good neighbors all!

Perhaps if there was a significant lesson on one side, the Americans have never launched an action against Canada again in any form except for a footnote that will be presented. The Canadian Militia, for its part, learned the rudiments of peacekeeping techniques for which Canada has become justifiably famous throughout the world. Conflict of consequence can sometimes be avoided if professional forces are kept out of the fray, unless they too are skilled in the arts of peacekeeping with Canadian "techniques" learned by accident during the Fenian incursions.

A force does not always have to fight; the Fenians were successfully turned back by confusion, part-time soldiers milling around, "pitchforks at the ready", pushing and shoving, with some spitting and swearing. This is the way Canadians have come to think the whole world should fight. To be perfectly serious, Canadians have discovered that, as often as not, it works. This could be an argument in support of the whole inefficient United Nations peacekeeping approach, modelled and nurtured by Canadians, as opposed to the American practice of going around the world with real fire power in an effort to dissuade people from rival political philosophies or promote America's economic agenda among other peoples.

In that final footnote to the Fenian raids, the Irish American leader of that cause, John O'Neill himself, determined to give it one last shot. Hearing of Native, French and Scottish unrest in the mixed race "Metis" society then dominant on the Canadian Prairies, he sent a force West to come up through St. Paul to invade the new Canadian Province of Manitoba. He hoped for better luck in the cause of Irish mischief in Canada this time and expected (and probably got) some American government support in the rush to occupy and control the West. The very idea that Louis Riel, the Metis leader, might join him was not far fetched.

His plans were thwarted by his adjutant, Henri LeCaron, a double agent for the Canadian government who had sold O'Neill on the idea in the first place. The Canadian government took action by dispatching a Joint Expeditionary Force of Canadian Militia and British officers and advisors from Eastern Canada. In true Fenian tradition, O'Neill and his small force arrived late, after many delays, so late that the Canadian forces had already left to return East after ceremonies celebrating the birth of the new province. The Fenians "attacked" a small Hudson's Bay post on the border, though no shots were actually fired. They were shortly surrounded and arrested by the Metis Militia of Manitoba sent by Premier Louis Riel, the very same malcontent from whom they had expected help.

The American government representatives, never far behind this band of mercenary dreamers, soon arrived to escort their citizens away with the eager compliance of the Canadian authorities. By now U.S. officials were thoroughly disgusted at Fenian blunders and would never again be even suspected of collusion in adventures into Canada. For that matter, as Canada was breaking its last ties with Britain, the Americans appeared to sever all but unofficial ties and sympathy for the Irish cause across the ocean as well.

9.

SANCTUARY

As Papineau and Mackenzie had taken refuge in the United States and as Brant and Tecumseh had come to Canada in earlier eras, the practice of providing sanctuary for each other's dissidents continued. The two governments had begun to trust each other and to cooperate in diplomacy. The harboring of dissidents was, as often as not, a favor, done to manage a difficult political situation. This is possibly the first actual example of the reciprocity for which these two nations became justifiably famous.

At an earlier time, General Benedict Arnold was seen as a traitor by Americans, since, after his experience in Canada, he did not stay with the revolutionary movement. Technically Arnold was the one obeying the lawful authority, since America had merely declared independence but had not achieved it. Legally it was the thirteen colonies that were "traitors" to the crown and Arnold who was loyal. For this he was granted a huge estate of over thirteen thousand acres in Canada. So much depends on historical perspective, however, and enough time has passed that none of this upsets either Americans or Canadians now.

This matter of perspective probably applies just as well to the Native Indian chief, Sitting Bull. He also received freedom and protective custody in Canada following his defeat of General Custer and the U.S. forces at the Battle of the Little Bighorn, as they advanced into Indian Territory. His restraint during a time of unrest on the Canadian Prairies a few years later assisted the Canadian government in putting down the brief North West Rebellion of Native Indians and a substantial community of Canadians of "mixed blood" called Metis, led by Louis Riel and his General, Gabriel Dumont.

These visionaries had proclaimed independent French speaking republics, first in Manitoba (which evolved into a Canadian province with Riel as leader and elected member of the Canadian Parliament), and then further West in Saskatchewan (resulting in creation of another Canadian province, though this time Riel was hanged). In both instances there was a remarkable vision of extending the Canadian West beyond the sphere of Anglo-Saxon control to make the area a sanctuary for semi-autonomous pockets of uprooted peoples from all over the world.

The Russian nobleman and author, Leo Tolstoy, for example, shared the vision and financed the establishment of Jewish settlements in this part of Western Canada, following a murderous series of anti-Semitic pogroms in Russia. That community remains scattered across Saskatchewan today, historically among the very first modern Zionist attempts to establish an independent Jewish homeland, a project that later focussed on Israel rather than Canada.

In between the creation of Manitoba and Saskatchewan, while "wanted" by the Canadian authorities, Riel took refuge, recovered his health and regrouped in the United States. However there were no attempts to extradite him and it appears that Canadian politicians were grateful that they did not have to bring Riel to trial at that time. Would that he had managed to escapt to the States a second time fifteen years later. When the second Metis or Northwest Rebellion was actually over, it was Dumont's turn to find sanctuary in the United States. There he joined Buffalo Bill's Wild West Show as a crack marksman until returning to Canada in 1888 after an amnesty.

10.

"FIFTY- FOUR FORTY OR FIGHT"

By 1818 the forty-ninth parallel had been established and generally accepted as the boundary between the United States and Canada from the Great Lakes to the Rocky Mountains. This gave America the huge watershed of the Mississippi-Missouri drainage system, everything draining to the south, and left Canada the vast territories draining north into Hudson's Bay and the Arctic Ocean.

Further west, especially on the Pacific coast, the jurisdictions were not as clear for some time. The British still controlled everything between California to the south and up through that tentative Canadian border at the forty-ninth parallel all the way to Alaska. The southern portion was an area known as Oregon and the Americans attempted to lay claim. For ten years a joint administration was set up to permit negotiations. In the absence of an agreement, this was extended indefinitely in 1827 but by the 1840's a flood of American settlers required a resolution of the question.

This time the Americans were not content with the forty-ninth parallel. They demanded exclusive jurisdiction along the Pacific coast as far north as the beginning of the Russian colony of Alaska at the latitude of 54°,40' known as "fifty-four forty." They had as yet little idea of acquiring Alaska from the Russians but, in retrospect, an advance to the Alaska boundary would have had tremendous significance for the future.

Gold fever was one of several considerations. Gold rushes in California and Colorado, and the giant Canadian Klondike strike were decades away, and Ontario is North America's main modern gold producer, but gold was already trickling out of Queen Charlotte Islands and Fraser River portions of this disputed area.

Feelings ran high. The phrase "fifty-four forty or fight" became a campaign slogan in the 1844 U.S. election. It appeared that the continuing withdrawal of the British would cause yet another war between the United States and Canada. However, at the higher levels of diplomacy, Canadians and Americans had learned to talk with each other and they each agreed to arbitration by the British who were on reasonably good terms with both parties for a change. For once, the messy pattern of fighting with each other was transcended by negotiation between states, demonstrating a new political maturity.

The matter was settled by the Treaty of Oregon in 1846, which indeed extended the prairie Canadian border at the forty-ninth parallel through the Rocky Mountains to the Pacific. This area became organized as two British colonies which eventually united to form the Canadian province of British Columbia. On the American side of this newly defined border the two territories of Oregon and Washington were then established and they attained the status of statehood in 1859 and 1889 respectively.

This avoidance of bloodshed set a precedent for resolution of other tense situations regarding boundaries through the Strait of Juan de Fuca and later in connection with the American acquisition of Alaska. Because of that later acquisition it is interesting to speculate how different the map of North America might look today if the Americans had been more insistent in attempting to acquire the territory of British Columbia. This have formed a contiguous land mass linking Alaska with the lower forty-eight states, giving America an even more pronounced Pacific character. The prairie provinces too were still in formation and might well have become states, followed by the Yukon and Northwest Territories.

As these two countries move ever closer together as one neighborhood of the Global Village, such questions become academic. For that matter, one reason the two parties managed to come to an acceptable compromise way back then was the growing anticipation that free trade and other measures of reciprocity were already on the fast track. However, should separatist trends in Quebec cause Canada to break up sometime in the twenty-first century, the scenario of British Columbia seeking statehood is not far fetched. In all probability BC would be followed, one at a time, by eleven other new States.

11.

KILLING FREE TRADE

While again no bloodshed occurred, the feelings around the "Alaska Boundary Dispute," as it was known, were so intense, especially in Canada, that free trade as it is known now, was delayed nearly one hundred years over this issue. The border between Alaska and Canada's Yukon Territory had been well established by the Russians and the British as early as 1825. Prior to that the Russians had attempted to establish activity in the Yukon as a penal colony. Evidently the Czars used Alaska and the Yukon for much the same purpose that the Soviet Regime used Siberia in the practice of slave labor.

The Whitehorse Star newspaper reported in its June 7,1907 edition that some "modern" miners had dug through the tunnel of an old Russian gold mine. The Russians had apparently not made any great strike but they had been close to an area that yielded rich seams of gold to those "modern" miners.

The timbers that shored the walls were old and rotted, and the tunnel looked as if it had not been worked for a century. At the end there were evidences of a tragedy. The bones of a couple of men were found past a cave-in which had evidently imprisoned them beyond all rescue, and on their legs there still clung the heavy manacles with which Russia in the old days hobbled her political prisoners.

The men had died miserably because of the cave-in and for some reason never to be known were not rescued. The irons on their legs had apparently hindered their movements, for the situation would not have been desperate to a modern miner, possessing full freedom of movement. Beside them were their century-old picks, heavy, blunted, and inefficient instruments. The remains were respectfully buried and the instruments and leg irons were saved, and will be a portion of the Russia exhibit in the Alaska building of the Alaska-Yukon Pacific Exposition.[6]

A boundary had been established between the Canadian Yukon and Russian Alaska in 1825 by an Anglo-Russian Convention. It followed the 141st meridian of longitude from the Arctic Ocean south for a thousand kilometres to the tip of Mount Saint Elias on the Pacific near the junction of the three territorial borders of Alaska, Yukon and British Columbia. Its purpose was to separate the mining, settlement and trading interests of the Russians from similar pursuits of the Hudson's Bay Company who had trading and commercial rights under the British.

The trouble was that neither party thought much or cared about the thirty miles from the tip of the mountain down the southern slope to the Pacific. The convention had generally agreed that the Russians would have "coastal rights" from Mt. St. Elias south to the "fifty-four forty" line of latitude, an area known as the "Alaskan Panhandle."

When the United States bought Alaska in 1867 from Russia for two cents per acre, they insisted on clarification of the boundary, especially since they had a natural interest in the southern region in particular. The Americans claimed the entire coastline, unbroken by the fjords of the region, some as deep as one hundred miles.

The Canadians protested vigorously that this would cut the Yukon off from the sea for the first time. The Canadians claimed that the border in the Anglo-Russian Convention had always been interpreted as running from mountain top to mountain top along the summits of a range that followed the general outline of the coast, cutting across all inlets and fjords.

This dispute became a powder keg during the Klondike Gold Rush in the Yukon beginning in 1896. Towns like Skagway and Haines were established over a hundred kilometers from the Pacific, around Hudson's Bay Company trading posts at the inland tips of the fjords. Canadian law was enforced, at least sporadically, by Canadian Mounted Police but suddenly the Americans were claiming the territory and the towns as theirs. Confusion reigned and large fortunes hung in the balance.

The matter was referred to a Joint High Commission which failed to find a compromise through meetings in 1897 and referred the issue to an International Tribunal in 1898. This body consisted of one British member, two Canadians and three Americans. The Canadians were confident since the British delegate, Lord Alverstone, was in the chair. He was Lord Chief Justice of England and would surely present a watertight defence of the historic British position on which the Canadian claim rested.

In fact, the opposite was the case. The whole tribunal was openly partisan and to buttress growing Anglo-American rapprochement in global politics, Lord Alverstone was instructed by the British government to support the American position. The Canadians lost by a vote of four to two and the Canadian delegates walked out after refusing to sign the accord. The Canadian press was apoplectic, the public was incensed and the government went ballistic. Anti-British feeling erupted across the country. There were two consequences to the Alaska Boundary Dispute which followed, both of historic proportions.

The Canadian Prime Minister, Sir Wilfrid Laurier, asserted that never again should Canada surrender its right to make treaties on its own behalf. Until then the British Empire was evolving towards a Commonwealth of Nations more closely associated with British control or leadership. Laurier continued his campaign all the way to a colonial conference in London in 1902 where he secured the support of Australia, New Zealand and others in reducing Britain's role in the world forever. The Alaska Boundary Dispute was the beginning of the end of the British Empire and Britain's role as a superpower.

Another consequence of this otherwise minor border dispute was to set back growing trade relationships between Canada and the United States by nearly one hundred years. Both countries were enthusiastic traders and each had a surplus of goods the other needed to import. Other possible trading partners were so far away that shipping costs and delivery time were problems. Entrepreneurs on both sides of the border had seen free-trade as an easy way to increase the volume of business and develop the economies of both countries.

Free Trade actually became the policy of the Liberal Party of Canada in 1902 in spite of the unhappiness over the Alaska boundary, simply because it made so much sense. They worked on the proposal with American counterparts until it was ready to present to Parliament and Congress in 1911.

"Reciprocity", as free-trade was then called, would have provided for the duty free exchange of raw resources and reduced tariffs on manufactured goods. The Conservatives opposed the plan on behalf of Canadian industrialists who were protectionist by nature. They accused the Liberals of leading the country toward political annexation by the United States. The Liberals called an election on the issue and suffered a crushing defeat on September 21, 1911. The Tories simply ran their successful campaign on the anti-American feeling which had smoldered for a decade since the Alaska Boundary Dispute.

The "reciprocity election" of 1911 in Canada had turned a natural and mutually beneficial proposal into political suicide for any Canadian political party for most of the twentieth century. Free trade was brought back by the Conservatives themselves in 1990, but even then at the very considerable political expense which contributed to the collapse of that party in the 1994 federal election.

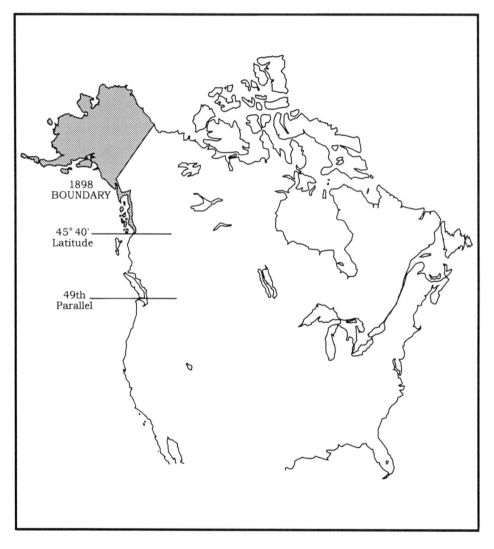

Fifty-Four Forty and the Alaska Boundary

12.

A BORDERLINE SITUATION

This is the law of the Yukon, that only the strong shall thrive;
That surely the weak shall perish, and only the fit survive.
Dissolute, dammed and despairful, crippled and palsied and slain,
this is the Will of the Yukon, - Lo, how she makes it plain![7]

The confusing situation on that last U.S. - Canadian border to be settled can be well illustrated by the activities of a young Canadian Presbyterian minister in the Klondike Gold Rush. The Rev. Robert Dickey graduated from seminary in Winnipeg in 1897 and was ordained for this mission. He reached Skagway in the autumn of that year and built a Presbyterian Church in that Canadian (soon to be American) city. The fact that the church was taken over by the American Episcopal Church "for interdenominational use" a year later, when Dickey headed up the trail, tells us something about blurry border lines that resemble a situation that has come around full cycle again today.

In three months after his arrival at Skagway, Dickey had organized a humane society for the pack animals (often flogged to death or permitted to freeze or starve), a school, and a hospital as well as the Church. He wrote letters back to Winnipeg pleading for nurses: "They ought to be physically very strong and more important still, of cheerful dispositions; they are needed more than mounties or missionaries."

Professional women were not the first of their sex to make their mark on the north, however. En route to the Klondike, Dickey had already met many women caught up in the gold rush fever. Some went north to seek a rich husband, find a good job or a career in entertaining. Others went with their husbands who held various positions. The less fortunate wound up as prostitutes, along with some who went north for that purpose. In Skagway, now an American port near the Yukon border, a bronze bust sits to this day on a monument with this inscription:

MOLLIE WALSH
Alone and without help
this courageous girl
ran a grub tent
near Log Cabin
during the gold rush
of 1897-98
She fed and lodged
the wildest
gold-crazed men.
Generations
shall surely know
this inspiring spirit.
Murdered, October 27th
1902

Mollie had come from Ireland as one of the "Irish Colleens" of the Irish Industries Village at the Chicago World's Fair in 1893. She came to Canada later on to work in a department store and when the excitement started in the Yukon, Mollie wanted to be a part of it. She had saved carefully and arrived at Skagway on October 9, 1897 aboard the S.S. Quadra. This was the same boat which carried the young Rev. Robert Dickey who would spend the fall and winter there before proceeding to the Klondike.

His friendship perhaps saved her from the ignominious experience of her friend, Priscilla, who arrived on a later boat to teach school. She was carted off to a brothel by Skagway's notorious gunfighter, Soapy Smith, who appeared to be "a kindly gentleman who offered to carry my luggage to a nice boardinghouse". Dickey hunted up a U.S. Marshal to help him rescue her. The presence of this officer of the law tells us more about the changing situation.

Mollie had been a Roman Catholic as a child but now joined in with Dickey and the Presbyterian group. She was in the thick of efforts to raise funds for the building of the church. Her group was called the "Muffin and Crumpet Society" and their socials not only raised money but served an important social function in a community where entertainments and activities were otherwise limited.

The women of Skagway were known as either "respectable" or "unfortunate", the latter being a euphemism for the prostitutes, of whom there were large numbers, typical of the times. Mollie was enough of a free spirit to be genuinely concerned about the welfare of both on the frontier. On one occasion she asked her minister to visit an "unfortunate" who was seriously ill at Clancy's brothel. Dickey tells the story in his diary:

Soul of virtue and honor herself, Miss Walsh was risking the censure of the respectable women of Skagway and indeed risking her own reputation, when she nursed the sick girl at Clancy's. She told me they were school-mates back home. A Roman Catholic, the prostitute had asked for a priest, but there was none. Seeing a Douay Bible on the bed-side table, I read the story of the lamb that was lost and was found.

While repeating the Lord's prayer, Miss Walsh anticipated the girl's wish and held the crucifix to her lips. The dying girl's eyes spoke her gratitude. The funeral service, two days later, was held in our church, which scandalized some people. Nearly fifty unfortunates were there, their painted faces and gaudy ornaments marking them from the respectables, some of whom sat aloof and disapproving.[8]

In the funeral Dickey read the story of the woman taken in adultery as the Scripture and chose as his text the verse "Neither do I condemn you. Go and sin no more". The thrust of the sermon was an urging of the unfortunates to leave their occupation and seek a less demeaning life. He promised to arrange whatever assistance they needed. More than three quarters of the young women responded to his invitation, and arrangements were made to find new futures for them.

71

A Captain O'Brien offered free transportation to Vancouver or Seattle for any of these women, inasmuch as boats were full coming north but empty returning south. Dickey arranged for the church trustees to give a letter of credit to Captain O'Brien for one thousand dollars, an amount equal to a couple weeks wages for each girl in 1898 when the going rate for prostitution was two dollars a trick. This was ample enough to get each girl settled in whichever city she chose as a place to make a new start.

The madame at Clancy's was furious of course, so Mollie and Priscilla went back again with the same U.S. Marshal to help the women get their belongings. The ladies of the Church, who were not all so lacking in understanding and sympathy, or perhaps chagrined at their earlier attitude, prepared a banquet for them all. The whole church saw the girls off on the *S.S. Shamrock* while Mollie and Priscilla went aboard to get the girls all settled in their cabins. Their eager response to an opportunity for a new start indicates that for many of them the northern adventure had not turned out happily.

Spring came and the "would be" miners began to flood over the White Pass into the Yukon, thousands every day. Dickey moved on with them and Mollie went part way up the pass to the village of Log Cabin where there was a North West Mounted Police station at the point where the Canadian border was later established. There she opened a grub-tent and was beloved for her kindness even as she prospered.

Two men vied for Mollie's affections, both mule skinners on the trail, both successful and popular. She evidently chose the wrong suitor because when she and her husband sold out both businesses for $100,000 at the height of the gold rush, they moved to San Francisco where he squandered the money. In a fit of depression, he shot and killed Mollie, the "angel of the White Pass" as she was to be remembered by her many friends on both sides of the Alaska - Yukon border.

Meanwhile, as American writers like Longfellow and Stowe before him had established certain Canadian images during the Expulsion of the Acadians and the Underground Railroad, Robert Service, a wandering Scottish poet then living in Canada, fixed forever the image of the north in his "Law of the Yukon" quoted above. On a more positive note, also from "The Spell of the Yukon" this bard concludes:

> There's gold, and it's haunted and haunting;
> It's luring me on as of old;
> Yet it isn't the gold that I'm wanting
> So much as just finding the gold.
> It's the great, big, broad land 'way up yonder,
> It's the forests where silence has lease;
> It's the beauty that thrills me with wonder,
> It's the stillness that fills me with peace.[9]

72

13.

GLIMPSES OF THE FUTURE

As previous centuries faded from the screen, the twentieth century came into view as the age of technology. The stage was set for a new level of inter-relationships between Americans and Canadians, a century of co-operation that many people on both sides of the border believed was certain to lead to free trade and other aspects of "manifest destiny." For many, especially expansionist American politicians, this even included the possibility of political reunification. Such a re-integration of the old United Empire was within grasp and has emerged as a possibility again, but in a new form. However, it was not to be at that time, despite all the positive predictions of pundits at the turning of that century.

The foundations for cooperation in a more technological century were laid typically by Thomas Edison, the American inventor of electricity, and Sir Alexander Graham Bell, the Canadian inventor of the telephone. No two inventions have been more critical to what would follow, and Canadians and Americans have been sharing each other's technology ever since. They shared with the rest of the world as well, but these two countries had an impact on each other at a level unthinkable elsewhere on the planet.

If television, computers and space age technology would come to dominate the second half of the twentieth century, there can be little doubt that the first half belonged to such inventions as electricity, radio and telegraph, airplanes and automobiles. The importance of each of these was clearly anticipated by cross border activity in the closing years of the nineteenth century on this continent, though like today, few ordinary people believed these wonders would come to pass.

Alexander Graham Bell had also been Canada's foremost experimenter in glider airplanes, anticipating power flight at his retreat on Cape Breton Island in Nova Scotia, and paralleling the work of the Wright Brothers in America who mastered powered flight prior to the turn of the century.

The first North American motor car, or "steam motor carriage" was built in Canada by Henry Seth Taylor in Stanstead, Quebec in 1867. Known as the Steam Buggy, it was followed by a variety of cars produced in America including the first gasoline model built by Duryea Brothers in Springfield, Mass. in 1894.

These early automobile and airplane models were but a prelude to things to come, much like Edison's first light bulb and Bell's first telephone. These glimpses of the future at the turn of the last century are similar in terms of hints and insights to the turning of another century at present. People could see the outline of what was to come, but they could scarcely bring themselves to believe it would all happen.

In reality, practically all these technological wonders that appeared like science-fiction to many, were accomplished in the very first few decades of the twentieth century. In retrospect, the most adventuresome predictors of the future now look conservative with respect to progress in the economy, technology and industrial development. However, they were wrong about the likely extent of Canadian-American reintegration and they were dead wrong in their pessimism about spiritual and moral issues.

On the spiritual front, things looked bleak, at least for organized religion. An economic depression lasting a decade almost up to the turn of the century led to mission cutbacks in new territories. The great era of church building was over and a new generation was less enthusiastic about maintaining these architectural wonders, many of which had forty year mortgages financed in Europe. Attendance at religious services was abysmal, leading to splits, attempts at reform, artificial unions and sects everywhere. Only new religions seemed to thrive, the Mormons managing to have their state of Utah recognized in 1897 and the Jehovah's Witnesses preparing for a whole new Kingdom to be established by God in the year 1914.

The seminaries of mainstream Christian denominations were almost empty, so congregations were often led by untrained lay leaders. These pretentious gentlemen frequently promoted simplistic beliefs resulting in a literal interpretation of scripture for the first time in the history of the church. They presumed to reveal the simple truth of the gospel which the corrupt church had conspired to conceal from the people for so long. Scholarship had once been the preserve of the church but now intelligent people were embarrased by the inability of the church to relate to science, history or social theory. It seemed obvious that organized religion was a spent force. As the twentieth century unfolded, nothing could have been further from the truth as churches rebounded and continued to flourish in every community of North America.

Before the actual turning of the century, the predictors were equally wrong about sexual and social mores and the future of family life. They had been too conservative about economic progress and technological advances, and they were also unduly pessimistic about the future of morality in society as a whole, though the trends of the times supported their pessimism.

For example, by the end of the nineteenth century the North American rate of alcohol consumption at over 100 liters per annum for every man, woman and child had far surpassed the European level. The gin drinking capacity of English children in London, England, was itself enough to spur the founding of the Salvation Army, but it was in North America that high bar stools were first installed to assist the younger patrons. Many of them were child laborers in factory and mine, and not all of them took their pay home, especially those who lived in gangs on the streets. There were no legal age restrictions governing the sale of alcohol in the Victorian era.

The Temperance Movement sponsored by the moribund churches had little impact, so the turn of the century predictions were pessimistic about the social and economic consequences of excessive alcohol consumption. Yet, though no one then could foresee it, the rate of alcohol consumption dropped a full 50% to less than fifty liters per person today. This came about through neither legislated controls nor outright prohibition, but through progressive changes in society itself.

Likewise, Victorian society believed sexual relations were a necessary but nasty business, especially in the home, even between loving and respectful spouses. The oafish, insensitive men had their needs, and the finer feminine creatures would have to indulge them from time to time, but the latter were to expect no pleasure. This social convention was supported by the position of the regressive churches of the time, Protestant and Catholic alike, who taught that the only purpose of marital relations was the procreation of children.

These dictums greatly affected the masses in North America and elsewhere, though the experience of the more licentious Queen Victoria herself was closer to the boudoir habits of the European aristocracy, who observed few restrictions, either at home in the palace or elsewhere in their social circle. The direct result of Victorian teaching on sexuality and its concomitant hypocrisy was an acceptance of, and an indulgence in prostitution to an extent that is almost impossible to imagine a century later.

At the time, there was no reason to anticipate more progressive teachings from the twentieth century church, or the advent of women's liberation. These and

75

other factors would change everything with respect to sexual expectations between loving partners in the home and in other responsible relationships. But prior to the turn of the century it was assumed that most sexual activity would take place outside the home as a favor to the lady of the house. In Europe this activity was discreet but in North America the resulting public licentiousness was flagrant.

There were laws against public bawdy houses but every city and town had a large number of them, a thousand in New York City at the turn of the century. The most reliable count had been published earlier by the Superintendent of Police in 1866, when there were only 621 registered brothels in New York. He was attempting to refute charges by Bishop Simpson of the Methodist Church that there were as many prostitutes in New York as there were Methodists. [10] With a half dozen girls in each place and perhaps twice that number free-lancing, that would be less than 12,000 "whores," or one for every twenty adult males resident in the city of 1,000,000 souls, a figure consistent with statistics gathered later in the nineteenth century at Cincinnati and Philadelphia. [11]

There were several hundred brothels in mid-sized cities like New Orleans and approximately two dozen each in small towns like Moose Jaw and Owen Sound. The impotent churches of the times fulminated against them in vain, unaware that their own teachings were fostering the problem. Of these examples, New Orleans and Moose Jaw have been documented most extensively because their reputations were among the most notorious, though they were not untypical.

Upon arrival, "You came out of the Moose Jaw station, turned left on River Street and you could have been in New Orleans. If it was early in the day you could see girls waving from the windows of the hotels across the street. If they caught your eye they'd call you up. By night the streets were filled with men roaming around, and the traffic down to the whore houses at the other end of the street was something to see. There was nothing attractive about any of the houses or in fact about most of the girls. But they were great places for railway workers, particularly if you happened to hit town on paydays." [12]

In Europe it had been estimated that during the last quarter of the nineteenth century one adult in three had contracted a major venereal disease at least once in their life. [13] By the turn of the century, some American medical researchers of this "social emergency" believed that 50% of North American males were infected with gonorrhea. [14] The changes that brought this figure to less than 0.2% for all venerial diseases a hundred years later had as much to do with a more mature sexuality as with the discovery of penicillin, neither of which was expected at the previous century's end. Pessimists in every era of transition aside, not all changes are for the worse.

At the end of the nineteenth century the going rate for the higher priced prostitutes in the bordellos of the Klondike and in San Francisco was five dollars. In most of middle America a "trick" with a regular whore at a hotel was $2.00, the price of a shave and a haircut, but not as time consuming. It is little short of amazing that this part of the normal landscape of that era has almost disappeared from consciousness, except on the fringes of society, in the completely different moral atmosphere at the end of the twentieth century.

Race too played a prominent part in the prostitution ethos of the previous century. Women on the margins of society were the most vulnerable and easily attracted into this trade. Immigrant women in many cases, but Native Indian women sold by their men all along the developing frontier, and impoverished Negro women in North American cities were especially available and popular among white male customers. At every level of society these men displayed a need to regard such women as both wildly exotic and also inferior to their "beloved" at home. Brothels in the Canadian northern prairie city of Saskatoon, for example, were actually organized by race: White, Black and Oriental,15 with no shortage of Natives free-lancing on the street. Needless to say, practically 100% of the patrons were White.

An ironic joke used to be, "What do you call a Black man in Regina, Saskatchewan (A part of Canada once more Anglo-Saxon than Wyoming)? Answer: "A tourist." The truth is that an historic co-mingling of races had reached the most remote parts of North America one hundred years ago via prostitution as attested by this press report of police raids one Valentine's Day in Regina.

"The first call was at Jack Webster's 'Nigger Club' at 1660 Osler Street. Raids followed at 1776 and 1802 Quebec St., 1932 Toronto St. and 1400 Rae St. as well as another back on Osler at the Regina Cafe. In each house the "tenant" was a Negro and most of the dozen prostitutes taken into custody were Negroes. When they appeared in court the following day and pleaded guilty, jail sentences without the usual option of a fine were imposed." Their lawyer, C.A. Wood, raised what was probably the first public outcry in Regina against racial discrimination. He charged that the police had raided the houses not because they were brothels but because they were Negro brothels.16

Given the history of co-mingling during the slavery era, it can hardly be assumed that America remained more racially "pure" in the matter of prostitution, with both the exploitation and the discrimination that went with the trade. The upshot of the racial factor is simply that the races of North America are probably more mixed than many people realize. It may be assumed that many of the ten million Hispanics are mixed White-Black-Native, and that a great majority of thirty five million Afro-Canadians and Afro-Americans are mixed, for a variety of reasons. The five million Metis, Native and Inuit are also largely mixed, and it may also be assumed that an equal number of Whites are mixed in some measure by now.

This suggests that as many as 100 million of the 300 million citizens of North America may be of mixed race. Though it is often in tiny proportions, this unrecognized but steady expansion of the gene pool in the average family over the centuries, may be a factor yet to be documented in accounting for the vitality of North American culture. In just one more generation this may produce a population in which the majority has mixed ancestry. Small in-bred groups can go on marrying their cousins but North American culture as a whole may be almost ready to move on to a broader "new world" identity.

At least one other salient development came out of the prostitution business. Large numbers of male immigrants found their life partners in such houses and either bought their women or wooed them, and lived happily ever after. Tens of thousands of such unions occurred in which both parties quickly buried and forgot the circumstances of their coming together. Their stories would be reminiscent of Gomer, the prostitute in the Bible who married the preacher, Hosea - except that most of these men did not neglect their partners, forcing them to return to the trade. This was a kindly generation of men and women, unlikely to share the judgmental attitudes of church and high society. After the turn of the century they would foster a new sexual ethic in the home.

Given the demographics of the times, the numbers of young single men, plus the numbers of prostitutes who did not stay in that profession into old age, it must simply be true that the great-grandparents of many people today had stories they never passed along. Careful examination of almost any family tree before the year 1900, however, reveals a large number of "illegitimate" offspring and other mysteries that are not otherwise easily explained.

Today there are approximately half a million prostitutes for 300 million people in North America. In 1900 there were 2 million prostitutes for the 100 million people on this continent, a figure 1,200% higher than the current rate. Is it that modern people have become more virtuous, or were there other changes? The century turned, and with it a new era of optimism and seemingly unstoppable progress, social as well as economic and technological.

This continued until 1914 and on through the twentieth century in North America, with only a few major interruptions due to the set-backs associated with the Great Depression and the World Wars. It would appear that, with certain adjustments, church and family are social institutions that survive and adapt to the turnings of the centuries. The question remains whether or not anyone has learned how to support and facilitate progressive changes in society, or will counterproductive measures be promoted again?

Pundits looking at the trends a hundred years ago were simply unable to identify the deeper currents of human aspiration that enable certain relationships to endure in spite of the many reasons to despair. Some of the same pessimism prevails today, while optimists and people of faith may choose to see, in the current turning of a century, an opportunity to extend the potential benefits of a new era beyond church and family to the community.

The purpose of examining the sharp drop in alcohol consumption by 50%, an improvment of the venerial disease situation by 96% and a 1,200% improvement in prostitution in the twentieth century is to suggest hope for the future again. For example, drug use could drop by 50% in the twenty-first century, AIDS can be controlled, and skyrocketing abortion figures at the end of the twentieth century may be 1,200% higher than they might be a hundred years from now.

People in the year 2100 may be amazed to learn of twentieth century drug abuse, and abortion as a frequent and crude means of birth control. Such changes appear to come more through progressive social developments which can be fostered, than through legislated prohibitions or condemnations in church.

The nineteenth century of conflicting border claims and confrontation, from the American War of Independence to the Alaska Boundary Dispute, was over but the North American Empire remained divided. A century lay ahead in which the potential partner nations would experience much cooperation together, along with deep divisions within. The twentieth century landscape would still be defined by cleavages along such lines as race, gender, language and religion. Yet hope endures, and, like the nineteenth century before it, the twentieth century concludes with opportunities for renewal. The jury is out on the question of what values will endure into the twenty-first century.

— Salvation Corners Is Still In Business —

One hundred years ago newspapers across Canada carried a feature about Owen Sound, the city with a glorious intersection known as "Salvation Corners" just east of a notorious intersection which was described as "Damnation Corners."

Because it was the seaport, rail head and highway terminus, in 1874 Owen Sound boasted twenty inns where hard liquor was not the only vice available for purchase. By 1886, there were also twelve taverns in the town licensed to serve liquor but not food; these were in operation twenty-four hours each day, seven days a week. Damnation Corners acquired its name because just a block away from Salvation Corners four of the most infamous of these taverns flourished. They were known by such names as Coleman's Tavern, The Blue Water, Pig's Ear and Bucket of Blood.

One block east on Division Street (now Tenth Street), St. George's Anglican Church, Division Street Presbyterian (now United), First Baptist and The Disciples of Christ (now Nazarene) were all sturdy stone structures that looked as if they were built for eternity. These four churches still offer the spectrum of Christian traditions: the power of ritual, a community of faith, evangelical zeal and fundamental convictions. They are representative of the spiritual vitality in Owen Sound from Roman Catholic through Lutheran to Pentecostal and Jewish in a swirl of ongoing spiritual dynamics that now includes everything from Orthodox to Eastern mystic and New Age spirituality.

The four taverns and houses of ill repute have all disappeared from Damnation Corners. That is not to say that sin, pain, heartbreak and exploitation have disappeared from the modern world. People still need the love of God in order to love each other. At the close of the century and the beginning of a new millennium, the four churches on Salvation Corners invite you to drive down Tenth Street to see for yourself who is still in business. If you are looking for spiritual vitality that is good for the long haul, join one of these congregations for Sunday worship.   © 1995 Dr. Brian A. Brown

80

PART TWO

WINDOWS ON THE PRESENT

(Americans and Canadians in the Twentieth Century)

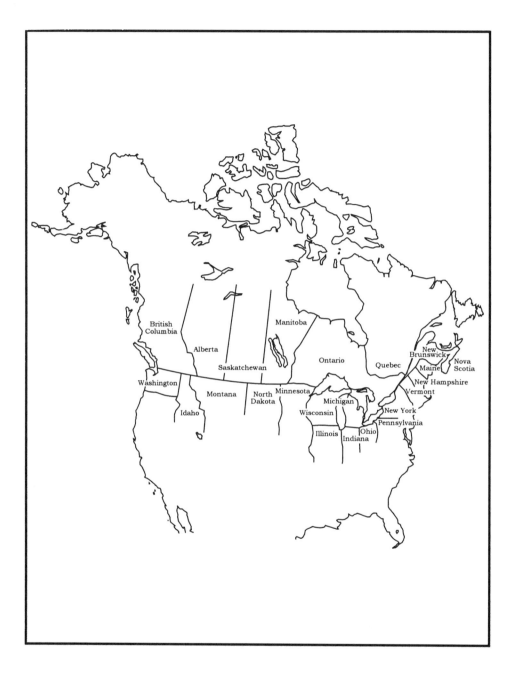

The Boozy Border
(Billions from contraband liquor now fund modern sports and entertainment)

14.

RUM RUNNERS AND DRUG DEALERS

Four and twenty yankees
Were feeling mighty dry.
They came across to Canada
And bought a keg of rye.

When the keg was empty,
They all began to sing,
To hell with the president:
God save the King![17]

It is little short of astounding that a virtual war, fought in the 1920's, within memory of a few who are still living, has been forgotten or blocked out by social historians. Along the US - Canada border more than 1,000 ships and airplanes at any one time were engaged over what was actually a thirteen year period. The action took place in more than one thousand ports and coves near the border along the eastern seaboard, up and down the St. Lawrence River, all over the Great Lakes and in and out of the bays and inlets that are so common on the Pacific coast. The confrontations took place on a thousand back roads and open fields along the border, dozens of railway crossings and at fifty-odd inland official border crossings.

This was the Prohibition era in which billions of dollars of profits were derived each year from an illicit trade in beverage alcohol in which several thousand crooks, gangsters and criminals of all stripes worked in collusion with a comparable number of corrupt custom officials, police, court officers and politicians on both sides of the border. The era has been trivialized and romanticized, but financial empires were established then which thrive today in legal alcohol trade, sports, media and other acceptable fields. Canadian Seagrams, the largest distillery operation in the world, and a corporation which is now buying up increasing chunks of the American movie industry, is perhaps the best known example, and that enterprise alone accounted for no more than five percent of the trade.

This story is bigger than any of the three recognized wars that had been fought along that border, bigger than all three together. The reasons it is so conveniently forgotten may have to do with the total futility of the undertaking, the legacy of organized crime that continues, and the shame of a corrupt era in the history of a society that prefers to glorify its past. Moreover, the "enemy" were conspirators who cooperated on both sides of the law as well as on both sides of the border. Documentation is almost as murky as the morality in question, though daily newspaper accounts, court records and government investigations of Customs and Excise officials provide as much information as needed. There could hardly be a better example of the adage, "Those who forget the lessons of history are doomed to repeat them," as America fights an almost identical War on Drugs on its southern border seventy five years later with much the same results.

The attempts at prohibition of the manufacture and sale of alcoholic beverages grew out of temperance movements led by protestant churches in the 1800's in an effort to combat crime and excesses on the frontiers, both north and south of the border. The momentum in this attempt to legislate morality reached its peak in Canada first, where prohibition was adopted by law in all provinces in 1915. It was repealed by federal statute in 1919 because it proved unenforceable.

Prohibition was then attempted in the United States over a longer period, from 1920 to 1933, with the same near total lack of success in enforcement. All this gave the era the nickname "the roaring twenties," referring to the well organized clandestine merriment and also the roaring inferno of violence. This was the very opposite of the result sought by those attempting to restrict the use and abuse of alcohol through legislated prohibitions.

The fact that Canada had finished its experiment before America started was significant. The population of each country accessed its supply of contraband from their next door neighbor. In the final analysis, it was the Canadians who made most of the money because of the length of prohibition in the United States and the much greater number of customers there.

The almost secretive history of this war is indicated by the personal story of America's most famous gangster, Al Capone, the archetype of the species. His typical story ends in dissolute tragedy in spite of his muscle and his millions. For years he managed to present a fictionalized version of his life and have it accepted as history.

Alphonso Caponi persuaded several biographers that he was born in Brooklyn, New York, whereas it is known now that he was an immigrant whose family came to America from Naples, Italy. This "crony evidence" is now regarded as primary and accepted as fact; the same kind of reassessment is happening now regarding his connection with Canada.

Capone had his henchmen establish a hideout of last resort across the border early in the twenties. Many of his underlings enjoyed their own periods of "R & R" in this not unlikely setting of Moose Jaw, Saskatchewan, on the western Canadian prairies. Moose Jaw was chosen because of its direct rail link with Chicago on the little used Soo Line, which only ever really flourished through smuggling during prohibition. Capone had no time or interest in his hideout for many years because the "underground" tunnels of Chicago sufficed and lent their name to the criminal movement.

Folk tradition, of the kind which ultimately established his name and birthplace, also has it that Moose Jaw became known as "Little Chicago" in Canada because of an underground tunnel the gentlemen from Chicago paid to have built from the railway to the Empress Hotel on River Street, a distance of about five hundred feet. "Scarface" Capone needed these elaborate arrangements on February 15, 1929 the day after he wiped out the Bugs Moran gang of Irish hoods in the Saint Valentine's Day Massacre.

He fled the combined forces of the law and underground foes, disguised as a woman with a couple of children, north to Canada on the Soo Line into Moose Jaw. Capone never emerged from the train station but went straight to the Empress where he planned to lay low until the heat was off. Unfortunately nobody had warned "Da Boss" that this most infamous "red light" district in Canada was rife with syphilis at the time. Capone contracted the disease from a Canadian prostitute and eventually died of it in Florida after a stint in prison.

Even Moose Javians have difficulty believing the rumors, as if this crime boss on the lam would have signed the guest book at city hall, but when questioned about his Canadian connection during a trial in 1931, old Scarface barely managed to control the twinkle in his eye. His typically evasive reply contained the usual mafioso hint that the speaker was not telling the whole story. He said, "I don't even know what street Canada is on." Reporter Ron Greenaway described the moment this way: "At this he showed all the satisfaction of a wit who had spoken memorably and was gloating over it."[18]

The Moose Jaw connection is better documented in the case of the Bronfman family from Brandon, Manitoba, owners of Seagrams. Once prohibition was repealed in Canada, the Bronfmans established a system of distilleries in the southern parts of every province. Especially in western Canada there was a string of liquor export houses in every town along the border, although none of it was "licensed for export" to the United States.

Head of the western operation during the prohibition years was Harry Bronfman. His brother-in-law, David Gellerman, lived in Moose Jaw, served as the principal Chicago connection and was the fall guy, going to jail on numerous occasions over import-export technicalities. It was not until months after the St. Valentine's Day massacre that Bronfman himself got arrested in Moose Jaw and briefly jailed in Regina before acquittal on a technicality with the aid of top lawyers and some "sympathetic" federal officials, rushed in from Ottawa.

Historians who maintain that there was no connection between all this activity and the thirsty customers in Chicago should compare these subtle indications of the Capone connection with even better known facts about Canadian sources of supply for Detroit, New York and San Francisco. The old mobster may have been smarter, but the legacy of organized crime and violence lives on in all those cities also. Or, perhaps people in Chicago simply drank less - if there is anyone who would prefer to believe that explanation.

Modern Moose Jaw, meanwhile, a city of not fifty thousand, in the middle of the Canadian prairies, remains architecturally the finest example of the Victorian era in the old west. There are a couple of especially fine Gothic churches that helped uplift the community once they got their own act together, and the Italianate Renaissance railway station of the CPR is also worth viewing. Today there is a modern health spa situated at a major natural hot spring, and other industries to supplement the grain farming and railway yards. Al Capone or his henchmen might be less at home at the modern Temple Gardens Mineral Spa or the Golden Nugget Casino than at the new Nevada Nickels Bar situated on old River Street in a hotel that has been there a hundred years. The tunnels under Main Street are a tourist attraction today.

A truer assessment of the size and scale of the illicit liquor trade in Western Canada in particular, and in the country as a whole, is seen in the western drinkers' preference for a particular whiskey, nearly a century later. The liquor trade finally became huge enough that it was requiring so much grain that there was little left for flour, bread and other cereal requirements, domestic and export. Millions of tons of Canadian grains of all sorts were being diverted to the export liquor industry each year at the height of US prohibition. The parallel today is the Colombian peasant family whose fields yield a bountiful harvest of cocaine while they must import vegetables to eat.

As a consequence, and rather than attempt to shut down the liquor trade entirely, the Canadian government absolutely prohibited the distilleries to use any food grains in their operations with the exception of rye - which is well suited for whiskey but less suitable for all other cereal purposes. Similar in taste to Bourbon, an American corn whiskey, rye whiskey sold well in the US during prohibition and has remained an overwhelming favorite in Canada ever since.

As trainloads competed with pickup trucks inland, shiploads vied with rowboats on both coasts and the Great Lakes. The waybill destination for the cargo was almost invariably "Mexico" but Bob Johnston, a modern day commentator for the CBC takes special delight in recounting his own research regarding the arrest and release three times on one night of a particular rowboat. It had a Canadian crew working on the Detroit River, and was laden to the gunwales with cases of whiskey, covered under bills of lading showing the destination to be "Peru".[19]

The abuse of alcohol was no doubt a severe problem in the early days of both countries as is the case with illicit drug use today. Without government regulation, poison brews were often marketed with deadly results. The distortions in the economy, the spread of violence and the establishment of organized crime left their marks on communities north and south of America's border with Canada, just as is happening again seventy five years later around another border in cities like Miami, Dallas, and Los Angeles as well as Tijuana, Monterey and Mexicali.

For those who agree that substance abuse is a moral issue, the problem is not leaky borders but empty lives. The solution is obviously not found in "blue laws" passed by religious conservatives on a moral crusade but a new public and private spirituality that offers meaning and purpose in life. The question of establishing ethics on the negative bases of restrictions, prohibitions and censorship cries out for a change to addressing problems with positive values such as meaningful employment, education and fulfilling lifestyles. The ethical issue thrown into stark relief by the prohibition issue will be revisited on a spectrum of issues in the next century.

Colombia is no more responsible for America's drug problem today than Canada was responsible for America's drinking problem in the twenties. History indicates that prohibition has the same chance of success in the issues of restricting gun control, racist hate literature, and abortion. Moreover, prohibition is a band-aid solution in each case which fails to address the problems. A new public spirituality may be required across the spectrum of social issues.

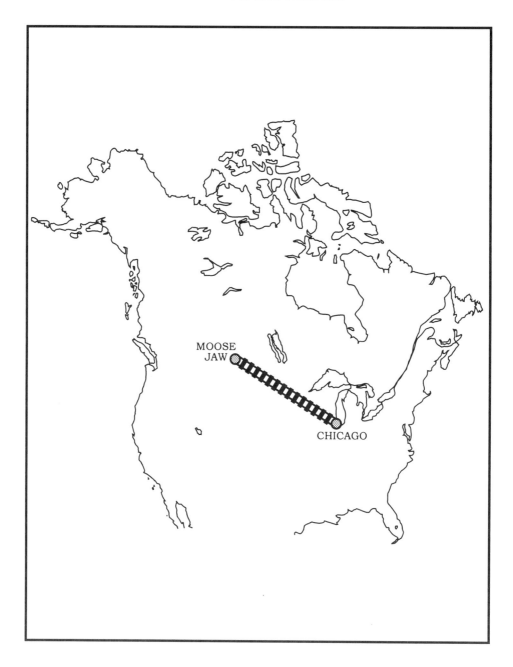

The Soo Line, 1920-1933

15.

CLEANING UP THE ACT

One of the first clear signs of this emerging new spirit was the organization of the Greenpeace Foundation in 1970. The concern was not entirely new but Greenpeace was among the first to address the environment with an almost religious zeal that would characterize many movements in North America and elsewhere toward the end of the twentieth century as people in many parts of the world grope toward futures with meaning and purpose.

Founded by David McTaggart in Vancouver, Greenpeace soon moved beyond the Canadian borders to become Greenpeace International, championed in the United States by John F. Kennedy Jr. and others. World headquarters are now in Amsterdam, and Greenpeace remains vigilant from rain forest to nuclear test sites and other environmental hot spots - in cooperation with dozens of other volunteer agencies it inspired or spawned as a movement.

From protesting abuses on the seal hunt in Newfoundland to old growth forest preservation in British Columbia, and around the world in ships like the *Sea Shepherd* and the *Rainbow Warrior*, Greenpeace has attracted a following from school children through the boomer generation to thoughtful seniors.

At the official level, such concerns were addressed surprisingly early in the United States and Canada by an international governmental agency that has earned the respect of many. With a name that should not be confused with any part of the War on Drugs, "The International Joint Commission" stood guard on many of the same issues since 1909, long before public awareness. This, the oldest of Canadian-American intergovernmental organizations, no doubt laid some of the groundwork for the birth of Greenpeace and others, illustrating that government initiatives can be altruistic, sensible and successful.

Established by the Boundary Waters Treaty of 1909 between the United States and Canada, the IJC was initially concerned with west coast issues as part of the fallout from the Alaska Boundary Dispute. It deals with the apportionment, conservation and development of water and related resources anywhere along the international boundary separating the two countries. Fisheries and Hydro-electric power have occupied the center of the commission's attention and since 1912 nearly one hundred contentious issues have been successfully adjudicated for the governments, other agencies, private companies or individual appellants.

There are three American and three Canadian Commissioners but voting and decision making patterns have been fairly bi-partisan for so long that the commission jealously guards this reputation on which so much of its success is founded. There are offices in both Washington and Ottawa which enjoy considerable independence in spite of a small staff and a limited budget.

The International Joint Commission was originally given many quasi-judicial powers and investigative authority and it was expected that it might become the court of arbitration for a wide range of other issues in the era before hopes for "reciprocity" or free trade were quashed by the Canadian election of 1911. This model had been used earlier on occasion by the British and Americans to establish Jay's Treaty after the War of Independence and the Treaty of Washington after the Civil War. Tampering with the formula led to less unanimity in Alaska but more recently the IJC has been used as the model for the dispute resolution mechanism for NAFTA which has only to establish a track record to earn similar respect and influence.

Whether prompted by secular concerns for "protecting the environment" for themselves and their children, or religious commitments to "respect for creation", this creation/environment movement ultimately succeeds among North Americans on the basis of an altruistic spirit, in both government and private agencies. It is this "spirit" which begins to inform us of the "spirituality" required in the future.

While exemplifying positive elements in many religious traditions, this spiritual quest is especially attractive to people who may have no formal religious "baggage," as they might call it, but who no longer see the earth as "ours," or even as God's gift to humanity alone. If anything, it is the other way around in both the scriptures and in modern sensibilities.

The quest to discover this spiritual balance may be the final challenge of the twentieth century. It is seen most clearly in issues like concern for the environment, peace and human rights. It must be extended to politics, media and entertainment and most especially business where the search for values and vision has come most into focus. As the century draws to a close "mission statements" emanate from every corporation, if not most local divisions and departments.

Unlike Americans, Canadians have difficulty with this because of a built-in bias against business, especially any business that is successful. Be that as it may, sometime around 1990 American business stopped looking to Japan or Europe for inspiration. Before the turn of the century, America's own business gurus, Alvin Toffler (Power Shift), Tom Peters (Thriving on Chaos and Liberation Management), Stephen R. Covey (Seven Habits of Highly Successful People), James Collins and Jerry Porras (Built to Last) and Peter Senge (The Fifth Dimension) had begun to write priority chapters on the spiritual dimension.

In terms of the business of doing business, America has come home at last. Along with technological "glimpses" into the future, at this century's turning there may be spiritual glimpses also. The challenge facing North American industry is to find ways for business to cooperate with governmental agencies and citizen groups in applying this new found awareness of spiritual values to the environment. The situation at the close of the twentieth century is serious as regards air and water pollution, endangerment of species essential for the fabric of nature's seamless gown, depletion of the ozone layer and other factors which could make life in the next century precarious.

If anyone in the world can find the way to do this in harmony with a healthy bottom line, it will be American business in concert with altruistic government policy and concerned consumer citizens. These factors may not all come together until the new millennium has begun, but the required elements were falling into place in the closing years of the twentieth century. The industrial complex of North America is already fully integrated, and while this newly re-United Empire does not stand alone in the ecosystem, this society has a crucial role.

Commemorative Postage Stamp

The Steam Buggy
(The first car in North America, built in Quebec in 1867)

16.

IN LOVE WITH THE AUTOMOBILE

The number one business in North America in the twentieth century was the automotive industry. It was also the first on this continent to become fully integrated through the US-Canada Automotive Products Trade Agreement of 1965, known as APTA, or more popularly, "Autopact."

In spite of the fact that a whopping 20% of North American cars sold in the United States are actually made in Canada, most Americans appear blissfully unaware of this arrangement, as they are in a number of other sectors of their economy in which the Canadian component is practically invisible.

The fact is that for every thousand cars the Goliath US imports from Canada, Canada as an industrial David imports a thousand cars from the US. Economies of scale plus the sharing of cheap sources of coal, steel and other raw materials make this integrated industry one of the most efficient in the world. With its predecessors dating back to 1904, Autopact is a major factor in making the motor car available to practically every family in these lands of vast spaces, helping to thus define North American society. For either country to withdraw from Autopact would be to further undermine the position of the North American automobile industry in the world.

It was the success of Autopact that convinced economists north and south of the border that free trade in other goods could also work well in this context. Politicians are loath to confuse people with the facts when more votes can be won with simple slogans like "America First" or "Buy Canadian" but even many of the most protectionist politicians were convinced by the weight of evidence of mutual advantage. When the North American Free Trade Association succeeded APTA in 1992, NAFTA was signed and implemented by President George Bush of the Republican Party and Prime Minister Brian Mulroney of the Progressive Conservative Party, the very political groupings who had most vigorously opposed "reciprocity" or free trade in any form for nearly a century.

The advantages of accessing each other's markets and serving the world together were made clear early on in the contest for dominance in the auto industry between General Motors and Ford. General Motors pulled enough competitors together and pioneered so many advances in technology that it became the largest corporation of any kind in America for most of the century. Ford, however, is the number one automaker in the world outside America, and has been so, right through the whole century, another fact little known by many Americans.

Ford achieved its dominant position overseas through Canada in 1904. Just a year after Henry Ford opened his first factory in Detroit, his company established Ford of Canada across the border in Windsor, Ontario. Parts were ferried across the Detroit River and assembled under the direction of Gordon M. McGregor in the facilities of the Walkerville Waggon Company. Not only did they sell well in Canada, this connection immediately opened up access to all parts of the then British Empire making Ford the most popular car in the British Isles, much of Africa, parts of Asia and everywhere "down under" in Australia and New Zealand. Ford has never looked back worldwide as a prime example of the value of free trade.

If the automobile has been a hallmark of North American lifestyle in the twentieth century, it has come at considerable cost to the environment. One major impact of privately owned vehicles, as opposed to public transportation on trains and subways, was the paving over of significant amounts of land in both countries, spreading out the cities, removing land from agricultural production and destroying wildlife habitat.

Earlier steam driven motorcars could not compete with gasoline powered internal combustion engines. Nor were "cleaner" electric or natural gas models able to catch on later. The petroleum industry became North America's second biggest business, a handmaiden to the auto industry and the largest single source of air pollution on the planet with a severe impact on larger cities.

The first commercial oil well in North America was drilled near Petrolia, Ontario, in 1857 by James Miller Williams. There the world's first refinery was built by Charles N. Tripp employing the technologies developed by Abraham Gesner, the Canadian inventor of kerosene. In the next seven years 27 refineries were established in the area. By then these wells were producing an unheard of 3,000 barrels per day. Two years later the first US oil industry got started in Pennsylvania when Edwin L. Drake made the first significant American strike near Titusville in 1859. The industry north and south of the border has been closely integrated from the beginning.

The love affair with the automobile has had such a hold on North Americans that many people have been willing to live shorter lives in an environment where they have difficulty breathing and sunshine has become a cancer threat, rather than accept limits on automobile ownership and use. However, this seemingly intractable problem is in the initial stage of resolution by the very combination of business, government and private efforts described earlier.

In response to public concern, the state and provincial governments of California and British Columbia were the first jurisdictions in the world to declare that zero emission standards for carcinogens from automobiles would be enforced by the end of the century. The auto industry has indicated that by exerting every effort, it can comply with these laws through new technology and manageable cost increases. Other jurisdictions have begun to pass similar laws and it is expected that the auto industry worldwide will be forced to comply if it expects to continue to have a share in the North American market.

In these ways the auto industry has become not only the model for free trade but also a leader in the efforts to enter the next century with a cleaner environment in North America at least. The fixation with the automobile has provided defining marks of this mobile culture, but it has also issued the greatest challenges in trade and the environment. These challenges and their solutions will be significant aspects of the history shared by Americans and Canadians in the twentieth century.

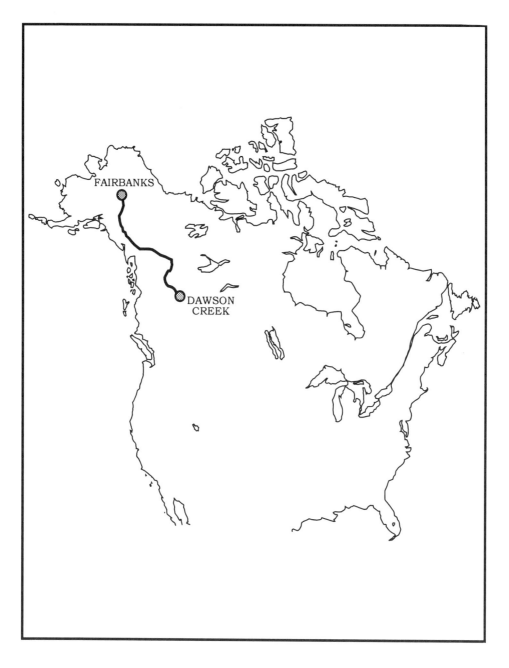

The Alaska Highway

17.

NORTH TO ALASKA

The two most grand construction "mega projects" in North American history are the Saint Lawrence Seaway and the Alaska Highway, dwarfing even the Panama Canal and the great continental railroads in many respects. The construction of the Alaska Highway was all the more remarkable because of the speed with which it was built and the circumstances that required it.

As it did through the first years of World War I, the United States attempted to stay out of World War II for important reasons that will be considered. However, on December 7, 1941, Japanese Vice-Admiral Chuichi Nagumo took a thirty three ship striking force to within 320 kilometres (200 miles) of the Hawaiian island of Oahu and the American Naval base at Pearl Harbor under cover of darkness.

The Japanese and Axis powers had been convinced that the US was about to enter the war on the side of Britain, Canada and their Commonwealth partners who were all that remained of the Allies at that point. The Japanese launched a preemptive strike of 360 airplanes from Nagumo's fleet against the American base, bombing eighteen US ships, destroying one hundred and seventy US airplanes and inflicting about 3,700 American casualties.

The immediate result was the American declaration of war, to the great relief of Canada and other democratic states. The American Pentagon quickly realized, however, that another US territory was vulnerable, as the subsequent Japanese invasion and occupation of parts of Alaska illustrated. Alaska was so vulnerable because it was huge and impossible to reach except for the coastal areas by slow ship and inland points by remote airstrips.

Canadian politicians became hysterical. Under the War Measures Act 20,000 Canadians of Japanese ancestry were taken from their west coast homes and placed in concentration camps far inland from the Pacific region when most of them lived. This racist activity occurred over the objections of the military who saw no threat from Japanese Canadians, and from the RCMP who made the point that, prior to this juncture of the war, no charges were laid against any citizens of Japanese extraction - regarding national security or any other matter! Similar prejudice was extended toward Ukrainian and German Canadians, without legal sanction but with political motivation. In Canada it is the War Measures Act that is invoked whenever the people panic and politicians need to appear decisive.

In a related, but more rational panic, the US pentagon requested Canadian permission to build an emergency road link to Alaska through two thousand kilometres of northern British Columbia and the Yukon territory, and the right to freely access that road through nearly two thousand kilometres more of existing Canadian highways in Alberta. The request was unprecedented and the two countries had a less than happy history of border disputes and occupations in that part of the continent. However, a war was on, Canadian resources were occupied elsewhere and the two countries had come a long way since "Fifty-Four, Forty or Fight" and the Alaska Boundary Dispute, so approval was granted.

From a security perspective, however, the highway project got started none too soon. While work progressed, Japan bombed the city of Dutch Harbor in Alaska and occupied the American islands of Kiska, Attu and Agattu. These were the only areas in North America to be successfully invaded by Axis forces in World War II. US forces recaptured them in 1943 after the Alaska Highway was completed when military personnel and supplies could be moved north.

If the road itself was not a marvel, its construction was a feat to rival the building of the pyramids. The original "passable track" road was rammed through five wilderness mountain ranges in only eight months during 1942. From the now famous "Mile Zero Post" at Dawson Creek, British Columbia it ran 2,333 km (1500 miles) to Big Delta on the Alaskan border. Then dubbed the ALCAN Military Highway, groups of US Army Engineers had worked from several staging areas at once, chopping, blasting and bulldozing up to 13 km (7 miles) per day.

In 1943 it became a permanent, all-weather, gravelled road eight metres (24 feet) wide and 2,451 km long (1600 miles) from Dawson Creek to Fairbanks, Alaska. Often referred to as one of the seven wonders of the modern world, this feat required the combined labor of eleven thousand American soldiers and sixteen thousand civilians, mostly Canadian. There were one hundred and thirty-three bridges and thousands of large culverts. The US bore the cost of the road and Canada paid for airfields, landing strips, telephone systems, buildings and other physical assets.

For the duration of the war, access to this military project was restricted but on April 3, 1946, Canada took possession of the portion of the road from Dawson Creek to the US border at Alaska and opened the road to unrestricted travel the next year. The US did the same on the American portion through Alaska. Small native bands paid a steep price in the overnight destruction of a stable lifestyle in one of the last areas of North America to be disrupted by modern culture and technology. The environment also took a savage beating and wildlife habitat was devastated.

Major environmental and human settlement issues remain in Alaska and Northern Canada, as they do elsewhere. The Alaska Highway ended the isolation of the north and integrated it into the life of North American society, though it remains distinct, as does each region of the continent. Certainly Alaskans and Yukoners have much more in common with each other than either of them have with the citizens of Ontario or Texas.

The Alaska Highway is all paved now and supports a huge commercial and tourist traffic. Maintenance costs have averaged over one hundred million dollars per year in the last fifty years, a five billion dollar tab for the annual effects of blizzards, floods and landslides in a land where -48 degree temperatures can cause a bulldozer blade to shatter like glass. Forestry, oil and mining are the principal industries at sites made accessible in every direction from the highway. Native self-government agreements on both sides of the border offer the hope that certain mistakes made elsewhere will not be repeated in the north.

Both the Yukon and British Columbia have experienced population growth and development since the building of the highway but the changes in Alaska have been even more dramatic. After the appropriate political process over several years, on January 3, 1959, President Dwight D. Eisenhower issued a proclamation declaring Alaska the forty-ninth state of the United States of America, the first new state since 1912 when Arizona and New Mexico achieved statehood. So much of the future of this continent may be determined by the rich resources of the north that the historical impact of the Alaska Highway on both Canadians and Americans is likely to be even more fully appreciated in the twenty-first century.

18.

HALF A CENTURY OF WAR

Even during the previous century of hostility there had been instances of military cooperation between the neighboring giants. A Canadian's rifle became US standard issue and the "gatling gun," the first effective machine gun, named after its American inventor, Richard Jordan Gatling, was first used north of the border in the Northwest Rebellion during the Battle of Batoche, May 9-12, 1885.

This first of a new generation of weaponry was given its field test in Canada by Gatling's eighteen year old nephew, Howard, known as "Gatling Gun Howard." He later accepted a land grant in Alberta from the crown for his contribution to the Canadian military and he became a Canadian citizen, farming northeast of Edmonton until his death in 1967.

In the twentieth century, such cooperation between Americans and Canadians became the absolute principle with only the rarest exception. In the early years Canadians were involved in the final actions worldwide of the disappearing British Empire: early "peacekeeping" undertakings in the South African Boer War and the intractable situation in the Sudan - neither very successful in the long term. Americans were still dabbling in hemispheric politics and gunboat diplomacy among their smaller neighbors to the south with equal lack of success or vision.

World War I, "The War to end all Wars" changed everything and made both Canada and the USA world powers on their own at a new level. At first Canada was perhaps too ready to respond to the call for assistance from Britain as "the mother country" and America was almost too reticent to get involved.

It is not the purpose here to review the entire history of that conflict, the bloodiest on the fields of battle in human history. It may have started as a quarrel among royal households in Europe but the fact that the first shots were fired in Sarajevo may indicate deeper currents of ancient hatreds. The war may have also served to sort out colonial empires in Africa and Asia but for many Canadians and Americans there seemed to be a clear distinction between the good guys and the bad guys, the British and French democracies versus the eastern European dictatorships.

The world changed as empires began to crumble, the communists took over in Russia, democracy stood the test, and the North American countries came of age on the world stage. The population of the United States was then half of what it was at the time of the Vietnam conflict in which the US lost 58,000 soldiers. The number of American fatalities was greater in WWI at about 60,000, twice the loss in proportion to the population. Little Canada was virtual cannon fodder for the war, suffering 60,600 deaths out of a population of one tenth the size of the US. Canadians have kept up their side of the partnership in even the most horrible circumstances.

In the old-style, counterproductive pattern of "making peace", the defeated were punished, restricted in future trade activities, and forced to pay steep reparations in cash and ships, and trains and anything else that could be moved to the lands of the victors. The practice seemed designed to ensure a future war in the next generation, though Canada and the United States were eventually able to see the wisdom in forgiving their portion of this "debt."

As a footnote to the First World War, a Canadian hero has become the feature of an American comic strip. It was Arthur Roy Brown of Carleton Place, Ontario, who shot down the famous German ace dogfighter, Baron von Richthofen. Captain Manfred von Richthofen flew a bright red Fokker Triplane and was known as "The Red Baron." On April 21, 1918 he was zooming down for the kill on the tail of a new Canadian flier, Second Lieutenant W. R. "Wop" May, when "Snoopy" Brown swooped in behind them in his "Sopwith Camel," an airplane supplied by the British RAF.

As Wop, the Red Baron and Snoopy skirted the tree tops in a line, Snoopy fired, causing the red plane to nosedive but it somehow landed upright in British held territory near Cappy, France. Richthofen must have hung on until then, but medical reports established that he died from just one bullet from Brown's mounted machine gun. Thus was born the favorite American legend of Snoopy and the Red Baron.

A second somber folk connection between the US and Canada from that sad conflict is a Canadian poem used by the American Legion and others at military funerals ever since. Dr. John McCrae of Guelph, Ontario, was a Major and First Brigade Surgeon in the Canadian Field Artillery. He wrote the poem in a scant twenty minutes of sorrow early in the morning of May 3, 1915 during the second battle of Ypres in Belgium.

> In Flanders fields the poppies blow
> Beneath the crosses, row on row,
> That mark our place; and in the sky
> The larks, still bravely singing, fly
> Scarce heard amid the guns below.
>
> We are the Dead. Short days ago
> We lived, felt dawn, saw sunset glow,
> Loved and were loved, and now we lie
> In Flanders fields.
>
> Take up our quarrel with the foe:
> To you from failing hands we throw
> The torch; be yours to hold it high.
> If ye break faith with us who die
> We shall not sleep, though poppies grow
> In Flanders fields.[20]

During the night McCrae had helped bury a young friend, Lieutenant Alexis Helmer. This poet-physician-soldier himself died two years later from pneumonia contracted in the trenches and lies buried in Wimereux Cemetery, Boulogne, France, but his inspired words point forever to both the futility of war and the hope for a better way.

The Second World War was as predictable as it was tragic. Somewhat fewer casualties on the battlefields were exceeded by a far greater loss of civilian lives, especially Jews, Gypsies and Russians, and again, years later there is the sense of futility. After five years of carnage, a radically different type of concluding settlement was implemented whereby, with American leadership, the victors assisted the defeated powers to rebuild, making permanent friends of former enemies. If they could sacrifice so much after the war to mutual advantage, could not governments and others find ways to circumvent such conflict in the first place at a great saving of lives and other costs?

Again there were many impressive examples of Canadian-American cooperation. Canadian conscripts fled to the States to escape the draft and American volunteers crossed the border to sign up early in the war, about five thousand each way. (A generation later a flow of twenty-five thousand American draft dodgers were likewise met by ten thousand Canadians signing up with the US forces *en route* to Vietnam.) Canada carried the brunt of the North American contribution early in the Second World War but, again, it was the US Cavalry to the rescue before the war could be concluded.

The causes of WW II seem to relate directly to the more typical conclusion of WW I, but by the time hostilities became unavoidable it was once again democracy against tyranny, even if democrats had not yet learned how to make lasting peace. Initially this was not a North American conflict. The spread of the war, loyalty to old alliances and the concern for democracy may have been the reasons the Canadian and American governments declared war, but those reasons alone do not explain the response in thousands of small towns and cities across this continent. Young Canadians and Americans were called upon and motivated by the necessity to prevent or stop a carnage in Europe.

A typical church group from Medicine Hat, Alberta or Missoula, Montana is therefore stunned on visiting "the Holy Land" to be confronted by the claim in huge letters at the Holocaust Museum: THE WORLD STOOD BY AND DID NOTHING WHILE SIX MILLION JEWS WERE MURDERED. The holocaust was unspeakably horrible and the racism unforgivable, and not exclusively Nazi. Canadians and Americans and their governments have been guilty of racism toward Jews and others at particular moments in history, but the old farmers go back to the bus and weep, not just for the Jews, nor even for the stupidity of humanity. They weep for brothers long buried in Europe and sadly missed. They see their names each Sunday on the brass plaque on the church wall and they always thought it was precisely to stop this inexplicable madness in Europe that North Americans got drawn into this war. True, it was not for the Jews alone, any more than for the Gypsies or the Poles, but the whole world did not simply stand by.

The large Jewish communities north of Chicago and Toronto and the tiny Jewish groups scattered all over the west are integral to life in North American society. They know the historic duplicity of North American governments in the plight of the Jews worldwide, and they are painfully aware of smoldering pockets of anti-Semitism on the lunatic fringe of this society. For them to feel completely secure for the twenty-first century it is important for them to somehow become more aware of the respect and affection in which they are also held in every community. It is time to move on together.

The debate over the "necessity" to finish the war with Japan quickly, after Germany surrendered, by the dropping of atomic bombs on the cities of Hiroshima and Nagasaki on August 6 and 9, 1945 endures. The fact of Western nations being the only people to have ever used nuclear weapons, dropped by "born-again Christians" on innocent civilian populations, stands as a searing counterbalance to other more altruistic actions at the conclusion of

WW II. Asia may never forget.

Then, before the world knew it, Russia had nuclear weapons (a necessary response to the West?) and the "cold war" was on. Canada and America shared an early warning defense system of some fifty radar stations across the top of this continent, mostly in Canadian territory. This venture involved some 25,000 civilians and service personnel. The two governments established the joint North American Air Defence Command in 1957 which became the North American Aerospace Defence Command in 1981. Both of these have functioned in giant bunkers, underground at Colorado Springs, Colorado where the American Commander always has a Canadian on hand as second-in-command of the combined forces.

Many of these developments have taken place with the usual assumptions and near invisibility on the part of the Canadians. As close as they are to the British, Germans and others in alliances, the US is unlikely to have any other "foreign national" as second-in-command of a nuclear submarine, far less the entire missile command headquarters.

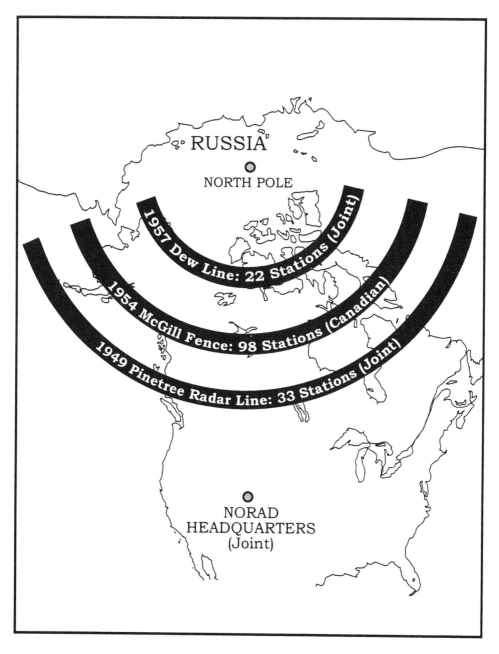

RUSSIA

NORTH POLE

1957 Dew Line: 22 Stations (Joint)

1954 McGill Fence: 98 Stations (Canadian)

1949 Pinetree Radar Line: 33 Stations (Joint)

NORAD
HEADQUARTERS
(Joint)

<u>NORAD And the DEW Line</u>

(In the "Cold War" the US and Canada integrated their defences along the
Distant Early Warning lines facing USSR ballistic missiles a few miles away.)

19.

HALF A CENTURY OF NO PEACE

In another respect of major importance, however, Canada and the United States have gone in separate, but complementary directions on the military front. Americans saw the Korean conflict as a necessary exercise to "draw a line on the ground" to circumscribe the expansion of the communist empire which had grown rapidly following World War Two. Canadians saw the UN action in Korea more in simple terms of smothering a nasty conflict while the world worked on ways to evolve politically without war. Both were correct but the difference in emphasis defined the divergent paths of foreign policy followed by the two nations in the pursuant fifty years.

As these paths converge again it is clear that defence from the bullying tyranny of communism was absolutely essential, to allow time for such an extreme, corrupt and misguided system to decay from within and collapse of its own weight. Its goals and ideals were worthy and inspired; its methods were disastrous. Communist agriculture produced scant food, communist industry produced shoddy goods while devastating the environment, and communist governments maintained control through an enduring reign of terror even long after the original ideals had disappeared.

As America had lead the cavalry charges that finally determined the final outcomes of two world wars, so it fell to America to lead the free world in the long "cold war" against communism. Others played supporting roles from time to time, and America frequently made her allies nervous that precipitous US overreactions might turn this potential nuclear nightmare into a hot war, the likes of which the world had never seen.

From the Bay of Pigs in Cuba to Desert Storm in Iraq, America was firm, if not always perfectly wise, in holding the line against communism and other forms of tyranny. The world winced when it appeared that the CIA was fighting the KGB with equally nefarious methods. If peace should ever come, would America be able to climb down from the barricades, or would the national psyche require another enemy, perhaps the Arabs or the Chinese? At the conclusion of the world wars, both the Allies and the Axis Powers were forced to destroy their canine units because these ferocious dogs could not be re-integrated into domestic life. Did the long standoff with communists turn America into the pit bull terrier of the world?

Most Canadians do not believe that for a moment, though the disorientation and flashbacks of veterans returning from Vietnam illustrates the stress that the whole of America experienced during the Cold War. Fortunately, friendly neighbors are right nearby and they are so trusted by Americans that the support needed to bring America more gently into a happier new era is close at hand.

The world will be forever in America's debt; her role in the twentieth century is certain to stand as one of the most definitive sagas in humanity's long journey to fulfillment of its destiny. However, the world has not reached that goal yet and in the meanwhile, Canada was spending the same fifty years preparing for the next phase of this shared pilgrimage. Canada's role in developing peaceful models for resolving conflict is as checkered as the American role in policing the world. There have been sterling successes, mixed reviews and abject failures. Moreover, the opportunity to develop an alternative means of security would not have existed without the security of the American shield. But as the method of the future, the alternative Canadian way deserves careful attention now, especially at the Pentagon.

As with American efforts in the other direction, Canadians were never alone in their attempts at peacekeeping. Some mental seeds may have sprouted in the United Nations during the Korean conflict. Canada also served along with

Poland and India in a 1954 International Commission for Supervision and Control in Vietnam, Laos and Cambodia, though, again, the time was not right and the appropriate methods were still undeveloped. The definitive beginning in conscious thinking and action in the new direction of peacekeeping took place in 1956.

In that year Britain, France and Israel had cooperated in an invasion of Egypt to secure control of the Suez Canal. World opinion, supported by the positions of both the United States and the Soviet Union, demanded that Egypt be given control of its own waterway, so there was need for the supervision of a truce. The Hon. Lester B. Pearson was then the Secretary of State for External Affairs for Canada and at the United Nations he proposed the idea of a large peacekeeping force to stabilize the whole region. He had the enthusiastic support of Secretary-General Dag Hammarskjold and the vision gained widespread acceptance.

Pearson offered a battalion of the Queen's Own Rifles, and the United Nations Emergency Force came into being overnight. To Canada's surprise the Egyptians objected to the uniforms, the regimental name and the Canadian flags displayed by the troops because they were virtually identical with those of the British invaders. To compromise, Canada withdrew from the front lines and provided service and supply troops only. It was this experience that convinced Pearson that Canada needed its own symbols and a flag distinct from Britain's Union Jack. He would address that task before long as Prime Minister.

Lester Pearson's leadership in the formation of the United Nations Emergency Force earned him the Nobel Peace Prize and gave Canadians a sense of identification with the peacekeeping ideal. The picture of unarmed Canadians standing in a line between two howling mobs of armed ethnic adversaries with the message, "you have to kill us before you can kill each other" is perhaps overblown but conveys an image that is amazingly effective in reality.

The techniques of peacekeeping are somewhat like sophisticated police tactics used in wearing down, seducing, jerking around, befriending and exhausting a hostage taker in a prison riot or domestic dispute. US police forces have cultivated this approach as opposed to the old method of bursting in prematurely and killing both the perpetrator and the hostage in the name of law and order.

Peacekeepers require special skills in moving unobtrusively, or using a "show" of force, massing in strength with "pitchfork at the ready" or befriending the crowd. Swearing or sweet talking, rough housing or romancing, starving or feeding, are all part of the peacekeeper's stock in trade. The goal is not victory but the perfect "sting" in which antagonisms are defused without anyone realizing how that took place.

When this happens early enough, further, more spectacular, military actions are often unnecessary. When a situation has gone beyond a certain point, some political, economic or military muscle is exerted to get the parties to the negotiating table. It is frequently frustrating and messy but both human and economic costs are only a fraction of the price everybody pays for a war.

Natural emotions sometimes dictate that a nation would rather lose 50,000 soldiers in a shooting war than to suffer the ignominious disgrace and the appearance of weakness displayed when half a dozen of its men and women are brutalized. This is especially difficult politically when national TV networks show their bodies being dragged through the streets of some city, the name of which the announcer cannot quite pronounce. The public needs to develop a new sophistication in this regard for the twenty-first century unless it is to be yet another century of war. Canada and The United States have so much to offer each other, not least from their differing military experiences in the last fifty years.

The American role is appreciated and has been acknowledged. By the same token, the Nobel Peace Prize awarded to Lester B. Pearson for his leadership in 1956 was awarded to the United Nations Peacekeepers as a whole some forty years later for its leading role in absolutely every United Nations peacekeeping mission in the world to date. Perhaps Canadians can be forgiven for the common assumption that this was their second Nobel Peace Prize.

As the US and Canada feel their way into the next century together, Americans may wish to rethink their cold war doubts about the United Nations and get beyond their paranoia about being taken over by a world government. Their security is now within the newly re-United Empire of North America, but both countries should be paying their bills at the UN and considering their roles in the permanent peacekeeping force that is certainly to be established in the twenty-first century. Canada and America can help make it work in the very different century and millennium now before the world.

20.

MEDITERRANEAN NORTH

The largest single construction project of the Second World War era was the Alaska Highway, stretching more than 2,400 kilometres or over 1,500 miles through the west and north of Canada into the heart of Alaska, from Dawson Creek to Fairbanks.

The largest construction project in the post war era is the Saint Lawrence Seaway-Great Lakes Waterway, permitting ocean liners to sail inland from Sept Isles, Quebec, to Chicago, Illinois, a distance likewise of 2,400 kilometers, or 1,500 miles. This is equal to the Alaska Highway but running from the Atlantic Ocean through the east and south of Canada to the American industrial heartland.

Through it, Detroit and Cleveland survived new patterns in world trade and Duluth, Minnesota and Milwaukee developed vast new markets for American agriculture. Before it was opened in 1959 the US and Canada combined were shipping only 18,000 short tons of merchandise through the same route by a system of small lochs and lake steamers, as compared to 180,000 tons of world shipping then passing through the Panama Canal. There are a number of factors involved, but present shipping tonnage at nearly 100,000 short tons through each of these two systems indicates the magnitude of the shift. The trend continues, making the earlier American dependence on the Panama Canal a thing of the past. US troops are out of the Canal Zone altogether as of 1999, with the cessation of direct American involvement and control.

Once regarded as one of the wonders of the modern world, the Panama Canal is only fifty miles long and lifts a ship less than 100 feet through six lochs, compared to the seaway's hundreds of miles in which a ship is elevated some 600 feet through several canals and dozens of lochs. The Welland Canal is one Seaway system which alone, near Niagara Falls, lifts each ship more that three times as high as the whole Panama system. It seems so typical of the invisible Canada-US relations that tourists still go to wonder at the engineering marvels of the Panama Canal, but hardly a soul has ever bothered to visit Welland, Ontario, where this massive lift system is merely regarded as "business as usual."

Of equal benefit to both countries, the Seaway follows the route of earlier shallow canals and small lochs built between 1783 and 1932 by Canadians for Great Lakes steamships. After ten years of discussion regarding a larger ocean going system, a 1941 treaty to proceed was signed by the Canadian parliament but left languishing in the US Senate for over eight years. A 1951 announcement that Canada was prepared to proceed alone and exert sole control over the project led to new negotiations, resulting in a successful treaty in 1954.

The monumental task of construction proceeded under the watchful eyes of the International Joint Commission (IJC) and took five years to complete. The Seaway permitted its first commercial traffic to enter the system in April of 1959 and the official opening took place on June 26, 1959 with Prime Minister John Diefenbaker and President Dwight D. Eisenhower in attendance, hosted by Her Royal Highness, Queen Elizabeth II of Canada.

Operational responsibility for lochs on the Canadian side is divided between the Canadian St. Lawrence Seaway Authority and Parks Canada, while the American authorities are the St. Lawrence Seaway Development Corporation and the US Corps of Engineers, all of whom report to the IJC. The fact that the public rarely, if ever, hears of problems with this relationship is merely typical again of Canadian-American relations.

The original investment of one billion dollars has mostly been paid off through user fees which have been used to retire thirty, thirty-five and forty year bonds sold on open markets or held by both governments. A further investment of nearly one billion dollars in hydro-electric facilities along the lochs has long since been retired and continues to make excellent profits for all concerned.

In addition to rescuing Detroit's struggling automobile manufacturing complex among other industries, and expanding the agricultural shipping capacity of both countries, new and cheaper supplies of raw materials such as timber, iron ore and other mining products also began to flow into the Canadian and American industrial centers from the forests and mines of eastern Quebec. More is expected especially from the Labrador Coast of Newfoundland at the turn of the century because of enhanced prospecting and recovery techniques, the presence of the Seaway and the free trade agreement.

In the nineteen-nineties Canada became a net exporter of iron ore, instead of an importer. More recent discoveries of nickel, copper, silver and cobalt at Voisey's Bay in Labrador have proven reserves that makes it the stainless steel "mother lode" of the world. As the new century opens, there is suddenly enough high-grade, low-cost ore accessible through the seaway to re-establish the competitive advantage of the industrial heartland of North America in one fell swoop.

The significant impact of these developments showed up first in a sustained rise in stock market investing in the whole Great Lakes region beginning in 1996. Prior to these discoveries, there was the fear that the advent of ocean-going super tankers would render the seaway obsolete, much as happened in Panama. As the cheap inland waterway of a re-invigorated North American continental industrial system, this concern is no longer of consequence. These days, no one talks any longer of the northern industrial states as the "rust belt."

The Great Lakes shipping season gets longer every year with the warming of the earth's atmosphere. With technological advances, the Seaway could remain open year round in the twenty-first century. Of a length approximately the same as the Mediterranean Sea, North America's own inland ocean has barely begun to fulfil its potential in the midst of one of the richest natural resource bases in the world. With a sizable population of ninty million people along its banks, a well trained labor force and an established industrial base, the system was only needing a free-trade agreement between Canada and the United States to continue its own elevation toward becoming the busiest commercial waterway in the world.

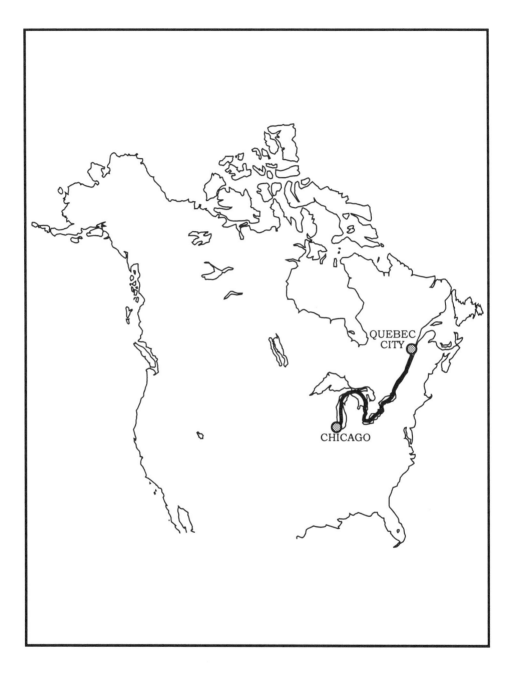

The St. Lawrence and Great Lakes Seaway

21.

OTHER EMPIRES

The twentieth century opened with the world divided into half a dozen empires and closes much the same except for who belongs with whom. Except for the Japanese and Ottoman empires, most of the others were headed by European powers, principally the British, followed by French, Spanish, Dutch and Portuguese. Several others had bits of empire. Russia's empire was contiguous and America was just getting into the business when the rules changed.

Those earlier empires were based on exploitation and domination and as the century opened they were doomed, though few realized it for a few years. As Spanish colonies threw off Spain's control, they were not about to accept America as the new master. So it went for the British and other empires all through the century until the collapse of the Soviet Union.

The loss of power by the Union of Soviet Socialist Republics over "satellite" states and client republics within the union, followed by the subsequent diminution of Russia's influence over its own "autonomous republics" was the final stage in the overthrow of the old style of empire system.

In the latter part of the century nations were faced with three choices: national isolationism, one world order, or new associations based on choice. The latter resemble regional empires and require some compromise of sovereignty in a new context accepted by the citizens.   Doubtless the world will be more interconnected than ever, at least in cyberspace.

There will also be nations that may choose to go it alone, whether Quebec, Chechnya or Rwanda, though life may be more difficult in isolation in the future than it was in past eras of nation states. However, by and large, the choice of new associations, or empires of choice, appears to be the overwhelming trend among the nations of the world at the close of the twentieth century.

The European Community is one such new regional empire, slowly growing out of the European Common Market toward one passport, a common currency, a single foreign policy, one army, labor laws in common, shared benefits like health care and mutual citizenship. This entire agenda is not expected to be fulfilled until sometime between the years 2010 and 2020.

By miracles unforeseen through most of the century, South Africa has become the economic engine for all of sub-Saharan Africa. This former pariah among nations is also now a dynamic leader in education and other aspects of life in a continent living far below its potential for so long. Not every little African nation yet shares this commonality, but prosperity and genuine progress seem proportional to participation in an as yet unnamed configuration.

So it goes throughout the world, in energetic southeast Asia, in the middle-east where trade may yet overcome longstanding animosities, and even in the former Soviet Union, where the members appear to have few options except to choose to reunite for trade if nothing else.

Each empire will be different and there will be various overlaps and multi-layered relationships. For historic, cultural and linguistic reasons, the Americas of the western hemisphere may be divided into two more integrated "empires", north and south, while increasingly united in trade and other matters. "Afta" NAFTA, as they say, these trade associations will no doubt extend from pole to pole and reach out creatively in many other directions as well.

The United States of America as a productive society can only thrive in such circumstances, once the feeling of paranoia disappears from some quarters. Trade will replace aid throughout the hemisphere and Canadian ice wines will be *numero um* on the Riviera in Rio de Janeiro.

For Canada and the United States, the more complete goals of mutuality, like those anticipated for Europe, are practically in place but are unlikely to extend uniformly south beyond the Rio Grande or the Panama Canal. In this manageable context, the old United Empire is destined to become one integrated new world culture across cultural, linguistic, religious and racial lines faster than any part of the world, including the other newer empires.

Why stop short of one world culture? No one knows why, except the herding instinct of the human species seems to set its own timetable. Reasonable expectations for the next one hundred years may include peace, prosperity and mobility in a restored environment. Nation states will continue to exist on the political level at least, and the world as a whole will build closer global relationships than ever in its history. Even so, the dominant pattern at the opening of the twenty-first century will be the new regional empires, regardless of birth-pangs and the struggle to survive.

22.

ARTS AND ENTERTAINMENT

Along with the facts of history, politics, economic realities and popular perceptions of these things, a question arises. Does art imitate life, or are there really some situations where life does imitate art? If the latter is the case, then in spite of the powerful ways in which Canadian and American cultures interact, the significant Canadian contribution to popular culture in the United States would be largely invisible.

The visible parts of the exchange includes Americans like Henry Wadsworth Longfellow and Harriet Beecher Stowe writing about Canada, and Canadian Mounties appearing in American movies, Paul Bunyon, Anne of Green Gables and the recitation of "In Flanders Fields" somewhere in America everyday.

The American contribution to Canadian culture is a given, because of America's dominant influence in world culture. Even here, however, there is an invisible element. It is sometimes said, somewhat unkindly as far as stalwart Vietnam veterans are concerned, that the finest elements of America's youth were not sacrificed on the killing fields after all.

Twenty-five thousand conscientious objectors who came to Canada between 1965 and 1975 applied for and were granted immigrant status. There were a few others before and after those dates, plus a large number who came to visit or study or who remained underground until it was possible to return to the United States. Those who stayed included some of the best educated young professionals and most sensitively gifted Americans of their generation.

These Americans are employed in lifetime careers in schools, clinics, libraries and research establishments all over Canada. They are not known in America because of the choices they made. Their spouses and children are Canadian and their contribution to the country is enormous, but they are neither well known nor adequately appreciated by Canadians because they started their careers in remote places and they have had too few of the personal connections that often lead to advancement. Moreover, enough of them experienced hassles even in Canada that they themselves rarely announce the circumstances of their citizenship.

However, their impact on Canadian life may be estimated by the fact that it is improbable that many Canadian school children of the present generation can get through the education system without one or more formerly American teachers. Not only is this an American influence, it is an influence of a particular stripe that has blended well into the fabric of Canadian life.

In their own invisible way, Canadians have repaid these significant debts of popular culture and community enrichment. Canadian authors, for example, include many who Americans do not think of as foreign. Every youngster in the world who has read Anne of Green Gables by Lucy Maude Montgomery would rightly assume the author is Canadian, but so is Leslie MacFarlane, who wrote the first twenty books in The Hardy Boys series. Margaret Atwood, author of The Handmaid's Tale, Robertson Davies with Fifth Business, and Margaret Laurence, The Diviners and Stone Angel are world class authors in anybody's books, and their work is also almost part of the American literary landscape.

Other Canadian authors too are well known, not as Canadians per se but as leading contributors in their fields. Educator Laurence Peter wrote The Peter Principle. Robert MacNeil (The MacNeil /Lehrer Newshour) wrote The Story of English and Wordstruck.

Marshall McLuhan, the media guru, gave the world The Global Village and The Medium is the Message among others. Leonard Cohen penned Beautiful Losers as an author, as well as his songs like "Suzanne". The jury may be still out on the writer who most influenced US economic theory in the twentieth century, but Canadian born John Kenneth Galbraith is certainly a giant in the field of economics and its relationship to society as a whole as indicated in his 1996 book, The Good Society.

Even comic books may be said to owe their popularity to a Canadian by the name of Joe Shuster who established their first superhero. It was he who invented the character of Superman and drew the first pictures of him in the form we all recognize, as acknowledged on this Canadian postage stamp.

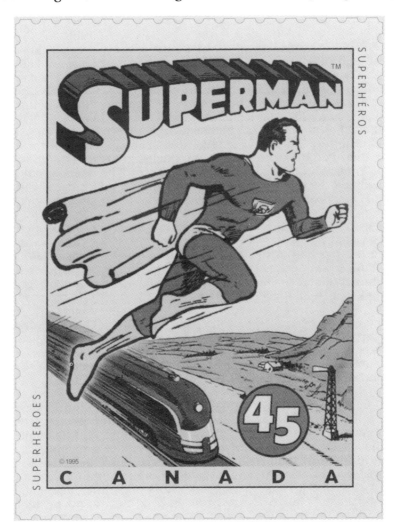

Superman is a Canadian

Canadian journalists often ply their trade south of the border: Peter Jennings of ABC, Arthur Kent, the "Scud Stud" of the Gulf War, J.D. Roberts, of CBS, Linden Soles on CNN, Morley Safer with "60 Minutes" and the aforementioned Robert MacNeil. Canadian CNN viewers are occasionally miffed when, during a world crisis, only commentators from La Stampa (Italy), The Guardian (Britain) and journalists from other countries are consulted for their views until they realize that the "American" interviewer is so often a Canadian. Indeed, Linden Soles has contended that CNN might as well stand for Canadian News Network.

Entertainers from Canada on American TV include Monty Hall, host of "Let's Make a Deal" and Alex Trebek of "Jeopardy," but even more Canucks are to be found on the comedy circuit. Years ago comedians Johnny Wayne and Frank Schuster set the record for most appearances on the "Ed Sullivan Show." Like Canadian Art Linkletter, most others are so well known that their credits need not be listed. Naming Rich Little, Dan Aykroyd, Dave Thomas (SCTV), Thomas Chong (half of Cheech and Chong), John Candy, Scott Thompson (Kids in the Hall), Gilda Radner, David Steinberg, Jim Carrey, Phil Hartman, Howie Mandel, Matthew Perry (Friends) and Alan Thicke, is to but scratch the surface of the list of Canadians doing comedy in the States. The writer-producer of the gender comedy hit "Grace Under Fire" is Pat Bullard, a Canadian who has also replaced Phil Donahue as host of America's long running popular talk show.

A complete list of Canadian popular musicians who Americans often think of as their own would be too long for consideration here. Skimming just the best known from the top half of the alphabet would give us Bryan Adams, Susan Aglukark, Paul Anka, Leonard Cohen, Celine Dion, Robert Goulet, k.d. lang, Gordon Lightfoot, Guy Lombardo, Joni Mitchell, Alannis Morisette and Anne Murray. Apologies to all the Shania Twains too numerous to mention.

There is significant reason to look at popular culture through each other's eyes. While it is easy for Canadians to see their shared culture through American eyes, it is equally important for Americans to see perhaps for the first time how much Canadian content may be influencing US culture. Nowhere is this more apparent than on Broadway and in Hollywood.

If Black or Asiatic actors, directors and producers had the role played in the American stage and screen industries by Canadians, it would look disproportionate. If Southerners, Italian-Americans or blonds dominated the industry the way Canadians do, this fact would be the subject of much commentary. The Canadian presence is virtually invisible because they play the American role so well. On the larger question of life imitating art or the other way around, this is a perfect example. If Canadians and Americans are one people in every way except politics, the proof is not found in an American movie about Canada but in the invisible Canadian influence in America's most definitive cultural industry.

The Canadian "Who's Who" in the American film industry goes back to the origins of the film industry when Canada's Sidney Olcott directed the first

122

classic production of "Ben Hur," in New York even before Hollywood produced its first movie. Canada's Mary Pickford was one of the four original partners who formed United Artists in 1919 to get the first Hollywood studio up and running. Other early Canadian studio executive producers include Jack Warner, co-founder of Warner Bros. and Louis B. Mayer, co-founder of Metro-Goldwyn-Mayer. The tradition has continued down through the years.

Canadian directors like Arthur Hiller (Love Story) and Norman Jewison (Fiddler on the Roof, Jesus Christ Superstar, The Cincinnati Kid, Agnes of God, and the all time favorite TV series "All in the Family") directed far too many movies and shows to count. The first century of cinema closes with Canadian directors and producers running all over Hollywood. Recent credits include James Cameron (True Lies, The Terminator, Aliens), David Cronenberg (Dead Ringers and Crash), Ivan Reitman (Ghostbusters, Meatballs, Stripes), and fast rising Graham Yost (Speed and Broken Arrow). Lorne Michaels writes and produces the popular "Saturday Night Live" which is modeled on the earlier Canadian version, SCTV.

There is also a significant Canadian film industry but that point is not germane to this argument. Canadians who wish their own industry was more robust should quit their carping and realize they are a very significant part of a continental media and movie industry.

Several thousand Canadian actors and actresses have lived and worked in New York and Hollywood in the last half century. Those who have become household names in America include actors like John Candy and Jim Carrey again, Raymond Burr, Glen Ford, Michael J. Fox, Graham Greene, Lorne Greene, Leslie Nielsen, Christopher Plummer, William Shatner and Donald Sutherland. Actresses of like standing include Yvonne De Carlo, Margot Kidder, Kate Nelligan, Catherine O'Hara and "America's Sweetheart" of an early era, Mary Pickford herself. America's latest globetrotting sweetheart, Anna Paquin (Piano, Emma and Fly Away Home) is originally from Winnipeg, Manitoba.

Others who may be recognized for their Academy Awards, frequent nominations, other awards and special dramatic roles are Dan Aykroyd, John Colicos, Hume Cronyn, Tyrone Guthrie, John Hirsch, Arthur Hill, Raymond Massey, Keanu Reeves, Jay Silverheels, Dave Thomas, John Vernon, and Al Waxman. "Baywatch" star Pamela Anderson, Jillian Hennessy on "Law and Order" and model turned actress, Monika Schnarre on "The Bold and the Beautiful" are as secure on TV as Genevieve Bujold, Tantoo Cardinal and Kate Reid are now on the big screen.

To add insult to injury, except that Americans are simply not offended in the least by such a Canadian presence, the trend established by the Canadian founders of United Artists, Warner Brothers and Metro-Goldwyn-Mayer continues. Garth Drabinski's Cineplex organization of Toronto is poised to dominate the theatre end of North American "stage and screen" while Edgar J. Bronfman of Montreal takes over much of the cinema production through controlling interest of MCA.

Such involvement, verging on control by a group more powerful than Americans from any state in the USA, including even New York or California, would be noticed and not tolerated if the foreigners were Russian or German. Sony comes and goes from Japan and dozens of British actors and actresses are currently in evidence in both leading and supporting roles. Americans note with pleasure the participation of Italian and French players and even film makers in the US industry. Yet it is unthinkable that any of these could become one of the two lenses in the spectacles through which America sees itself. This is what the Canadians have become. Strangely, nobody who wears glasses notices them unless they do not have them on.

Perhaps a clear example is in order. The comedy series "All in the Family", featuring Archie Bunker, was a watershed in race relations, as Americans learned to laugh at their ridiculous prejudices. The actors were American but the whole enterprise was conceived, largely written, entirely produced and directed by Canadians headed by Norman Lear. Only Canadians know America well enough and yet remain sufficiently objective to perform this service. Only a Canadian could produce and direct a biting comedy with such a social impact without some question of the propriety of a foreigner attempting to meddle in such a sensitive area of American life. The question was never even raised.

The Canadian presence in the US film industry in particular demonstrates that in the media which most reflects American life, the international border with Canada has already vanished in certain important respects. Canadians are the trusted co-interpreters of North American culture and the invisibility of their presence is no threat to Americans. To the contrary, as the relationship becomes more acknowledged, Americans will welcome an enriching Canadian articulation of a shared concern for peace in a new era, business ethics and the protection of the environment, evolving structures of family life, racism in North American society and other aspects of life in the United Empire of the twenty -first century.

There may be more British, Italian or French stars than Canadian on the US stage and screen at any given moment, depending on the *flavour de jour*, but the infrastructure is largely Canadian. The record of seventeen Academy Awards for Canadian sound engineer, Douglas Shearer, says it all. When Canadians communicate, Americans pay attention, even if they do not realize that it is these "foreigners" who are making the sound. Marshall McLuhan would be proud.

23.

LET THE GAMES BEGIN

Sport is big business in North America, ranking just behind religion and the movies in public leisure activity. Sport tells us less about this society than the other two, but it does delineate again the difference between this old United Empire, including Canada and the United States, and the rest of the world.

Back-to-back World Series Championships by the Toronto Blue Jays in the nineties proved that the American game can flourish well in Canada. Hockey does just as well in the United States, where the Stanley Cup, presented by Canada's Governor-General, seems to reside at least every second year.

Both these national sports had their origins in the early 1800's, baseball in either Massachusetts or Cooperstown, New York, and hockey in Windsor, Nova Scotia. Cuban and Japanese teams have developed good baseball; Russia and various European countries now have excellent hockey programs but in both cases their best professional teams still do well to beat North America's top amateur clubs.

Of the "big four" of North American sports, it is the origins and history of baseball, the only one of US origins, that is best known. The other three deserve special attention at last, to release them from the obscurity of northern mists and Canadian fog.

Kingston, Ontario and Montreal, Quebec have both attempted to present themselves as having the frosty ponds and the frozen lakes where hockey may have had its North American debut, but research[21] leaves no doubt that the honor goes to Windsor, Nova Scotia in 1799 or 1800. The famous New England writer, Thomas Chandler Haliburton, creator of *Sam Slick,* had been born in Windsor in 1788 and referred to hockey as "playing ball on ice" in his 1836 best-seller, *The Clockmaker,* a sport he later related to activities played on Long Pond at King's College in Windsor when he was eleven or twelve years of age.

Long after its popularization throughout Nova Scotia, James Creighton took the game from Halifax to Montreal in 1873 from whence it became popular in Ottawa at about the same time that soldiers introduced the "Halifax Rules" of this game to the military establishment at Kingston. Some debate over the origins of hockey remains in Canada among those unfamiliar with the research. Suffice it to observe that Micmac Indians of Nova Scotia were the first on record to sell hockey sticks commercially and by 1865, Starr skates from Dartmouth, N.S. were world famous at 75 cents per pair. Moreover, the goal of a hockey game is not a trap shoot but a fish net from the Maritimes.

Attempts to establish the Canadian Football League in major American cities have been less successful than the expansion of the US National Basketball Association to Toronto and Vancouver. However, both these games came to the United States from Canadian sources also. In fact, of the big four North American professional sports, namely baseball, hockey, football and basketball, three are Canadian in origin.

In 1874 McGill University in Montreal was invited to send a team to Harvard University in Cambridge, Massachusetts for a football match. It was only after the teams assembled on the field that it was realized that the Canadians were prepared to play a North American version of English rugby while the Americans expected to play soccer, which most of the world still calls football.

A friendly solution to the impasse was found in the decision to play two matches, one of each, learning the other team's rules as they went along. Soccer enthusiasm soon died out in the States and never did catch on much in Canada but the upshot of those matches at Harvard University was that the Americans were enthralled with the Canadian game. Harvard sent to England for the official rugby rules, adopted most of the Canadian changes and within a year organized matches with other eastern US teams in what they called the Ivy League since most of them were based at ivy covered universities.

Basketball is one of the few sports that can be said to be actually "invented." It too began in the American setting of Massachusetts where a Canadian psychology student at Springfield College responded to a need for indoor recreational activity in the winter season. James Naismith decided to design something that could be played in teams and easily picked up by students in need of exercise. In the indoor setting he decided to make it a non-contact sport and to use a ball that should be thrown with skill instead of force. Naismith devised the first set of rules in 1891 at this college associated with the YMCA where it became a favorite, spreading to Ys throughout the United States and Canada within a decade.

Like baseball and hockey, basketball is played by identical rules in both countries while football has remained slightly different. However, American players dominate the Canadian Football League, despite having only three "downs", a shorter playing field and higher scores. Canadians are more typically involved with management and ownership of American football teams, like the Washington Redskins where the flamboyant Jack Kent Cooke is the owner and boss. There might be enough Canadians on all teams in the National Football League to field a single team at most.

The evolution as a single North American sports culture is illustrated equally well by examination of certain athletic activities that are enjoyed by many players in both the United States and Canada, but which have never caught on with the public in either country. Rugby is "too confusing" and cricket is "just too boring" - all in the minds of North American spectators, as sports fanatics from every other part of the world will attest.

Soccer is only beginning to catch on with the North American public, largely at the expense of the older sport of lacrosse and with an enthusiastic nudge from immigrant communities. It is also something more of a social phenomenon, like horse racing and other activities to be viewed later through a window on everyday life, since they represent entire subcultures of society.

Outrageous ticket prices are among several reasons why the public may be shifting its interest in "spectator sports" to various forms of participation in the twenty-first century. All such trends happen in North America simultaneously north and south of the US-Canada border.

The one area where Canada has taken a lead is in women's sports, which is a growing phenomenon worldwide, with an emphasis on participation. At the 1996 Olympic Games in Atlanta, Canada became the first major participant nation to send a team with a majority of female athletes. This fact had a direct positive impact in reversing Canada's previously dismal medal count, giving the Canadian team it highest standing ever!

However, the American sports media is one area of the communications industry not dominated by Canadians. This ensures that America will always have the fastest runners in the world. When Americans win the 100 meter sprint or the 400 meter relay, for example, these are regarded as the races to establish who are the fastest men in the world. When someone like Donovan Bailey and the Canadian relay team win the Olympic Gold Medals in these events, *Time Magazine* and late night US talk shows decide that these are not the definitive events after all. The really important races are which ever ones are won by American runners. This unnecessary petulance is unworthy of a great sporting culture.

More uplifting is the growing enthusiasm for Special Olympics all over the world at the turn of the century. The lack of professionalism harkens back to the original spirit of the Olympic Games played by amateurs, for the love of sporting achievement. The next logical step is to include wheelchair athletes and others with handicaps in their sports at the regular games.

24.

GOD SAVE THE QUEEN

In the future Canada might have dropped its connection with the Royal Family for the sake of French Canada, newcomers and old Scots and Irish, all of whom have been ambivalent about the monarchy for years. The occasion might have been the passing of the beloved "Queen Mom," mother of Elizabeth II and the last direct connection with the Scottish line. However, to Americans, royalty is part of the Canadian mystique so the monarchy may remain as an acceptably benign token of distinctions between the two countries in the United Empire for some time.

The Monarchist League can relax. An essential ingredient for successful reunion of this old United Empire is the maintenance of separate political structures and symbols. Rather than acting as walls that divide, these elements of an emerging continental culture, which is becoming more evident daily, simply serve to highlight what each has to offer the other.

The US Declaration of Independence upholds the right to "life, liberty and the pursuit of happiness" while the Canadian constitution offers "peace, order and good government." The first are values that protect individual rights and the second represent communal rights.

Far from being antithetical to each other, these are complementary values, opposite sides of one coin, and perfectly matched for the mature balance North American society will need in the twenty-first century. The Canadian community might have benefited from more individual initiative in the twentieth century and America has sometimes suffered from lack of community.

On the world scene, the recent collapse of absolute communism on the political left was actually matched earlier in the twentieth century by the collapse of the political right with the defeat of Nazi fascists. The world has been working out a political balance between these twentieth century extremes ever since, especially in North America where the entire debate between liberals and conservatives has been a struggle to control the dynamic center of the political spectrum. Socialist economics of state intervention in the marketplace do not work; laissez-faire capitalist justice is always suspected of an "everybody for themselves" ethic.

The economic principles elucidated at mid-century by John Kenneth Galbraith seem at century's end to maintain the balance between production of wealth and its distribution in a manner that is both just and capable of stimulating further production. This is the balance sought through a full century of worldwide experimentation from Russian Communism to Germany's National Socialism. ..

This Canadian born economist was personal economic advisor to US Presidents Roosevelt, Truman, Kennedy and Johnson. John Kenneth Galbraith stands equal with media guru Marshall McLuhan as the most important Americans Canada has produced in the twentieth century. (A Canadian twist turns this around to say "John Kenneth Galbraith and Marshall McLuhan are the two greatest modern Canadians the United States has produced.")

Regardless, Galbraith, who now calls himself "an advisory Canadian rather than a practicing Canadian" maintains that Canada was the first country in the world to implement Keynesian economic policies which became so influential in the United States at the time of the greatest economic expansion in North American history. Both countries tinker with their economies, seeking the balance together now, with continuing hints from this elder statesman of the economic realm.

As a new era dawns in North America these two mature political cultures offer each other the benefits of slightly different experiences that may continue. Though the two North American systems are distinct, they are so close on the political spectrum that cross pollination is taking place more and more in the natural course of events. Areas where this can be easily identified include changes in social services, health care and government regulation of media, banking and the environment.

This hybrid synthesis of balanced economic theories and the spread of democracy is evolving throughout the world as the harbinger of true globalization. It is in maintaining and adapting institutions like the monarchy that Canada can illustrate that world culture will not be merely warmed over American culture.

The Monarch will pay taxes to "the people", as represented by their government, instead of the other way around. This is a complete revolution on a spiral, true movement that history may see as genuine progress.

The Monarch will be permitted to fail in marriage and in other ways as long as constitutional responsibilities are maintained. The Royal family, instead of serving as the hypocritical pinnacle of a class system, may be like other families, broken, mended, blended and extended - more like the Biblical model than recent artificial constructs.

Instead of a figurative role as head of one church, the worldwide Anglican communion, the Monarch will have a title change from "Defender of the Faith" to "The Defender of Faith," perhaps almost an ombudsman safegarding the freedom of religion.

In addition to troubles in Britain, the Monarchy as an institution has been on quicksand in Canada in recent times, partly in deference to Quebec (that mood has changed) and partly because of the ethos of the times. Ironically, it is free-trade and the closer association with the United States that has insured the continuation of the Monarchy in Canada into the twenty-first century.

25.

THE INFORMATION SKYWAY

As mentioned, the inventive genius of Thomas Edison produced electricity and that of Alexander Graham Bell the telephone, an American and a Canadian inventor respectively. The two nations have been borrowing each other's inventions ever since, especially in media and communication related technologies, from Canadian IMAX film technology to Disney's virtual reality.

Predictions by Canadian media philosopher Marshall McLuhan that television would turn the world into an electronic "Global Village" may have to wait to be fulfilled by the internet but that era has begun. As automobiles and telephones came on the scene in the late 1800s as a prelude to the twentieth century, so the internet unveiled the twenty-first century even before it began.

In its ultimately refined form early in the century the Internet may render other media antique except insofar as they adapt to Internet format or rely on public gatherings. Publishing industries may adapt but broadcast networks will continue disintegrating into narrowcast formats. Satellites spinning the World Wide Web may produce a new firmament on high, but consideration of the social and ethical dimensions of the new "cyber culture" in North America can be left for consideration through Windows on the Future.

Canadian fears of cultural domination via the new technologies may be as ephemeral as the notion that the American Civil War would make Yankees out of Southerners, or that education would cause the wild west to lose its free spirit. If Canadian culture is not secure by now, perhaps it never will be.

At the close of the century it may be reassuring for Canadians at least to recognize how much of cyber technology is Canadian in origin. Admittedly, the Corel Corporation, the Canadian owner of WordPerfect, does publish its annual financial report in American dollars, but that merely reflects its main customer base. (Or is printing an annual report of a Canadian based North American corporation somewhat akin to the quaint practice of continuing to employ British spellings such as "colour" and "labour." Some Canadians have stubbornly adhered to this practice long after international English usage dropped it, as if this tokenism could somehow insure the survival of a distinct Canadian culture.)

In a related field, the highly successful computer animation program at Sheridan College, in Ontario, has spawned an adjunct to the Canadian film industry which does the computer simulations for many of the major motion pictures produced in Hollywood. Disney Studios has established its main computer animation facility in Toronto primarily because of the well trained talent there. As the border diminishes in significance, particularly in business, it should be no surprise that the media and communication industries are among the first to flourish in Canada in concert with American partners.

Tim Collin's Canadian "V-Chip" is in every American home television manufactured after 1996, put there by the Communications and Decency Act of Congress and a presidential decree. He developed it primarily for American use, but since Canadians have traditionally been equally keen on censorship, it will no doubt be used in many Canadian homes as well, without legislation.

The "Java" Internet language, developed by another Canadian inventor, James Gosling, offers free net software to everyone with a home computer. This leakage of programing onto the Internet is rapidly transforming the computer itself. The sophisticated models at the end of the twentieth century, which had every capability built in or attachable, are being replaced for the twenty-first century with simple, cheap models that can do even more by just bringing everything they need down from the sky. This revolution has only been possible since Java broke the corporate monopoly on programs that were protected by complex computer languages which were protected by copyright. Developed over a cup of coffee, Java has become *the* computer language.

134

Indeed, much of the stuff of everyday high-tech life in North America is Canadian in origin. Cultural industries were the one main exemption Canadians sought under free-trade, but if Canadians are unable to defend their own culture using their own technology, perhaps it is time to move on in this regard.

26.

EVERYDAY LIFE IN THE UNITED EMPIRE

Service clubs cross the US-Canada border every day and also attempt to see themselves as global. But like the trade figures and Hollywood productions, these community building networks are primarily a North American phenomena involving the United States and its invisible partner. There are Lions, Moose, Rotary, Kiwanis and Loyal Elk now in many parts of the world but there is a difference.

No one should denigrate the global connections of these groups or their value in creating a sense of world community, but with rare exception, the service clubs of Thailand, Russia, Ethiopia and Spain are limited to North American ex-patriots and the business elites in the capital cities. Those neighborhoods certainly have indigenous expressions of community service and fellowship but these typically take their own forms. Service clubs are a North American phenomenon, with but a few important exceptions.

In Canada, for both historical and current reasons, there will continue to be a bit more cachet to belonging to the "Canadian" branch of Rotary or a 4H Club, and the same is true for Americans in their national associations. Such fortunate groups may maintain both officially separate status, like the New Zealand branches of the same organizations, for example, and also function everyday in an essentially North American neighborhood.

Former national associations like the American Dental Association and the Canadian Medical Association are becoming North American in scope with the Canadian section holding a regional status like the New England Medical Association or the Western Livestock Breeders. An annual meeting of The American Psychological Association in Toronto is an "everyday" business-as-usual event, not a visit to a foreign environment. There is nothing remarkable in any of this; it is just the way things are in the evolution of a single continental culture.

Everyone has seen Candice Bergen (Murphy Brown) on TV Sprint system telephone ads that begin with the announcement that on weekends a person can place a long distance call to any state in America for just 10 cents per minute. Then the viewers are informed that it costs just thirty -five cents per minute to call certain countries in Europe and sixty-five cents to many parts of Asia. It costs seventy cents per minute to Tokyo and to Mexico City, and 10 cents to any province in Canada ... just like any state in America. This ad tells people a lot more than the price of long distance Sprint calls! Even as the internet changes the way people communicate, these telephone ads at the end of the twentiety century symbolize the way in which technology contributed to the making of one society in North America.

Car racing is one of those cross border leisure activities that has an entire subculture attached to it. These people belong to a fraternity or community that sometimes seems more important to them than nationality, religion or earning a living. Except at the very top, it is said that one could win every race in a season and still not meet car expenses. This is an "ama-ture" sport in the true sense of that Latin word - people do it for the "love" of it. They live and breathe such a sport for the love of cars and the association with peers.

In car racing the primary interest is at the minor level, as opposed to sports where the minors are little but a reflection of dreams, and a preparation for the major leagues. Because older styles of neighborhood community have broken down, people are increasingly prepared to commit more to such associations of choice, most of which are North American in scope, as opposed to global or national. Car racing is only one example of this general trend.

These changing times are also illustrated in horse racing. The phrase "sport of kings" is applied to mounted racing of "thoroughbreds," an elite activity which may soon practically disappear. Betting on horses was the only legal form of gambling for many years and the masses kept thoroughbred racing going for the last century in this way. The proliferation of casinos and lotteries has changed all that, and except for "Triple Crown" events, who is even interested, except for the Queen and a few rich folks who think of themselves as an aristocracy of North America? This elitism is as anachronistic as nationalism itself.

Meanwhile, the sport of "harness racing" with "standard bred" horses, while not as glamorous, is flourishing. Though closer to the people, there are million dollar purses here too: "The Little Brown Jug" which is run in Delaware, Ohio, the "Hamiltonian" at the Meadowlands Track in New Jersey and the "North American Cup" each year at the Woodbine Track in Toronto. These trotters and pacers get less media attention than their galloping cousins, but this sport grew out of rural districts and small towns all over North America. It remains a family activity, and accessible to the middle class, as opposed to a diversion for the rich and famous.

Licensing, shots and fees make cross border thoroughbred racing difficult without lawyers, agents and bankers. Standard bred racing moves freely back and forth across the border with reciprocal licensing. There is a United States Trotting Association (USTA) as well as a Canadian Trotting Association, but, interestingly enough, the USTA includes the four Atlantic provinces of Canada.

North Americans now have an increasingly comfortable everyday identification with each other whenever they find themselves abroad. A popular image of Canadians and Americans working together abroad was an incident during the Iranian hostage taking affair in 1979-1981. Six American soldiers and diplomats managed to hide out in the Canadian Embassy for some months in what was later called the "Canadian Caper." On January 28, 1980, they were successfully smuggled out of Iran using Canadian passports in the company of Ambassador Ken Taylor, his assistant, John Sheardown and their wives. Americans and Canadians may be both similar and distinct in various respects, but the rest of the world can still barely tell them apart.

The principal Canadian technical contribution to the NASA space program is the so-called "Canadarm," an arm-like device used on practically every mission for the work outside the spacecraft. There has been a token person from a dozen countries blast off into space with American crews but only the Canadians equal the Russians in numbers, and the latter have a whole space program to contribute. Such a fact is only remarkable in its lack of news-worthiness since the Canadians are simple part of the North American program as opposed to some US foreign relations gesture.

A bit of futurist trivia also shows Canada's usual dominance of Hollywood's depiction of the space frontier. Canadians William Shatner as "Captain Kirk" and James Doohan as "Scotty," on Star Trek's USS Enterprise, commanded an essentially Canadian cast including John Colicos, Saul Rubinek, Kim Cattral, Andrea Martin and even Christopher Plummer on occasion. Leslie Neilson and Walter Pidgeon starred in The Forbidden Planet. Arthur Hill and Kate Reid starred in The Andromeda Strain. Lorne Green and John Colicos starred in Battlestar Galactia. Do these "aliens" represent a coded message for the future of the Canadian presence in North American high-tech industries or have they already taken over?

PART THREE

WINDOWS ON THE APOCALYPSE

(Race and Religion at the Millennium)

27.

WALLS THAT DIVIDE

In 1989, after two generations of symbolizing the bitter divisions within the human community as well as the German people, the Berlin wall came crashing down. Pressure against it had been building since protests led by Protestant churches in the German Democratic Republic (East Germany) became as articulate and determined as the similar movement in nearby Poland led by the Roman Catholic Church.

The Communist regimes in Hungary, Czechoslovakia, and even Romania, as well as Poland were liberalizing after years of repressive laws, including travel restrictions. This meant that East German citizens were increasingly free to travel west through neighboring countries, but both Germany and the world were stunned when the Berlin Wall was successfully breached and then demolished. Souvenir chunks of cement from the wall found their way to every corner of the globe.

The destruction of the Berlin wall was indeed "the writing on the wall" of the Iron Curtain itself. The communist governments in Eastern Europe collapsed like dominoes and the Union of Soviet Socialist Republics was shaken to its foundation. A hard line coup attempted to block liberalizing reforms in the USSR and was itself overturned by courageous citizens who surrounded the parliament to protect it, and by courageous army officers and soldiers who refused to move against their people.

The picture of liberal communist foreign minister Eduard Shevardnadze mounting a tank facing the Russian parliament building, with a socialist idealistic dreamer, the poet Yevgeny Yevtuchenko, and defiant Government Leader Boris Yeltsin, risking their careers and their lives to effect monumental changes inspired both Russia and the world. The course of world history was changed and it became evident that walls that divide could be broken down despite all the evidence to the contrary.

Who knew where it would stop? The oppressive tanks did prevail that same year in Tiananmen Square in Beijing and the tide of reform in communist China was temporarily stemmed or rechannelled. Meanwhile, walls began to tumble that had bitterly divided Jews and Arabs in the Middle East, Blacks and Whites in South Africa and Protestants and Catholics in Northern Ireland. Tremendous challenges still confront all these peace processes and liberation movements but maps have changed in the last decade of the twentieth century and hearts have dared to beat high with hope and determination.

At the same time, there is the sorry spectacle of new lines of demarcation in Bosnia, as well as frustrated aspirations along gender lines almost everywhere in the world, and unresolved rifts between labor and management, and between producers and consumers, to mention a few continuing divisions. Creative responses to these questions may occupy the human race for much of the next century but there are some items remaining from the twentieth century agenda that cry out for more immediate resolution in the North American context at least.

Is the issue of native land claims and recovery of native dignity in society capable of resolution? What is the future for a black president of the United States? Can French Canadians find a secure place within North American society without finally separating into a nineteenth century style nation state of their own? Can the mostly white Christian Coalition escape the siege mentality of "Fortress America"?

The latter in particular is largely identifiable in classic categories of race, religion, language and culture, a dangerous combination. The Christian Coalition is a powerful force on the right wing of American politics but it is also dangerous because of the feeling of disenfranchisement among its members. They indeed inhabit a mental Fortress America with the strength of their convictions. Along with the Blacks, French and Natives, the Christian Coalition has concerns that must be understood, addressed and appreciated for their powerfully positive potential rather than written off because some of them are born in negativity and insecurity,

Each of these four groups have sensible concerns or genuine grievances as once did the warring factions of Serbs, Croats and Moslems in the European context of Bosnia. While not currently as newsworthy, these situations in North America appear as intractable and as incapable of resolution as the position of Catholics in Northern Ireland, Arabs on the West Bank or Blacks in South Africa less than a decade ago. Ending the isolation of these sizable and important North American ethnic groups is the last great hurdle of the twentieth century.

Racism has brought this century closer to the brink of apocalyptic self-destruction than even wars, poverty or attacks on the environment. The Book of Revelation pictures four horses in its vision of the apocalypse. In a certain tradition of prophetic application of Biblical imagery to contemporary events, the four horses of the apocalypse could have frightening application as a warning regarding continuing racial tensions in North America.

When the black horse came out, its rider held up a pair of scales in the search for justice. The pale horse had death as its rider and all hell followed him. The red horse was permitted to take peace away, so that people would slaughter each other. The white horse had a bow and a crown and came out to conquer.

The history of the twentieth century would present this as a warning concerning Black Power, French Power, Red Power, White Power or power centered in any ethnic identity. That century with its racially defined killing fields from Auschwitz to Hiroshima is over. Its residue should have no place in the future.

At the turning of this century there appears to be a "window of opportunity" in North America to face these and other divisions with creative solutions to longstanding difficulties, in concert with trends elsewhere in the world. To lose this chance through pessimism, inaction or the wrong approach is to allow racist infections to fester in this society in a manner which could yet spite all the hopes and dreams for a truly more abundant life in the new century and the next millennium.

The ethnic mix first so prominent in New York and Toronto is now common throughout North America. Variant views, cultural distinctions, the babel of tongues, the spectrum of colors, ancestral rights and traditions are all to be welcomed and should flourish in an emerging common culture of the future, but there is important unfinished business from the past as it has been shared by various groups in North America.

West Indians and Asiatics in Canada and Hispanics in the United States are arriving in substantial numbers. In spite of the publicity, the assimilation of these new immigrants seems to be less of a challenge than finally dealing with ancient injustices among citizens who have unfulfilled aspirations dating back hundreds of years. Each new wave of immigrants has had to almost fight their way into North American society. Haitians and Filipinos will have greater difficulty than the Irish and Ukrainian before them only because these new minorities are more visible. These modern problems regarding integration of more recent arrivals will only be successfully resolved when the more ancient divisions are healed.

Without ignoring other divisions and difficulties, the four areas of concern delineated above, Red, Black, French and alienated White deserve careful attention and special consideration in the North American context before North Americans can all get on with the future. These ancient ghosts simply must be exorcised at last! Do Americans and Canadians have the political wisdom and the spiritual resources to cause these borders to vanish and these walls to crumble before the new fault lines become substantial and permanent? Within this emerging twenty-first century neighborhood these resources must be found or North American society will fail to achieve its own potential, far less contribute to any constructive trends toward globalization.

28.

THE BLACK HORSE

America has always had a mixed ethnic population. The Natives who first welcomed the crew with Columbus met European whites, Jews and at least one African, a certain Pedro Alonzo Nino. Negroes were also with Balboa when that expedition first sighted the Pacific Ocean, with Cortes and Pizarro in the Americas, and with De Soto in Mississippi and Florida. The expedition of Cabeza de Vaca into New Mexico and Arizona was partly facilitated by a black Moor from North Africa named Estavanico who may have explored as far north as Canada.

The number of black Americans is approximately equal to the entire population of Canada, a mere accident of history with no particular significance except to convey a sense of proportion. At the end of the twentieth century, both stand at a little over thirty million. Black influence has been traditionally marginalized in North American culture, ironically because of the visibility of black Americans as opposed to the invisibility of Canadians.

In the era when Hispanics and blacks were first opening up the American South and Mid-west, slavery was not at issue. Negro slaves were brought into America in small numbers at first by the Dutch and the English in the Northern States but at the time it was expected that ample cheap labor could be supplied by the native Indians and by "indentured" white labor from England. Later the high demand for larger numbers of cheap laborers for Southern Plantation operations happened to coincide with a growing and nefarious Arab and European trade in black slaves which flourished in response to the demand.

The lamentable story of African slaves in America is well known and the long aftereffects on the nation are well recognized. It is one of those areas of unfinished business in which tremendous strides have been taken in the last fifty years but, as was the case in the USSR, South Africa and the Middle East, there also remains a profound pessimism in some elements of American society who believe things never really change.

While the Civil Rights movement that brought about the dramatic changes of the last half of the twentieth century had origins and an energy of its own in the American context, it is also instructive to see the developments affecting black Americans in a global context. The movement identified as Black Power in particular has a relationship to the end of colonialism and the rise of independence movements around the world both in timing and in methods.

The Civil Rights movement itself, with its greatest successes achieved by non-violent means, was related to the leadership of Mahatma Gandhi who led a nation of nearly a billion people to independence without violence in the face of British guns and jails. Gandhi's Hindu philosophy of *ahimsa*, or non-violence, was neatly compatible with traditional Negro spirituality centered on the cross of Jesus with its emphasis on the acceptance of suffering in confidence of a resurrection. The Biblical story of the escape of the Hebrew slaves from Egypt to the "Promised Land" was a powerful spiritual model but it was Gandhi who inspired black Americans in the quest to attain their goals here and now on earth instead of by and by in heaven.

Minor progress in the advancement of negroes toward equality in American society took place as a result of their efforts during the World Wars and through the courts and the federal political system in the first half of the twentieth century. But progress was so slow that it sometimes appeared to be moving in reverse as white America boomed into a prosperity that black America did not share in the 1950s. Pent-up black aspirations exploded in a seemingly minor incident in 1955 when a tired black woman was arrested for refusing to give her seat on a crowded bus to a white passenger. A boycott of the bus company organized by The Rev. Martin Luther King turned into the mass movement which galvanized America for more than a decade.

Mature political and community leadership of the civil rights movement was provided for many years through the National Association for the Advancement of Colored People (NAACP) , The Urban League, the Southern Christian

Leadership Conference (SLCL), the Congress Of Racial Equality (CORE) and the Student Non-violent Coordinating Committee (SNCC). Black intellectuals and public figures not directly involved, like author James Baldwin and singer Mahalia Jackson, lent prestige to the movement but the storm was gathering.

A series of "freedom marches" across the country climaxed on August 28, 1963 when a quarter million people, including many whites, took part in a "March on Washington" and heard the Rev. Dr. King make a stirring plea for justice and share his dream that someday his children would live in an America where a person would be judged by character rather than by skin color.

Also in 1963, President John F. Kennedy asked the American Congress to pass a law legally prohibiting segregation in public places. Whether it was a contributing factor or not may never be known but that bill was still bogged down in the political process when Kennedy himself was gunned down in Dallas on November 22, 1963. His successor, President Lyndon B. Johnson saw the bill through and made it stick.

However, a series of non-violent voter registration drives and protests against black exclusion from the political process, led by King, caused tensions that frequently resulted in violence. The world watched as State Troopers attempted to turn back marchers at Selma and Montgomery, Alabama, using tear gas, whips, electric cattle prods and dogs. White clergy and others stood in solidarity with King and his followers and together they prevailed.

This led to a series of random violent incidents in 1963 which resulted in death. Medgar Evers, Mississippi Field Secretary for the NAACP, was shot to death. Four little negro girls were killed when a bomb exploded in a Birmingham, Alabama church. In 1964 automobiles and houses belonging to black citizens were blown up in various cities. White civil rights workers, clergy and seminarians assisting in black voter registration were killed in Mississippi, Georgia, and Alabama but the voter registration drives continued with great success through 1965.

Even after these advances it was apparent that a significantly powerful number of Americans were unwilling to accept the changes. The residue of crime and growing drug use associated with a background of poor education and unemployment in black ghettos offered little short term assurance to nervous whites who feared the disintegration of their neat and orderly society. These fears combined with blind prejudice in many police forces and other areas left many thoughtful blacks with a feeling of futility which led to the next phase in the evolution of the situation.

In the twentieth century the world has learned again the true meaning of the word "revolution", namely, winding up back where you started. This happened when communist dictators replaced the Czar in Russia and when revolutionary dictatorships replaced colonial administrations in parts of Africa and South America. However, the revolutionary impulse can play a constructive role in the cycle of political evolution if it is wisely managed, so that when a complete revolution has been accomplished, the people are not just back where they started, but at the same part of the cycle on a spiral leading up, rather than simply revolving in a circle. Such has obviously been the case in the revolutionary impulse which was known as Black Power in America.

The Civil Rights movement from 1955 to 1965 advanced the cause of black Americans in search of justice and dignity, but only so far. In 1965 the Rev. Dr. Martin Luther King Jr. was awarded the Nobel Peace Prize for his non-violent leadership through these tumultuous years, but while organizing a "poor peoples" march on April 4, 1968, in Memphis, Tennessee, he was shot to death.

By this time many black citizens had concluded that, progress notwithstanding, the breakthrough in which they sought to attain genuine equality would require either a new approach or a more direct form of action. Black nationalist groups like the Nation of Islam (Black Muslims) favored separation of the races rather than integration. Elijah Muhammad and Malcolm X (Malcolm Little until he dropped his "slave name" even without knowing his family's original African name) taught that civil rights activities were a demeaning form of cooperation with White structures of authority.

In the late 1960s CORE and SNCC both endorsed the principles of Black Power under a new generation of leaders including Floyd McKissick and Stokley Carmichael. They urged their followers to form political blocks within black communities from which they might force economic change. Blacks were to be responsible to their own political leaders and purchase from black merchants exclusively. White civil rights workers were urged to change their focus to deal with the racist attitudes of their fellow citizens and support the new division of society.

With its own enforcement agencies, Black Power hoped to curb lawlessness in black communities without reference to white police forces which seemed inherently racist. Moreover, to protect its people, Black Power was prepared to meet violence with violence. They believed that in America a person commands more respect with a gun in hand than kneeling helplessly before the oppressor.

Black Power advocates also glorified things black to instill pride in the black population. They were responsible for the adoption of the term "black" which replaced "negro" in popular usage. They used the slogan "Black is Beautiful" and encouraged the use of African motifs in clothing and hair styles. In a welcome twist of irony, as blacks ceased to straighten their hair, whites took to tight perms in Afro style. Signs continued that there was hope in America.

The assassination of Martin Luther King strengthened the movement toward Black Power for a time and its militancy soon had some of its leaders in trouble with the police, who were inclined to brook no rivals in law enforcement and security. Before it had finally made its point, the Black Power movement reached the height of its influence among young black radicals, and in terror among whites due to the activities of the militant Black Panthers.

The Panthers were founded in Oakland California in 1966 by Huey P. Newton and Bobby Seale as a response to perceived police brutality. The Black Panthers also subscribed to classic Marxist-Communist theories of revolution. In their zeal to establish a black political identity they approached the United Nations to monitor and insure the freedom and independence of black communities in the United States.

Several shoot-outs with police ensued in various locales. In 1969 a police action against a Panther apartment in Chicago resulted in the killing of two Panther leaders. A Federal Grand Jury investigation revealed that the police had pumped at least 82 rounds of ammunition into the place while the Panthers had replied with only a single shot throughout the fracas. This report aroused considerable public support for the Panthers.

Also in 1969 the police in New Haven, Connecticut, charged Seale in the death of a suspected informant, but a Connecticut Supreme Court Judge threw the charges out after a mistrial. In another highly publicized trial, in 1972 Professor Angela Davis was accused of purchasing the guns used by Panthers in a fatal shoot-out at the Marin County Court House in California. Tried for conspiracy, kidnapping and murder, she was found not guilty by an all white jury.

To set things again in the global perspective in the early 1970s, the African National Congress had turned to violence at last in its long struggle and the Cuban Revolution had been successfully exported to Chile. The "troubles" erupted in Northern Ireland, PLO terrorism was at its peak in the Middle East, and the Front de Liberation de Quebec had turned to kidnapping and murder in Canada. America had just pulled out of the war in Vietnam as the communists took over.

But then, almost as quickly as it began, the revolutionary movements in America died down, quite possibly in response to the winding down of the Vietnam War. It was ironic that a nation which exhibited its faith in force expected those in its midst who felt oppressed to remain at peace. However, in 1973 Bobby Seale ran for mayor of Oakland. He lost by sixteen percent of the votes but another, more political era had begun in the African American struggle.

That era, characterized in the dramatic campaigns of the Rev. Jessie Jackson for the US presidency saw the payoff for earlier voter registration programs. It became apparent to the major parties that the African American vote could determine the outcome of any close election. By the end of the century both parties were courting an African American, General Colin Powell, the top military leader in the country and former Head of the Joint Chiefs of Staff to be their presidential candidate. While all polls indicated he could win, he declined to run at that time. The point was clear; there would be an African American president before long and he or she would be elected on the basis of merit.

151

As small independent nations have discovered, freedom itself is not the end of the road. Independence and self-esteem are but necessary way stations en route to fulfillment as equals in a wider human community. The American experience in race relations in the twentieth century has left this unfinished business remaining, but it stands as an inspiring model to the world. The classic expression of the finest American and human ideals in connection with the long and ultimately successful struggle by African and other Americans is found not in the speech "I have a Dream." In a longer and less known letter of Martin Luther King Jr. written from his cell in the Birmingham jail to fellow clergy who were lukewarm toward the cause he appeals to all that is ultimately right in America. That letter is appended to this book in its entirety.

29.

THE PALE HORSE

Marshall McLuhan's vision of the world as a global village brought together electronically may come to pass eventually through the interactive connections of the internet, but television alone could not fulfill that vision. Perhaps because information flows only one way on TV, instead of being drawn closer together, people learned more about a world of distinctions. Anyone who had an important sense of identity seems to have clung to it more tightly in recent years and "separatist" movements sprang up in Scotland, Indonesia, Kashmir, Spain, Sri Lanka and a dozen other places where ethnic identity coincided with any sense of historical grievance or alienation.

This was taking place at the same time that economics, environmental concerns and other factors were indeed drawing people into one world. The negative reaction may have been a natural human response to the fear of ethnic identity loss among those to whom, for whatever reason, this was of primary importance. The Canadian province of Quebec has long nourished just such a sense of uniqueness as the cultural and political bastion of the French "Canadien" community. There are also more than a million members of the French community in the Acadian regions of the Maritime provinces, Northern Ontario and flourishing pockets in Western Canada. Some viable French culture also continues in Maine, Louisiana, but Quebec remains the heartland of French culture in North America.

In spite of dramatic strides to preserve and extend French culture elsewhere in Canada in the last quarter century, many Quebecers feel that their heritage is under siege and may not be able to survive as a functioning culture in the present political framework. The greatest fear of some Quebecers is that they may become Louisiana North as far as a functioning French society is concerned, a quaint curio for tourists like the New Orleans "French Quarter." The Quebec motto, *Je Me Souviens* means "I Remember", not "I am a souvenir".

Cultural retention in the home and in voluntary associations may be fine enough for Polish, Jewish and Chinese immigrants who came to North America expecting to give up much. It will not do for French Canadians who were "here first," who have retained French as a public culture for over four hundred years and who form a population with a robust majority in a geographical area that looks like a country and has the natural resources to be one.

The trouble is that the French were not here first and the natives that make up a similarly robust majority in the sparsely populated northern half of the province are determined to remain as part of Canada rather than become part of an ethnic French political enclave.

Native territories were not part of the original Quebec at the time of confederation, which established the Canadian nation in 1867. Natives and others cannot imagine why these former Northwest Territory lands should become part of any independent Quebec. The Canadian people might insist that the federal government defend the interests of the natives and it is doubtful that Quebec would attempt to use force to compel native compliance or to expel federal authorities from native communities.

Once a major exception is made in the case of Northern Quebec, the clangor among a million other non-French Canadians might also be impossible to ignore, especially in a province where at least a third of the French speaking population itself is diametrically opposed to separation. If a referendum favoring separation were to pass someday, most of the world would follow Canada's lead in recognizing a new state just somewhat larger than Switzerland or Chechnya in size and population. This is not a vision of the confident young giant of a nation featured in the dreams of ardent Quebec separatists but it represents the emerging reality.

Quebec can leave Canada if it wants to, but that prospect is finally unlikely, given those and other realistic costs of separation. For starters the new country would start off with a proportional share of the Canadian national debt. In addition, hopes of trade and business with the rest of Canada would be foreshadowed by a sorrowful enmity with Canadian neighbors that would exceed any bitterness over the Alaska Boundary Dispute which already held up free trade for a hundred years.

If Quebec is not to leave confederation then, is it a given that the "French fact" in Canada is to be reduced to functional equality with other ethnic groups? For important historical and constitutional reasons, it is not the view of the majority of Canadians that this should happen. A backlash against the constant threat to divide the country is growing, however, because of the economic uncertainty which affects every Canadian's mortgage rate, and also because of the growing resentment of Canadians who feel an attachment to the whole of Canada.

Quebec's store of political capital is beginning to run out in certain parts of the country just when Quebec may be turning back from separation, as Black Power advocates in the United States and Scottish Nationalists in Britain have done already. That era in the world is over, even if it has taken a little longer in Quebec because of the strength of the separatist movement there. In the referendum of October 30, 1995 Quebec nationalists came as close to staking their claim to total independence as may ever happen, in spite of ongoing dreams of nationhood of one kind or another.

An appendix to this book, titled "What Does Quebec Want?" is included as a sympathetic exposition of a Quebec nationalist leader's aspirations. It was presented by then Premier of Quebec, the Hon. Rene Levesque, as a foreword to another book by the author in 1976 in the search for common ground at the height of separatist trends around the world.

Meanwhile, the first thing for Quebecers to recognize at the end of the twentieth century is that, while their culture may always occupy a unique place in Canada and therefore in the world, Canada is changing in other ways. Quebec's historic and cherished parity with Ontario in population and power is history, and neither separation nor constitutional amendments can change that. The gap is large and growing, and it will continue to do so unless Quebecers dramatically increase their birth rate or several million French citizens move to Quebec from France, neither being likely prospects.

British Columbia is now the confident young giant within confederation and Native Indians are next on the agenda to receive recognition for their uniqueness and some sort of constitutional standing as a distinct society within Canada. Canadians as a whole do not mind celebrating uniqueness as long as equality is maintained. To belong to a "distinct society" does not confer "special status" that is superior to the status of other Canadians.

Canadians as a whole were ignorant and insensitive toward Quebec's past history and future aspirations for far too long but this has been deliberately remedied in the last quarter century. The position of French culture outside Quebec has been strengthened among the one million "francophones" that have not been assimilated elsewhere, contrary to out-of-date statistics still circulating in Quebec.

Moreover, the one million English ethnics and others (referred to in Canada as Anglophones and Allophones) who have remained in Quebec despite threats of separation are now able to function in a French environment. Many of them are actually as inclined to do so happily in public as are most francophones. Indeed, Quebec's language laws restricting the use of other languages in business and on the school yard are needed as much to stem the tide of North American English among young francophones in some parts of Quebec. In Montreal at the turn of the century a slim majority have mother tongues other than French for the first time in history and the current government of this French province is sensitive to that fact.

Finally, in this regard, the highly successful French Immersion program in other provinces now includes nearly half a million students from English speaking homes who are obtaining their entire education in French. This is a gesture of good will with few parallels in human history, though completely written off as meaningless in circles of extreme Quebec nationalism, where one must be born French as well as speak it.

While English Canadians were unappreciative of the French fact in Canada for so long, they are left now with a realization that much of French Canada does not know them very well either. A simplistic notion accepted by many Quebec nationalists holds that Canada is made up of two parts: descendants of the hard working *habitant* pioneers of Quebec and the children of privilege descended from an elite English conquering class.

The truth is that the rest of Canada was populated in early times mainly by Scottish and Irish who were deported by the English during the "highland clearances" in Scotland, and starved out of Ireland in a deliberate reduction of the population during the "potato famines." In many cases they suffered horribly in frozen backwoods areas of the Canadian wilderness where their babies died and their dreams were shattered. Yet they too broke the land and learned to cherish it.

French Canadians all know the story of the English General Wolfe who defeated the French in Quebec at the Plains of Abraham in 1759 and many of them presume that so-called "English" Canada revels in the story. The bitter truth for other Canadians, whose history goes back equally as far, is that this same English officer commanded the English troops against them in Scotland a dozen years earlier. The Battle of Culloden Moor in 1746 sealed Scotland's fate as an independent state and accounted for far more executions and deportations than Quebec has ever known under any circumstances.

At one point Canada was half French-speaking and half English-speaking but the English half had little of the diehard English ethnic identity ascribed to them by French Canada, except in tiny pockets of mostly poor English immigrants and in a very few elite neighbourhoods. Consequently the next waves of immigrants from Eastern Europe and more recent arrivals from Asia and the Caribbean found acceptance and even assimilation easier in "English" Canada. Some of the latest groups are still struggling to find their places, but their integration into the English speaking environment is a foregone conclusion, since there nobody cares much what they speak. The streets of Toronto, for example, are a babble of tongues while the people on the street in Montreal are required by law to communicate in French in an obviously self-defeating effort to build up the French speaking population.

Whenever they are out of power in Quebec, the separatists picture French Canada as the courageous little figure in white standing alone in front of the tanks in Tiananmen square. As soon as they achieve their occasional victories at the polls in a provincial election, they become the drivers of the tanks. Indeed, their electoral successes have taken place by convincing the voters that it may be possible to have what entertainer Robert Charlebois has described as "A free and independent Quebec, within a strong and united Canada."

The news flash for French Canadian nationalists is that "English" Canada they fear and resent has not existed for years, if it ever did exist. Ignoring the Natives who really were here first, of the two "founding races" so often described in Quebec as responsible for developing Canada, only one remains and that is the French. It must soon decide whether it wishes to become even more of an anachronism or adapt to maintain its distinctive character within the North American Empire, albeit with certain historic advantages guaranteed within the Canadian political framework. Because of the complications involved in separation described above, the conclusion may be foregone but it is still to be hoped that this choice may come about in a positive way.

In 1978 a brash Quebec teenager was chosen by his school for a Canada Youth World cultural exchange program that would take him for a month to Meaford, Ontario to experience life in a part of Canada where there were few French in a small town otherwise much like his hometown. Bruno Lacombe accepted on a dare, almost as a prank. He was as bitter against *les anglais* as an imaginative teenager could be and just as utterly committed to the cause of Quebec nationalism.

Bruno saw his chance to make at least some of the English oppressors realize how many Quebecers felt about them and to acquaint them with the justice of the separatist cause. The Parti Quebecois had come to power in 1976 with the promise of a government sponsored referendum on independence and young Lacombe saw his chance to preach the gospel next door and make some points with the neighbors in Ontario who surely did not understand the situation.

People in Meaford today remember the pugnacious young student who refused to stand for the Canadian national anthem at school or to bow for the Lord's Prayer. In class he argued passionately against the injustices French Canadians had experienced over the centuries.

The eventual 1980 referendum failed to gain a majority of Quebecers in favor of separation and the PQ lost power before long. Nearly twenty years later, under another PQ administration, at the beginning of another attempt to pass a government sponsored referendum in support of separation, Bruno Lacombe offered words of affection for Canada in a letter to the editor of the Meaford Express newspaper.

Editor:

In 1978 I was part of a youth exchange program and spent three weeks assisting in French classes with Mr. Chalifoux, the French local teacher at Georgian Bay Secondary School. Most of "my" students have now grown up and settled down, and may even have kids in that school. At that time I would stay sitting down while the national anthem was being played. (I was a little bit hostile and surprised they tolerated me.) I had the privilege to share my views with many history classes also on the topic, "What does Quebec want?"

Now a few months before another referendum, I still think of those Canadians who kept on loving me although I was blinded by my nationalistic pride. Now I stand for a strong Canada and you guys from Meaford High opened my eyes. When French Canadians tell me that English Canada hates us, well I have news for them. I have the opportunity to speak out often since one of my jobs is with the Government of Quebec.

Life is so funny. I did eventually vote "Non" to separation in that first referendum of 1980. Again in 1995 my answer will be the same and for many more reasons than only national finances which alone would be quite valid. As the United Nations recently declared, Canada is truly the finest country in the world in which to live.

Bruno Lacombe,

Laval, Quebec[22]

Today the Rev. Bruno Lacombe is pastor of a French church in Laval, Quebec and in 1996 his congregation entered into a twinning arrangement with the English speaking United Church in Meaford in an attempt to foster further exchanges of people at the grassroots level.

There is something so deeply touching to all Canadians in the story of the *pur laine* (pure wool) old stock French settlers who helped established the country of Canada. Canadians know that this was once the most open and generous element of North American societies. Among New Holland, New England, and New Spain, only New France refused to permit the slave trade at any time. The French explorer, Samuel de Champlain proposed to the Natives that "Our sons will marry your daughters and we will be one people" leading toward the establishment of a North American *Metis, a* mixed population that was dominant in certain parts of Canada in early times. Without doubt the richness of the French Canadian culture and heritage is an essential element in the soul of the whole nation, which explains a passion for a Canada including Quebec in the rest of the country, that some Quebecers find hard to recognize.

A reason for that may well be the long standing insensitivity on the part of the growing majority toward French culture and language, but one that is in process of redress. At the same time, it is still a world where people are sometimes unable to surmount their history of ethnic divisions, a situation which too often leads on to the Bosnian style of conflict. It has been unnerving to hear otherwise respectable nationalist politicians in Quebec calling for the *pur laine* to produce more white babies who would grow up French, and to hear referendum losses blamed on what are presumed to be non-French "ethnic" votes and (Jewish) money. If anything called the fairness of recent referenda into dispute it was the total lack of neutrality on the part of the provincial government, a democratic government of "all the people", that worded the ballot, put the question and campaigned blatantly on one side with all the power of incumbency.

After the 1996 referendum, officials of the governing Parti Quebecois were charged with rejecting huge numbers of ballots in ridings known to be federalist strongholds. Eighty six thousand ballots were rejected in a close vote that federalists won by only a 50,000 vote margin. Canadians never dreamed that deliberate fraud would be attempted in their country, but if two or three additional votes had been invalidated from each of the twenty thousand ballot boxes there could have been a new country on the map.

When explaining what life in an independent Quebec would be like, the respected former premier, Rene Levesque once said, "One thing sure, is that Quebec will not end up, either soon or in any foreseeable future, as the anarchic caricature of a revolutionary banana republic which adverse propaganda has been having great sinister fun depicting in advance." Those who loved him can only be glad he did not live through the racist indignities and attempts at vote rigging in 1996.

As the consequences of separation become clearer, growth in support for total independence diminishes. The rest of Canada is still prepared to accommodate and encourage a unique society in Quebec, and most Quebecers would prefer to be part of a large province rather than become a tiny country.

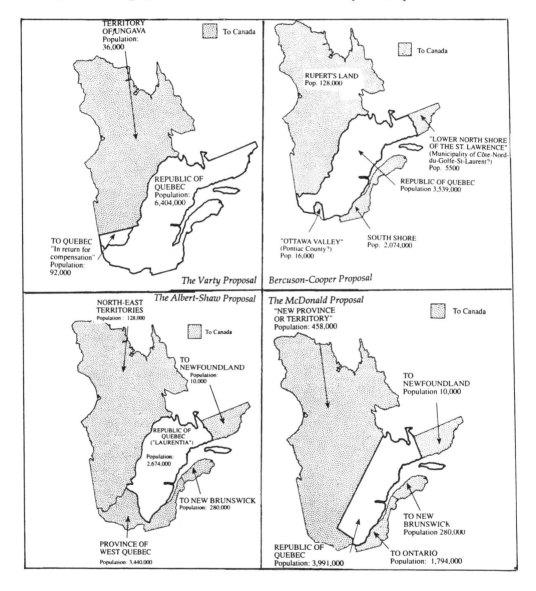

Proposed Maps of an Independent Quebec
(Bibliography see: Varty, Bercuson-Cooper, Albert-Shaw and McDonald)

160

30.

THE RED HORSE

The United States has about as many French citizens as there are African-Canadians, so it is appropriate to treat the North American French minority in the Canadian context alone, and the Black minority primarily in the American context. By contrast, the native Indian communities make up almost two percent of the population both north and south of the border, approximately five million in all - a figure similar to the French population of Quebec. They are separated by a border which, incidentally, many native groups have never officially acknowledged, and do not wish to recognize now.

The natives are still sometimes called "Indians" by themselves and others in both countries, and are technically Aboriginal Americans anywhere in North America. The term "Native" is used more generally to describe anyone of aboriginal ancestry, including those called "Native American Indian" and "Eskimo" in the United States, and in Canada those designated as "Status Indian", "Non- Status Indian" (with or without treaty rights), "Metis" (mixed race but officially recognized) and "Inuit" (in the north).

Natives are the fastest growing ethnic group in North America which partly accounts for the attention they have begun to receive in government circles and for their own growing political activism. This is a dramatic reversal from the situation of a declining native population in the several centuries following the invasions of native lands by Europeans. Indeed, at the time of first contact in 1492, there were 100 million natives in the Americas as a whole which, by coincidence, was the same as the population of Europe. The rapid decline in native population was primarily due to the introduction of European diseases, a greater factor than battlefield losses.

Well organized aboriginal "countries" were well established among the natives of South and Central America before Columbus arrived. They made treaties and traded with each other. Their well laid out large cities and their advanced engineering and mathematical sciences are well known. The devastation of those societies is documented elsewhere but it may be noted that these populations are growing rapidly again and are reclaiming political power in several Central American countries in particular, including parts of Mexico. Native societies north of Mexico were generally less developed, though sizable cities existed as far north as present day St. Louis, Missouri, which, with a population of 40,000, was the same size as London and Paris in the time of Columbus.

One of the ironies of history is that as the native population declined in numbers through contact with generally less healthy Europeans, the latter began to flourish and improve in health upon the introduction of native foods. This was true in the colonies and even more dramatically so in Europe itself. It is sometimes thought, for example, that the introduction of the potato changed the course of modern German history more than any other single factor, through an essential expansion of what had been a cereal based diet. Likewise for the turkey, brought to Spain from America, exported to England and returned to America where it became a reliable staple in the early New England colonies, without which many settlers might not have survived.

Rather than remembering it as the occasion when kindly colonists invited natives for dinner, Thanksgiving in both Canada and the United States might better be recalled as Native Foods Day. Everything on most tables is native in origin on that holiday. The key elements of turkey, cranberry and pumpkin pie are all native as are the potatoes and yams, the beans, tomatoes, pepper, corn and squash. Even coke or hot chocolate and cigars afterwards are all native in origin and were unknown to Europeans. It is difficult to imagine the North American diet today without these foods developed by native horticulture.

The accusation that European Christians brought diseases and gunpowder to these natives, and received food and lands in return, is believable after reading a proclamation from shipboard, similar to the "Requiremento" proclaimed by Columbus on his first contact with native communities.

REQUIREMENTO

I request and require you to recognize

THE CHURCH

as your mistress and as governess of the world and universe, and the high priest called the pope in her name, & their majesties

KING FERDINAND AND QUEEN ISABELLA

as rulers and sovereigns in her place.

And if you do not do this, with the help of God I shall come mightily against you and I shall make war on you everywhere and in every way that I can, and I shall subject you to the yoke and obedience of the church and their majesties, and I shall seize your women and children, and I shall make them slaves, to sell and dispose of them as their majesties command, and I shall do all the evil and damage to you that I am able.

I insist that the deaths and destruction that shall result from this will be your fault.[23]

The great reduction in native population, which took place through epidemics of European diseases, happened both by accident and by design. These were diseases against which the healthy natives, in their relatively germ-free environment, had little or no immunity.

At the same time, most modern people have scant knowledge of the extremes of brutality exercised by the first Europeans with their superior fire-power. Christopher Columbus himself recorded occasions when, as an example to others, he would cut off the hands of native slave laborers who were panning for gold too slowly.

In North America, natives continued to roam freely for some centuries, although their settlements were frequently uprooted or burned down. They tended to move west to avoid contact, but they certainly did not observe the niceties of national or colonial borders for some time.

As late as 1864 the Alberta warrior Maskepetoon was apparently in Mexico where he appears in the diary of Maximillian, the ill fated puppet Emperor of Mexico under the brief French Empire regime there. The contention that the natives of North America have always been citizens of the continent as a whole has much historical validity.

Attempts to redress ancient wrongs might be addressed jointly by Canadians and Americans. As both countries learn to better appreciate the native cultures they may discover more about themselves and find one more reason to reunite this old empire with native participation.

The famous speech of Chief Seattle, in the era when control of the Pacific coast was still disputed between Canada and the United States, has been discredited in some quarters because, while not a forgery, it has been edited by both native and white promoters of its ideals. However, as modern as it sounds, it has existed for a century in its present form and faithfully conveys long standing native concerns in a style the chief would have used, judging by other native documents of the time.

The authorship of the speech which follows is communal in many respects, much like the authorship of the first five books of the Bible, said to be "written by Moses" and revered as if they were. Neither is a forgery, as such, any more than a recent political program published by the Progressive Conservative Party of Canada under the affectionate title "The Policies of John A. Today," a full century after their popular founding leader, Sir John A. Macdonald had died.

The original Seattle speech was given to federal emissaries in the presence of many natives in 1854.

Chief Seattle's "Speech"

The Great Chief in Washington sends word that he wishes to buy our land. He also sends us words of friendship and good will. This is kind of him, since we know he has little need of our friendship in return. But we will consider your offer. We know that if we do not sell, the white man may come with guns and take our land.

How can you buy or sell the sky, the warmth of the land? The idea is strange to us. If we do not own the freshness of the air and the sparkle of the water, how can you buy them? Every part of this Earth is sacred to my people. Every shining pine needle, every sandy shore, every mist in the dark woods, every clearing and humming insect is holy to my people. The sap which courses through the trees carries the memories of the red people.

The white people's dead forget the country of their birth when they go to walk among the stars. Our dead never forget this beautiful Earth, for it is the mother of the red people. We are part of the Earth and it is part of us. The flowers are our sisters; the deer, the horse, the great eagle, these are our brothers; the rocky crests, the juices in the meadows, the body heat of the pony and humans - all belong to the same family.

The shining water that moves in the streams and rivers is not just water but the blood of our ancestors. If we sell you the land, you must remember it is sacred and you must teach your children it is sacred, and that each ghostly reflection in the clear water of the lakes tells of events and memories in the life of my people. The water's murmur is the voice of my father's father. The rivers are our brothers, that quench our thirst. They carry our canoes and feed our children. If we sell, remember, and teach your children, the rivers are our brothers, and yours, and you must henceforth give the rivers the kindness you would give any brother.

The air is precious to us, for all share the same breath - the beast, the tree, the people. The whites do not seem to notice the air they breathe. Like a man dying for many days, they are numb to the stench. But if we sell you our land, you must remember the air is precious to us and shares its spirit with all the life it supports.

If we decide to accept, I make one condition: the white people must treat the beasts of this land as their brothers. I am a savage and do not understand any other way. I have seen a thousand rotting buffaloes on the prairie, left by the white man who shot them from a passing train. I do not understand how the smoking iron horse can be more important than the buffalo that we kill only to stay alive.

What is man without the beasts? If all the beasts were gone, the people would die of great loneliness of spirit. For whatever happens to the beasts happens to the people. All things are connected. This we know. The earth does not belong to the people; the people belong to the earth. This we know. All things are connected like the blood which unites one family. Whatever befalls the Earth befalls the children of the Earth. The people did not weave the web of life but are merely a strand in it. Whatever we do to the web we do to ourselves.

It matters little where we spend the rest of our days. Our children have seen their fathers humbled in defeat. Our warriors have felt shame, and they turn their days in idleness and contaminate their bodies with sweet foods and strong drink. A few more hours, a few more winters, and none of the children of the great tribes that once lived on this Earth or that roam now in small bands in the woods will be left to mourn. The whites too shall pass; perhaps sooner than all other tribes. If you continue to contaminate your bed, you will one night suffocate in your own waste.

One thing we know, which the whites may one day discover - our God is the same God. You may think now that you own God as you wish to own our land, but you cannot. God is the God of all people and God's compassion is equal for the red and white people. This Earth is precious to God, and to harm the Earth is to heap contempt on its Creator.[24]

165

Native works of art are among the cultural delights of the twentieth century. In the United States the native art form known best is the artifact, principally jewelry, typically made of silver with inlaid turquoise stones. In the arctic regions of both countries, soapstone carvings have become an important industry with substantial revenues accruing to Eskimo and Inuit artisans.

One of the more interesting art stories of recent times has come out of southern Canada. Kept from European immigrants for hundreds of years by a successful, unspoken, instinctive conspiracy until the 1960s, a tradition of native graphic arts has recently captured the interest of university art faculties from Rome to Tokyo. Until the first public exhibitions in Toronto in 1962 by Norval Morrisseau, native art known by the Canadian public was little more than bead and trinket souvenirs. He revealed two native styles that had been seen previously but their significance had remained unrecognized.

The ancient art of "rock painting" originally employed colors in bright ochre outlines with subtle interior shadings compatible with the natural environment. This style is particularly adaptable to modern acrylics and gives a stained glass window affect, but except for ancient weathered examples, it was seen little and basically ignored outside native communities.

More exciting still to the art world and others is the work of the shamanistic tradition, often called the "X-ray" technique. A native shyness, an inferiority complex induced by centuries of ridicule, and, to some extent, an outright conspiracy among natives kept this marvel away from public awareness until Morriseau's first exhibition. In this particular and unique art form, the faces and limbs of human or animal figures display an x-ray like transparency which evokes an eerie sense of the interior life of the subject. Even inanimate objects like the features of the earth itself are imbued with life in this way.

Within a few years a number of native artists were exhibiting in the shamanistic style. In spite of humble acknowledgments that they stood in an ancient tradition, it was assumed by many that this engaging style was new. It appeared destined to be a hit, the southern equivalent of the soapstone carvings. Then it was learned that the Royal Ontario Museum in Toronto had drawers stuffed full of paintings in the shamanistic style on birch bark parchments, hundreds of years old.

Jungians and other depth psychologists were especially enthralled. The Queen and the Pope were presented with shamanistic art works by some of the best, newly authenticated, native artists. Many of them are from the Manitoulin School, a native artistic community on an island between Lake Huron and Georgian Bay that has become a mecca for American tourists who come to view the work of Bell, Simon, Trudeau, Shawana, Debassig and Cheechoo.

Other noteworthy facets of the modern interface between natives and the dominant culture relate to time management and finances as well as substance use and abuse. Centuries of a perceived native lack of punctuality at the work place have been reassessed. Well organized, even "driven" white executives and workers alike are now being taught to slow down to be more wisely productive. Workaholics are being introduced to the virtues of "flex time," formerly known in derision as "Indian time."

For many years individual natives have been unable to finance their business aspirations in a credit/capital economy because use of private property as collateral was impossible under treaty arrangements that gave the whole band communal title to property on North American reservations (or reserves as they are termed in Canada). The reason for this has been traditionally ascribed to a perceived native inability to manage money. Ironically, north and south of the border governments are now increasingly turning over the management of gambling casinos to native bands with little or no especially adverse consequence, to the natives at least.

A reversal of understanding with respect to substance use and abuse has also been overdue. Europeans introduced the practice of alcohol consumption to natives who have often displayed a variety of physiological and socio-psychological difficulties with its use. The increasing awareness of the derelict effects of the native gift of tobacco to the non-native community, which is used with less negative effect among natives, is the parallel of interest. Neither group seems able to forswear the vices introduced by the other.

In the matter of Indian Wars and alliances, the American record is more straightforward than the Canadian. That which was taken from the natives in the United States was acquired by brutality in "acts of conquest", usually legal, unsavory as that may appear in retrospect. The British in Canada never fought a single war against the natives, nor has the Government of Canada. Everything acquired from natives north of the border has been acquired illegally by stealth and political deception of Canada's most trusted native allies.

Prior to the British era, and in spite of good beginnings earlier, there were bitter wars between the French and the natives, a legacy that has come back to haunt modern Quebec. However, the British were at pains to carefully cultivate alliances with the natives in conflicts with the French and later against the Americans, as has been noted. Without these alliances it is doubtful that the British could have acquired Canada or that the Canadians could have kept it.

These treaties basically offered secure land titles and natural resources (usually including fishing rights but rarely minerals) to native bands and tribes in return for alliances in battle. It would appear from historical records that the natives upheld their end, even at great cost, but that the British and Canadians exercised every deception imaginable to avoid keeping their part of the contracts.

This results in a basic difference between modern native claims for redress north and south of the border. In the United States the claims are primarily moral claims pursued through the political process, with some legal aspects to support the claims - and the natives rarely win. In Canada, the claims are almost entirely legal claims pursued through the courts with a moral argument thrown in - and the natives almost never lose. However, in both countries there is substantial unfinished business to be concluded with native citizens before North American society is made whole in terms of its history.

It will never be known exactly what traditional native spirituality might have looked like without its five hundred year interface with Christianity. It has not been supplanted as completely as were African religions but what remains of native spirituality has co-opted so much from Christianity that it is a new hybrid religion with many of the best elements of both. Some Christians have great difficulty with that, especially the many devout native Christians who outnumber the native traditionalists. Given the history of conversion by force and European cultural imperialism, it may be difficult for others to understand the continuing attraction of Christianity to native communities, but the same phenomenon could be observed in Africa after the missionaries departed and also in primitive Europe at a much earlier time in history.

While the weight of spiritual influence has been one-sided until the modern era, many churches, including Roman Catholic and Protestant "mainstream" denominations have more recently recognized the power, truth, and beauty found in native spiritual imagery. They have begun to adapt and adopt native traditions in the context of worship in native communities and also in non-native congregations. This trend has been especially helpful in the search for new imagery celebrating God's goodness in the environment of creation.

Natives believe that their fresh contribution to arts and spirituality in North America is no mere accidental prelude to native hopes for a more effective role in political life. The violent standoff between "Red Power" natives and US federal officials at Wounded Knee in 1973 was similar to events at that time involving the Black Panthers in the United States and the FLQ in Canada.

This type of confrontation involving natives continued into the last years of the century at Oka, Quebec and other parts of Canada. It is urgent that legitimate land claims be settled so that Red Power, Black Power, French Power and perhaps even White Power issues be moved into political resolution. Natives in particular have a political "self- government" objective that may be attainable at the municipal level in many parts of the continent.

Unlike African Americans, natives are not so dispersed in the population that self-government would seem like a state within a state. On the other hand, unlike French Canadians, natives are not so concentrated in one area that they often aspire to an independent country. Such options have been indeed contemplated by African, French and Native North Americans, not to mention white "Fortress America" advocates in the United States, but walls that divide would take everyone back in time, not forward. A proliferation of independent, new political states would be an indictment of North American civilization.

Municipal style government for reservations and reserves could give authority for native court systems which would remain responsive to state/ provincial and federal laws and charters on the larger issues. As with other areas of life previously considered, it is increasingly realized that native justice traditions, such as the victim sharing responsibility with the judge and jury in "the sentencing circle", may also have value for society at large. The municipal model is of interest to native leaders in both countries, but two departures from this model have already occurred in Canada at the end of the twentieth century and each has potential for wider application.

In Saskatchewan, a western province slightly larger than Montana and with a population of a million people, natives are still a decided minority. But the children of this fast growing group have been the majority of primary school registrants in the province since the mid nineteen nineties. The trend will continue and possibly appear in a few other parts of Canada and the western United States. In the course of time this will give natives a stake in city, provincial and state politics not previously contemplated and without any of the special status which, like quota systems, seems unfair to many people.

The situation in Nunavut is even more dramatic and has caught the imagination of natives and non-natives alike. Officially coming into existence in April, 1999, Nunavut is a new Canadian Territory which represents the first change to the map of North America since Newfoundland became a province or Alaska and Hawaii became states. Nunavut is also of interest because of creative adaptations of the normal democratic institutions. Nunavut is likely to have a most significant impact on the twenty-first century.

The ancient and gigantic Northwest Territories acquired by Canada from Britain and the Hudson's Bay Company, have previously provided expanded territory for Quebec, Ontario and Manitoba and have spawned the provinces of Alberta and Saskatchewan. Now, after local plebiscites, federal legislation has created the new territory (and province in waiting) known as Nunavut. Located in the eastern Arctic region, with a size and resource base similar to Alaska, Nunavut has a native Inuit majority of eighty-two percent.

Issues of "special status" were disposed of in the settlement of native land claims which give the Inuit a suitable economic base. Nunavut does not claim to be a "distinct society" either, it simply is one. A reasonable provision for longer residency requirements may prevent transient resource workers from exerting undue influence in territorial political life but no such provisions are based on race or linguistic distinctions.

While avoiding quotas, Nunavut is the first jurisdiction in North America to achieve gender parity in its Legislative Assembly. Each constituency will be represented by two members, one female and one male, and all citizens regardless of gender will have two ballots to cast in elections with two gender balanced slates of candidates.

The legislation establishing these and other creative twenty-first century solutions to questions of residence eligibility, gender, courts, and resource development all came out of traditions of native wisdom. Some of them have been tried experimentally in Alaska. It always helps to have someone else try things out first to work out the bugs. Now all of these areas are subject to wider application in North American life. For that reason the text of most of these provisions to establish Nunavut are included as an appendix to this book.

Other prospects in the area of native advancement into the United Empire of North America might include the possibility that natives be the first group of citizens in both Canada and the United States to have dual citizenship recognized. For most Americans and Canadians a simple full recognition of each other's existing citizenship will suffice for travel, employment and other exchanges, as happens at present for the most part. Recognizing natives as citizens of both countries, exercising their franchise wherever they happen to live, could be one of the first significant steps marking a new era in the relationship between Canada and America. It would also solve at last the problems associated with governing reserves/reservations that straddle the existing border between the US and Canada, and their long history of administrative difficulties.

Native integration into the society of the United Empire would heal old wounds and give North American culture some roots that go back into the mists of time. Shared traditions then will be as ancient as those of Egypt and as instinctively wise as those of the Orient. To complete this unfinished business is to lay a more complete foundation for political and social life for the twentieth century than North America has known heretofore.

31.

THE WHITE HORSE

Is the "religious right" indeed an unholy alliance of mean spirited, racist bigots who actually hate their neighbor, or are its members vigilant and concerned Americans seeking to rid their country of self-administered poisons to which the rest of the culture has become addicted? Both are possibilities and both may be true in some measure. This may help to explain much confusion, some panic and widely divergent views about this phenomenon on the conservative wing of American political and religious life.

There is an urgent need for mainstream North American society to appreciate and encourage the truly legitimate aspects of the Christian Coalition agenda. This is part of an appropriate political debate and a genuine quest to re-establish a spiritual foundation for this society.

In the first place, these citizens have every right to views which are thoughtful and even provoking, whether popular or not. If a broad spectrum of ideas can be encouraged in democratic debate, extremist elements will fall away and search for another vehicle for expression of their frustrations.

Secondly, it just could not be possible that such a mass psychosis could arise to sound these alarm bells about the pace and direction of changes in society unless the underlying causes were substantial, even if sometimes unconscious. It may be time for the liberal elements of North American society to get over their panic and sincerely ask what may be at the root of all the passionate concern.

For example, whether or not abortion is murder, might there be genuine substance to a deeper, inarticulate instinct that the finest sensitivities of the human spirit are being killed? Is it possible that the present massive rate of abortions is a dreadful "root canal" of the communal womb, not to mention the specter of individual psychic damage at a level not yet fully appreciated? For a society that accepts repeated medical flip-flops on the advisability of eating chicken eggs, it is passing strange that there is so little flexibility in the various positions on aborting human eggs.

Among "extremists" who insist that the individual's right to own guns is intended as much to protect them from the state as from hoodlums, could there be a correct instinct in their fear that big, impersonal governments can become Orwellian big bullies? If so, how is that concern to be addressed, and how is it related to security against random violence?

If the world truly benefits from free trade, and North America prospers in the switch to high-tech, high-pay industries, is it right that working class Americans alone should bear the brunt of the dislocations and temporary distortions in the economy? As they lose their homes to the mortgage companies, their howls of protest may be inappropriately directed to foreign factory workers who are pleased to have the smoke stacks relocate to neighbourhoods outside North America. This does not make them "red-necks." The callous manipulators of this process and the academic critics of the religious right rarely share the pain.

Moreover, racism aside, it may simply be impossible for America to absorb huge and unprocessed masses of cheaper immigrant laborers in exactly the same era in which the working poor are asked to bear the brunt of the above transition. The religious right may lack a certain sophistication in articulating an instinctive reaction to these profound phenomena, but they are sometimes alone in forcing these issues onto the political agenda of North American society.

If the religious right sometimes uses inappropriate rhetoric in its failure to articulate the fears it cannot express, the liberal churches, media, universities and other critics are just as guilty of visceral reactions in place of reasoned comment. It is equally difficult for both sides when emotions run high on issues as controversial as sexuality, racism, religious rights and the remedies for crime.

It is simply ironic that those charging the religious right with extremism do so in such shrill voices. Hyperbole and even crude attempts at humor, while typical of political and media cultures, are obviously tinged with an unhealthy level of anxiety on both sides. People who would do and say extreme things should examine themselves to determine what it is they really fear.

On the other hand, simple good people who merely wish to protect their children from violence, promiscuity and drugs cannot understand why their movement is seen as so insidious by so many African Americans, Jews and a liberal establishment with a long memory. The Christian Coalition does not support gay bashing or the shooting of abortionists. To them it is merely an unfortunate coincidence that extremists are attracted to their wholesome movement.

In this respect, the religious right too needs to reassess its rhetoric. Those favoring a conservative ethic need to bend over backwards to avoid code words designed to appeal to religious bigots and racist extremists or else accept the reality that they will be seen as guilty by association.

On both sides of this great conservative-liberal divide there is naivete, misrepresentation and self-serving distortion of the views of others that is neither Christian nor democratic. This debate is capable of arousing the most base of human emotions unless it is developed with greater intelligence and sincerity than has been in evidence heretofore. The extremist genie has been put back into the bottle several times in the twentieth century, but it should be exorcised once and for all in a public process that involves a respectful quest for a moral consensus that is both wise and acceptable to the broad spectrum of citizens.

The white supremacists and Christian fundamentalists attracted to the religious right are perhaps immature and emotionally unstable, but they may be no less legitimate as extensions of instinctive grievances than were the Black Panthers in the ghetto, the Mohawk Warriors at the barricades or the FLQ terrorists in Quebec. All three of these latter were at least understood by the liberal intelligentsia. In some cases they were almost patronized.

However, Christian Coalition leaders should understand by now that people who disagree with positions of the religious right actually fear the extremists identified with that particular movement. Extremists of the religious right are less likely to be patronized, embraced and finally engaged politically as was done successfully in the other cases. French Power can be voted upon. Red Power can be negotiated. Black Power can be understood in the context of American history. White Power turns the stomach and strikes fear in the heart for most people.

There may be two reasons for this. The first and most obvious is the potential size and power of a movement associated by its own rhetoric with Nazi, fascist and Klan precedents which attempted to separate races, dictate morals and restrict freedoms in a manner intended to favor a particular social order. The second reason may be a subconscious awareness that the Christian Coalition could ultimately be vindicated in some of its harsh critiques of dearly loved liberal sacred cows, such as welfare entitlements and affirmative action.

To open Pandora's box is to risk changes that could materially affect the whole of society, not merely those forced to bear the brunt of transition thus far. However, of all the spirits set free in the Pandora myth, the final one to flutter forth was Hope.

Only a more honest and less self-serving discourse can defuse this dangerous impasse. North America may be ready to move on to that next stage as part of the final legacy of the twentieth century. If not, a hundred years of struggle with these issues may have been in vain.

The conservative ethics of the pioneer Agricultural Age in North America, which were often more form than substance, gave way in changing times to a liberal social ethic more suited to the Industrial Age which characterized the twentieth century. That ethic has now collapsed in the face of changes in the Information Age as the twenty-first century unfolds.

The conservative ethic of the Agricultural Age was based on a literal Biblical theology and supported by the authority of the church. There is still an important place for spiritual beliefs and institutional churches but they are by no means in control.

Liberal ethics of the Industrial Age were based on social science and implemented by governments through social policy and state supported systems such as health care and education. There is still a role for government but people have found social science inadequate. It is frequently neither sociable nor scientific, and social engineering of any sort is ineffective at any rate, as citizens of the former USSR demonstrated to the world.

Ethics for the Information Age may build upon spiritual foundations and there needs to be a common denominator of social consensus, but the new ethical element will be greater individual responsibility. The role of the church or any other spiritual community will be to equip people to assume their responsibility. The role of the state will be to provide a secure context for this much freedom.

The debates over sexuality are illustrative of these principles. At first there appears little room for compromise between diametrically opposed positions on abortion, for example, but a society requires a workable consensus. Because it appears so clear cut, an extensive consideration of the abortion issue may serve to highlight the need for a new approach to ethics in general, and the concerns of the religious right in particular vis-a-vis the liberal left.

One side argues that abortion is always wrong and tantamount to murder. Whether that conclusion is reached on emotional or intellectual grounds, or a combination of both, it is clear that anyone holding such a view will take a strong stand in opposition to the practice. They deliberately use the evocative phrase "pro-life" to describe their position, inferring that those who hold another view are obviously "pro-death." Some pro-lifers will grant that cases of rape or situations where the mother's life is in danger represent legitimate exceptions, but some see even this as an improper compromise on the sacredness of life.

On the other extreme are advocates for freedom of choice, usually on the part of the woman, with respect to bringing a pregnancy to full term in all or most situations. Their "pro-choice" terminology likewise demeans those who are thereby represented as giving up their choices and God-given responsibilities. These persons believe that while the fetus is "alive," and may look like a tiny human, it is not a human life, legally or morally, in and of itself. Such advocates range from a few who may believe that no abortion is of particular consequence to many who believe that all abortions are unfortunate, or even tragic, with profound consequences, but not quite murder.

The waters are murky with medical and psychological evidence pro and con in reference to the mother's health. Legal arguments often revolve around the responsibilities and rights of the father. Moral arguments frequently center on a desire to have every child born into a loving and supportive environment.

The Bible teaches that while "life" may begin at conception, it was when God breathed the breath of life into Adam's nostrils that "man became a living soul,"[25] and not until. This ancient Christian doctrine of "homination" is also related to the "viability" argument which holds that the fetus is human if it has reached the stage where it could survive on its own outside the womb.

While modern medical science has changed the rules considerably, most of the earlier doctors and teachers of the church differed only in the timing of those abortions that may be permitted. While none of them "favored" abortion, in the fifth century St. Augustine counseled its permissibility until hominization had taken place and viability was assured.[26]

St. Thomas Aquinas, in the thirteenth century, taught that abortion is a sin against marriage, and as such he opposed the practice. However, he did not regard it as homicide until after the fetus had been ensouled, which he believed was completed several stages after conception.[27]

The position of the Roman Catholic Church in the post-reformation era became modified at the Council of Trent in the sixteenth century and firmer in opposition to abortion as the years went by. Any opposition in favor of earlier Catholic positions went underground.

Most Protestants maintained the more permissive position of the earlier church until a similar split in the twentieth century between liberals and conservatives. Most other religious and secular groups in the United States and Canada permit abortion but neither favor nor promote its general availability.

Then in the 1960's medical science opened the "choice" issue further both by ensuring greater fetus viability and also making abortion cheaper and safer. This coincided with another earthquake on the Richter scale of evolution, the liberation of women. Women working outside the home rated with the social impact equal to the industrial revolution, when a majority of men left the farm for the first time, with all the social and familial change that followed in the wake of that upheaval.

The abortion debate took center stage in the struggle between those who longed for a world that was, and those who determined that women should never again be restricted to the single choice of a domestic role. The debate raged ostensibly between people who were sensitive to enduring old human values and those determined to create a world of greater freedom and justice, for children and women in particular.

The opposition to abortion is strongest among males, inside certain churches especially. The right wing extremists who shoot doctors and bomb clinics also appear to be males in every case, determined that a social order in which they held a privileged position should not change.

Both sides have their own supporting casts of medical, legal and theological authorities. All the while, both sides also know full well that the other has arguments that are logical enough, so the debate has been conducted primarily at the emotional level for some forty years in the ethical wilderness toward the end of the twentieth century.

Then the landscape shifted just as dramatically again. The very feminists most eager to promote the freedom to choose were confronted by the deeply disturbing statistics of gender imbalance in abortion. The realization grew that, with medical technology advancing again, the century was closing with twice as many abortions of female fetuses as males in many North American clinics as well as elsewhere in the world.

The consequences of unlimited personal choice came into focus in a new light. Could it be that members of the religious right were correct in their instinctive reaction all along? Perhaps abortion is a callous attack on what makes people human. Even if it is not murder, it may indeed be an offence to God in many situations.

Moreover, at about that same time it became increasingly apparent to some[28] that perhaps a disproportionate number of unmarried teenage females obtaining abortions were from Roman Catholic and conservative Protestant families. The doctors responding to the pleas and demands for abortions were mainly liberal Protestant, Jewish and secular/humanist physicians. Ironically, their own daughters and the young families from these latter traditions

Ironically, their own daughters and the young families from these latter traditions required such services less frequently themselves. Rates of sexual activity appear to be about the same in both groups but, in a strange twist, contraception is the preferred method of birth control in a liberal environment while abortion is frequently the only recourse among Roman Catholics and fundamentalist Protestants.

For example, Quebec, the only province in Canada with a Roman Catholic majority, is now the province with the lowest birth rate. This is not because of contraception but because Quebec has the highest abortion rate in Canada. In the United States there are more abortion clinics to protest against in the "Bible Belt" than in more liberal California, for the same obvious reasons.

In a reversal of what the religious right might expect, the fewer the choices, the greater the reaction. Human history is replete with such examples. Religious and political demagogues continue to pander to their constituencies, but is it not time for the real debate to move on from abortion, pro and con, to abstinence, contraception, safe sex, health and social responsibility?

As will be seen in other ethical questions, there may be few options except to move forward in the twenty-first century. At the end of the old century, surgical abortions were being replaced by pharmaceutical abortions in the final shift on this vexatious issue.

In Canada, the legal drug misoprostol, used to treat ulcers, was being prescribed in combination with the cancer drug methyltrexate in a safe, effective and private method of early abortion. No visit to hospital or clinic is required; a cooperative physician can merely prescribe over the phone.[29]

A New York non-profit health organization was the first to acquire the American marketing rights to the European abortion-inducing drug RU486,[30] or "mifepristone" as it is known in North America. Its approval by the federal Food And Drug administration for general use beginning in 1997 has suddenly moved abortion procedures beyond the range of extremist guns and bombs.

This has forced the religious right to belatedly commit itself to more positive options in a new "alliance for life." On the other side of the equation, however, there is as yet nothing more than token rhetoric about the tragic nature of abortion from the "pro-choice" liberal mainstream.

"Banning" abortions has been no more effective than "prohibition" of liquor or censorship of "dirty pictures" but in each case a higher ethic is available through education, the spiritual life and a compassionate public policy. As pharmaceutical abortions in the doctor's office or at home replace surgical abortions in clinics and hospitals, it becomes essential for "pro-life" programs to move above and beyond "anti-abortion" activities.

This is happening, with less traumatism than expected, but to achieve the desired and permanent shift in social mores, it must be done in concert with others who recognize the dehumanizing consequences of all forms of abortion. Even many who hold the view that abortion must be an option in any particular case are concerned when the numbers of abortions are as high as they were in the last years of the twentieth century.

As the nineteenth century had a morbid preoccupation with death in its poems, songs and literature, but could never speak of sex without hypocrisy, the twentieth century has been equally immature in the opposite direction. One hundred years from now, students of this era will be amazed at the twentieth century fixation with sex in every popular song and story, and its peculiar denials of the reality of death. But in spite of all this interest in sex, the level of debate on the ethical issues remains low.

At the turn of this century, the number of abortions stands at one million per year in the United States and one hundred thousand per year in Canada, identical figures in proportion to population. This itself is interesting since abortions are controlled by a variety of legislative restrictions in the United States, and by none whatsoever in Canada.

Like prostitution, the practice of abortion is unlikely to disappear entirely, but the sheer gross numbers may be surprising to people one hundred years from now, in much the same way that modern people find it hard to imagine the sheer volume of the prostitution business one hundred years ago. That will happen only if there is a significant shift away from current understandings of sexuality and reproduction, as well as in the lifestyle modifications that would follow.

The extremely high number of abortions itself might lead an objective observer to conclude that something is seriously amiss in the sensitive areas of human reproduction and sexuality. Learning from the example of church teachings leading to prostitution at the end of the nineteenth century, might it not be equally obvious that church teachings are a major contributor to the abortion epidemic at the end of the twentieth century?

Some Roman Catholic leaders fear that the availability of birth control devices will lead to promiscuity and sex, even in the home, for reasons unrelated to procreation, such as the mere expression of love. Abuses are possible, but do these spiritual guides need reminding that it is God who already took the chances by providing the basic equipment for sexual activity to almost everyone in the first place?

Some Protestant leaders fear that providing complete and graphic sex education in the schools, or even at church, might actually teach young people how to engage in sexual activity. Perhaps it is not obvious to them but their own young people are already figuring out how, all by themselves, with an urgent nudge from nature. "How" has never been a problem; the problems arise when nobody is willing to talk about "why" in a frank and honest manner.

In this century, the media and the courts have made the whole world painfully aware that many of the most shrill of these moral leaders are hypocritical. This fact is doubly tragic because it undermines the ministries of many wise and compassionate spiritual leaders. What is missing in both the Catholic and Protestant cases above is a mature awareness of the beauty of sex and its value in loving relationships.

Moreover, neither of these church situations takes realistic account of the amount of sexual activity in a society fixated on sex, and where the major spiritual communities make little or no contribution to limiting unwanted pregnancies. In dealing with children and teens in particular, this position is assumed in an almost "Victorian" spirit of false modesty.

As a result, the teachings of churches are a prime contributor to a rate of abortion 1,200% higher than it might be when more mature attitudes to human sexuality prevail. A reduction in the abortion rate of this magnitude is a reasonable objective for the twenty-first century, once churches and other social agencies discover again the ways to support and encourage progressive social change. It may also happen without their involvement as individuals take more responsibility and scientific advances are factored into other social changes.

The need for more mature public debate on abortion, and genuine communal efforts, not to merely prevent abortion but to make it unnecessary, are paralleled in other areas, sexual and otherwise. The tactics of the religious right appear to many to have the opposite of the effect they desire in areas of promiscuity and homosexuality also. The tragedies of right wing intolerance and reverse results are only exceeded in their negative impact by the lack of ethics or even much concern in more liberal quarters.

Relationships among young unmarried couples are still sometimes destabilized by church and family in modern society, whereas a Biblical culture would have sanctioned many of them in premarriage betrothals and thereby deprived the merely licentious of a social acceptance they now enjoy. Is it time to add a betrothal ritual to engagements for those who wish to delay the formalities of the marriage ceremony, for instance?

To offer another example, the AIDS epidemic spreads from the gay community to society at large precisely because that society itself requires such relationships to be furtive and unstable. These are but two further areas crying out for more mature public discussion with less hysteria on the conservative side and less irresponsible, blase attitudes on the part of liberals.

The religious right is correct that North American family life is in deep trouble. Mobility, consumerism, high rates of "illegitimacy," as well as abortion, the changing roles of women and male intransigence are among the changes that have placed the institution of the family under stress. The rate of marriage dissolution seemed to have peaked and reversed toward the century's end but it remains high. Perhaps the most fundamental change in the twentieth century family was the separation of generations.

In the prosperity which followed World War II, for the first time in history, the younger adult generation did not need their parents' financial support. Until then almost every household had three generations under one roof. Moreover, because of post-war medical advances, the older generation lived longer and was healthy. Since they were no longer financially assisting the two succeeding generations, and because they were healthier, they too had more disposable income and independence. This phenomenon may have contributed more to the decline of "family values" than has been realized.

Grandparents in the home have not only passed on traditions and provided stability to the third generation. They also, by their presence, modified the behaviour of the second generation. Without them the rise in alcohol abuse and domestic violence in even good families has destroyed many households. There are a few signs that the generations may be reconnecting for the new century, but even the most conservative families are unlikely to turn the clock back completely. Here again some new thinking is required across the social and religious spectrum.

It may be helpful for some to realize that the "nuclear family" of the post-war era was itself an aberration in both its isolation and its size, as compared to "traditional", pioneer or Biblical models of family life. For example, there is not a single example of a nuclear family consisting of two original spouses with two children of their own anywhere in the Bible.

Adam and Eve had many sons and daughters according to the Bible in the book of Genesis. This first family was a dysfunctional unit in which one son was murdered and another ran off. Jesus himself was born to an unwed teenage mother whose "betrothed" partner died not many years after they were married. This left the young Jesus in an almost impossible position as the male head of a household, which may have included a number of siblings or been limited to himself and his mother.

Indeed, the modern amalgam that passes for the family, including in-laws and outlaws, second wives and other women, absent dads and "sugar daddies," half-brothers and step-sisters, "maiden aunts" and "funny uncles" resembles nothing so much as the Biblical family, as depicted in the stories of Abraham, Isaac and Jacob.

Those families too needed guidance, often in the worst way, but to restore family values does not require a return to the nuclear family of Leave It To Beaver or Father Knows Best. Those of the religious right who think it does should be reminded that the family vision they sometimes promote is neither traditional nor Biblical. They miss the mark of what values need to be upheld for the seething and searching amalgam described above.

What is required is a recovery of true family values, replacing hypocrisy with honesty, exploitation with integrity, and sex with love. These are the kinds of values so sadly missing equally from the judgmental religious context and from the various "do your own thing" humanist environments. The role of the spiritual community in the future is to inspire and encourage these values rather than to condemn their absence and prohibit their opposites.

Both Canada and the United States are governed and led by liberal establishments that have drifted far too long on principles developed for an industrial society that has largely disappeared. To that extent, they are reminiscent of communist functionaries who governed Russia long after the communist vision had died.

The religious right is indeed correct to challenge the old assumptions and point to the sore spots on the body politic. A change is overdue. Solutions that appear reactionary to some liberals should be met with refined convictions of their own that relate to present realities, as a contribution to a future consensus.

The religious right has shown itself to be prepared for this discussion and is rightly offended by the lack of identifiable ethical positions among others who have so much to say. A thoughtful address by Ralph Reed, Executive Director of the Christian Coalition to the National Press Club in Washington in 1994 is appended to this book to make the point in fuller detail.

The principles of reverse effect, seen in the changing of some positions on both sides of the abortion question for example, can be illustrated in many other areas of concern to the Christian Coalition. The right to bear arms to obtain security, and punishing criminals to make them behave, both may be counterproductive in practice. Trade barriers as a means to protect jobs, and racial inbreeding as a means of strength, are oxymoronic by nature or open for discussion at least.

Of a more positive nature is the concern of the religious right for workers and income distribution in the post-industrial era. The political left has lost its monopoly on the union vote as the religious right quarrels openly with the business right over protection of workers' incomes.

The first information driven robot was introduced in the United States in the early 1960's. The President of American Motors, George Romney, reportedly taunted labor leader George Meany at the opening of the world's first fully automated assembly line in 1962. "Mr. Meany, I want to see you go down the line and see how many union cards you can sell!"

To this the union leader acidly replied, "Mr. Romney, I want to see you go down the line and see how many automobiles you can sell!" The two-edged sword of industrial automation was seen for both the benefits and the problems it would bring, but the issue has not been satisfactorily resolved in spite of the fact that by 1982 there were 32,000 robots in use worldwide, By the end of the century the figure reached twenty million and it is still climbing.

The right wing reaction, spurred by the unemployed older workers and the less educated members of its constituency, may not have the answer in erecting trade barriers against smarter Japanese robots and cheaper Mexican hand labor but, again, they alone seem to have heard the cry of superfluous workers. The work place has changed dramatically and there are ethical issues to do with access to training, family life, retirement security and other matters that are being temporarily and tragically ignored with important consequences for the twenty-first century.

The religious right may be dead wrong on all counts but they are sometimes the only ones raising the questions needing to be faced at the end of the twentieth century. Liberal ethics designed for the Industrial Era may be of little value for the twenty-first century, but the question is whether a return to the conservative ethics of the Agricultural Era will serve society better. Can the people of this neighborhood work together to establish a new "coalition" or consensus including Christians and others to build an ethical foundation for the Information Era? This is the challenge of the times.

Futurist Alvin Toffler has delineated three "waves" of human civilization. Agricultural society was the first wave, in his view. It was then that religious foundations were established. Next came industrial society, with a whole new ethic for applying those eternal principles to a radically different social context. That second wave has now crashed leaving a moral vacuum which some would fill by reverting to the only other known model, the old ethic of the Agricultural Era. Its application appears "conservative" because it seeks to conserve or salvage what is left of society after the collapse of "liberal" adaptations of ethics in the Industrial Era. The underlying principles are fine but neither model of application is particularly Biblical and neither may be adequate for the challenges of the third wave of civilization in the Information Era. Examples of these challenges will be apparent in consideration of ethical issues unique to the twenty-first century which follow.

The Christian Coalition does function as an alliance of Catholic traditionalists, Protestant fundamentalists and other moral conservatives. It plays an invaluable role in doing so. As its concerns are met, addressed or at least engaged, the religious right may become less of an ethnic rallying place for the fearful and angry among the white American working poor, and the true debate may proceed in earnest. Wars and negative campaigns in the name of morality have largely failed. The adoption of higher ethical standards for the whole of society, and across the spectrum of ethical issues, is a goal worthy of a new beginning in a new century. The religious right is capable of assuming its legitimate place in the discussion.

This is a more likely development than any expectation that substantial numbers of Jewish, African or Native Americans will ever feel at home in the Christian Coalition. It is equally unlikely that Hispanic and other immigrants will be attracted to the religious right in droves any time soon. Homosexuals and other marginalized peoples are not expected to join that coalition, and people from the liberal Protestant mainstream are unlikely to convert to the cause.

However, if the liberal ethics of the Industrial Era are bankrupt and if more than a simple return to conservative ethics of the Agricultural Era is desired, citizens of the Information Era will have to communicate better with each other and with their children. The goal is to establish positive ethics appropriate for a new era which are in harmony with values that are eternal. A rigorous and robust ethic is sorely needed, open-ended but not devoid of content - one to which Christians can fully subscribe and which others can also share without compromise.

The issues range from the domestic use of guns to reservist participation in a new form of integrated armed forces, from the environment to health care. From the impossibility of censorship on the internet to the shift from surgical abortions to pharmaceutical terminations there is the need for a new and higher ethic of personal responsibility and greater consensus in public policy.

The role of "religious authorities" in forbidding certain actions is being increasingly ignored, but the spiritual dynamic of enabling the good rather than forbidding the bad may meet with increasing acceptance. Because of the intensity of its moral convictions, the religious right may be ready to leapfrog the liberal center to address such concerns, as the issues of the new century become more clear. Through the leadership of the Christian Coalition, the religious right has moved from the lunatic fringe to become one of the few arenas of vigorous thought on social, moral and political issues.

The lazy, liberal left needs to get over its paranoia and self-destructive disengagement in order to contribute more to a new ethical framework for the future. Again, on the liberal side of the ethical spectrum, for whatever reason, it is people of religious faith who may take the lead. The first signs of constructive ethical engagement for the new century took place in 1996, prior to the last US presidential election of the old century.

On September 13-15, 1996, thousands of Roman Catholic activists, mainstream Protestants, liberal theologians and Black ministers met in Washington to found Call to Renewal. To avoid acrimonious conflict with the Christian Coalition, they did not endorse candidates. Rather, the intention is to focus on issues and attempt to raise the level of ethical debate.

Call to Renewal principles try to assist Christian voters to evaluate the candidates for themselves, to determine whether their platforms uphold dignity for the poor and disadvantaged, peacemaking and methods of law enforcement, economic justice and compassion. Call to Renewal is also attempting to set up "Higher Ground" coalitions through cooperation with Jewish activists, responsible gay organizations and others.

"The old categories and polarities - of left and right, Republican and Democrat-have failed us," says Jim Wallis, editor of *Sojourner* magazine and a leader of the Call to Renewal. "We must rejuvenate the moral values and political will to rebuild our disintegrating family systems, our shattered neighbourhoods and our divided nation."[31]

The religious right has sounded a wake up call for North America in the face of an ethical vacuum. The liberal left within the Christian community has become engaged. Is anyone else responding to this timely alarm? A new century and a new millennium are before this society. Citizens of North America may contribute much to world culture but they have unfinished racial business and a spiritual agenda to attend to at home as the new era begins. These goals may be addressed by religious leaders taking political positions and by church committees producing thoughtful position papers, but a spiritual renewal of the whole of North American society may also be required. This will be undertaken by individuals who may then freely affiliate in new or established spiritual communities of their choosing.

PART FOUR

WINDOWS ON THE FUTURE

(A Re-United Empire in the New Millennium)

32.

THE HEART OF AMERICA

America enters the twenty-first century as the most generous and outward looking nation on earth, critics, second thoughts and self-doubts aside. In reference to the previous century, a Canadian broadcast editorialist, Gordon Sinclair, known as a curmudgeon on every other issue, wrote an ode-like piece which he read to violin accompaniment on a Toronto radio station.

This paean summarized and rebutted criticisms of the American situation in the world at a time when the United States was still mired in Vietnam. The news references may be dated but the names and places can be changed for twenty-first century equivalents. Sinclair's appreciation of America is as appropriate today as when first aired in 1973.

"THE AMERICANS"

(A Canadian's Opinion)

The United States dollar took another pounding on German, French and British exchanges this morning, hitting the lowest point ever known in West Germany. It has declined there by 41% since 1971 and this Canadian thinks its time to speak up for the Americans as the most generous and possibly least appreciated people in the world.

As long as sixty years ago, when I first started to read newspapers, I read of floods on the Yellow River and the Yangtse. Who rushed in with men and money to help? The Americans did. That's who. They have helped control floods on the Nile, the Amazon, the Ganges and the Niger. Today the rich bottomland of the Mississippi is under water and no foreign land has sent a dollar to help. When distant cities are hit by earthquake, it is the United States that hurries in to help. Managua, Nicaragua is the most recent example. So far this spring, fifty-nine American communities have been flattened by tornadoes. Nobody has helped.

Germany, Japan and, to a lesser extent, Britain and Italy, were lifted out of the debris of war by the Americans who poured in billions of dollars and forgave other billions in debts. None of those countries is today paying even the interest on its remaining debts to the United States. The Marshall plan and the Truman policy pumped billions upon billions of dollars into discouraged societies and now newspapers in those countries are writing about the decadent war-mongering Americans.

When the franc was in danger of collapsing in 1956, it was the Americans who propped it up and their reward was to be insulted and swindled on the streets of Paris. I was there; I saw that. These days I'd like to see just one of those countries that is gloating over the erosion of the United States dollar even build its own airplanes. Does any country in the world have a plane equal to the Boeing Jumbo Jet, The Lockheed Tristar or the Douglas 10? Why do all international airlines except Russia's fly American planes? Why does no other land on earth even consider putting a man or a woman on the moon? You talk about Japanese and German technology and they give you radios and automobiles. You talk about American technology and you find men on the moon, not once but several times, and safely home again.

You talk about scandals and the Americans put theirs right in the window for everyone to look at. Even the draft dodgers are not pursued and hounded. They are right here on our streets in Toronto and getting American dollars from Ma and Pa at home to spend up here. When the Americans get out of this bind, as they will, who could blame them if they said "the hell with the rest of the world."

When the railways of France, Germany and India were breaking down through age, it was the Americans who rebuilt them. I read now that the Pennsylvania Railroad and New York Central went broke but nobody loaned them even an old caboose. Can you name me even one time when someone else raced to the Americans in time of trouble? I don't think there was outside help even during the San Francisco earthquake.

Our neighbors have faced it all alone and I'm one Canadian who is damned tired of hearing about them being kicked around. They will come out of this thing with their flag high. When they do, they are entitled to thumb their noses at the lands that are gloating over their present troubles. I hope Canada is not one of those, though there are many smug self-righteous Canadians. The American Red Cross was told at its 48th Annual Meeting in New Orleans this morning that it is broke. Does anybody out there plan to help?

Gordon Sinclair[32]

That said, the United States itself still has both citizens who would rather cower in "Fortress America", and others who are deeply troubled by legitimate concerns about American life at the dawn of the third millennium. Violence at home, on the street and in the classroom, the residual effects of racism, the need to fill the spiritual void which followed the decline in organized religion, and America's place in the very different world of the twenty-first century are all concerns of more than passing interest.

America was born in revolution, raised on the six-gun, torn apart by civil war, and became accustomed to both communal and domestic violence in the twentieth century. However, there are signs that America is developing a new maturity in the wake of that century which ended with a decade of apocalyptic violence. Cult violence and overkill symbolized by zealous officials at a religious compound in Waco, Texas in 1993, the trial of the World Trade Center bombers in New York in 1994, and domestic terrorism in the explosion of the Federal Building in Oklahoma City in 1995, kept the issue of violence before the public and required America to take a long, hard look at the supposed "right" of citizens to bear arms at the close of the twentieth century.

This chain of events plus the last rounds of race riots, the bombing of Black churches by Ku Klux Klansmen,[33] activities by "militia" volunteers and drug cartels required a fresh approach to law enforcement, civil disobedience and domestic violence as reflected in the media and experienced daily in real life America. The peaceful resolution of an eighty-one day stand-off between the FBI and a Montana "posse" of Freemen in 1996 was in such remarkable contrast with the aggressive tactics of federal officials at Waco that hopes were raised in many quarters that America was turning a corner to a new level of maturity in civic life. Subsequent law enforcement endeavors have supported this analysis with remarkably few exceptions.

American males, whether in law enforcement agencies or vigilantes, are unlikely to wimp out on the tough-guy image any time soon, but the tragic proportions of recent violent activity have engendered an openness to new ideas. With one of the largest proportions of citizens imprisoned of any country in the world, a million Americans live behind bars at public expense. This is four times the rate in Canada and twice the world average, keeping the United States in a select category which also includes Iraq, Iran and Turkey. The answer cannot be once again to build more and bigger jails in America, or even more lenient sentences. The spiritual renewal that is required in the heart of America has less to do with conversion to God and more to do with the relations between neighbors, though the two are not necessarily as unrelated as they have been in the past.

The "War on Drugs" can never be won by helicopter raids into South and Central America as long as so many heart-weary Americans provide a lucrative market for the very drugs that their government outlaws. The parallel with the whole American crime scene, with its related violence, is that prisons, like helicopters, are merely expensive but unnecessary surgery on the body politic. These situations merely require better preventative medicine.

Politicians, educators, spiritual leaders and private citizens will all play a role in rethinking the issue of violence, its causes and context. Differing Canadian experiences with the Royal Canadian Mounted Police, respect for the law and international peacekeeping techniques may be a small part of the mix for America in a future in which the two cultures contribute more to each other.

American fears of being swamped by poorer immigrants from the south in whatever comes "afta NAFTA" may be balanced by the stability of the Canadian presence in a dynamic new North American community. Americans will need to get beyond their simplistic images of Canadians as peace-loving and law-abiding rubes who drink milk, eat apples and breathe pure air, but these old neighbors have much to offer each other in this critical era when both countries face transitional challenges of unprecedented proportions.

Andrew Carnegie's classic assertion that Scotland has indeed taken over England was based on the historical facts of another era. A Scottish King actually did accede to the throne of England upon the death of Elizabeth I in 1603 to bring the modern monarchy into being. When James VI of Scotland also became James I of England, the Presbyterian Church became the British state church for a brief period of rigorous spiritual discipline. This led to puritanism and the pilgrims who were among the founders of America. Carnegie was referring to more than political power. It was moral leadership, work ethics, business acumen, personal frugality and a broader international world view which the Scots contributed to the union. These virtues are akin to what Canada offers America.

People like to remember America as "great" in its more conservative Agricultural Era, when the spiritual and political foundations were laid, the blights of slavery, alcohol abuse and prostitution notwithstanding. In its more recent Industrial Era, America led the world through two world wars, the "cold war" against communism, scientific advances and material prosperity - all this in spite of domestic violence, international debacles, drug abuse and the abortion epidemic. Any criticism of those eras now is merely with the benefit of hindsight, and offered in comparison with an illusionary perfection. It is neither unpatriotic nor unfair to acknowledge what was wrong in the past, but America's best years are still ahead, and Canada may share in that future.

There will be no particular political change to effect the reunion of the United Empire of North America. No constitutional amendments are required to recognize that which is desired and is already in effect in many ways. Canada merely needs to get over a long standing national inferiority complex and America needs only to acknowledge who is her partner. America may always stand larger and more powerful in proportion to Canada, as England does to Scotland, but needful of a conscience, an alter-ego, a trusted soulmate in a partnership far deeper than any military alliance or trade deal.

The heart of America is sound but weary. The present heartaches over America's place in the world abroad and heartbreaks over domestic terrorism at home are capable of resolution in this positive new context. The fact that so

190

many Americans care about these things is again a measure of the greatness of this nation.

As far as the relationship with Canada is concerned, while most Americans hardly ever think of it, a significant cultural and economic re-orientation is taking place in the Northern states. US border states will be enthralled with the new relationship. It enhances their own ethos, which moves now from status as a fringe element among Yankee, Southern and Western cultures to become again the dominant culture in North America for the first time since the old United Empire.

Aligned with three new territories and ten Canadian provinces, this dozen Northern tier, small and mid-sized states from Washington to Maine will have a key role in the twenty-first century. The population within one hundred miles of the US-Canada border, on both sides is one hundred million. Americans affected by this shift in identity live in Washington, Idaho, Montana, North Dakota, Minnesota, Wisconsin, Illinois, Indiana, Michigan, Ohio, western Pennsylvania, upstate New York, Vermont, New Hampshire and Maine. While some observers have suggested that Canadians are practically Americans anyway, it could be said that these Northern Americans are practically Canadian in many respects.

As indicated, at the end of the twentieth century, while America was preoccupied with defining its new relationship with Mexico, and while Canada was focused on the Quebec situation, an event of even greater significance for both took place without notice. As the twenty-first century begins, North America is becoming one American society with several related cultures, one of them being Canadian. Like a love affair that begins before either party realizes what is happening, or even like a childhood sweetheart one has always loved without realizing it, America has taken Canada to heart. From the media to trade, from the quest for peace to ethics for a new era, and from environment to cyberspace, "the Empire is back".

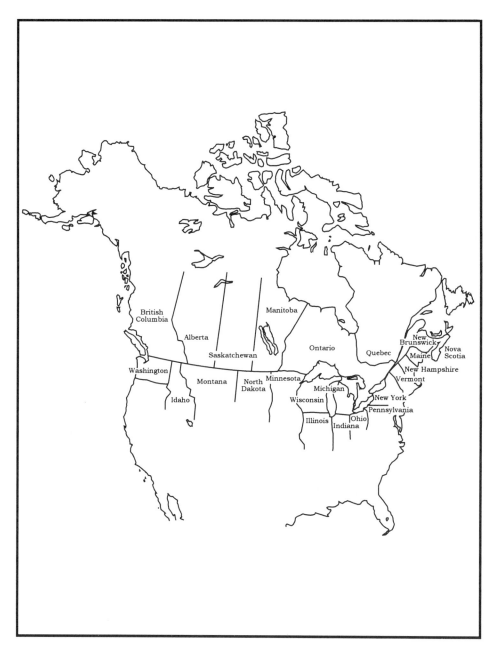

Border States and Provinces
(With 100 million people, the border area will redefine North American culture.)

33.

THE SOUL OF CANADA

The soul of Canada is troubled. Nearly one hundred years ago, Prime Minister Sir Wilfred Laurier predicted that the twentieth century "belongs to Canada" because of the country's seemingly inexhaustible supply of natural resources, its democratic institutions and a population that was both skilled and hard-working. As things turned out, the twentieth century belonged to America and Canada's sense of being overlooked has led to a national inferiority complex.

Canadians now insist that they did not want to see the country "ruined" by development anyway. This is sour grapes, or a retrospective view at best. Canadians, normally generous in spirit, also exhibit an occasional anti-American prejudice that is unworthy and immature.

At the same time, most Canadians are heartsick and mystified that nearly half the residents of Quebec are not enthusiastic about belonging to a country with such potential. Years of social spending have produced a dynamic culture and inclusive health and education systems, but federal and provincial governments have such a debt load that recent cut-backs have soured the electorates. Canada has become a nation of complainers.

This is in spite of Canada placing first, year after year through the 1990's, in repeated United Nation's surveys of all its member countries, ranking them according to education, health care, longevity, living standards and environment. Canadians are not always the smartest, healthiest, longest living, richest or most environmentally conscious people in the world, but they are either first or they rank so close to the top in each of these categories that it can truly be said that Canada is the best country in the world in which to live.

What Canadians need most is a more positive attitude. Such a development seems ready to burst upon them in spite of themselves. History points to a recurring theme of optimism in every country at the beginning of a new century. Toward the conclusion of an old century pessimism abounds, especially if a millennium is drawing to a close. Religious fanatics are sure the world is coming to an end, but they are merely reflecting a general uncertainty or angst in the human soul at a time of reflection and transition. Then the century turns and an era of optimism breaks forth with faith in progress, rising property values and new initiatives on old problems.

These hopeful factors are about to come into play in Canada as elsewhere, but there are additional reasons for Canadian optimism. Scottish frugality in the banking system, careful development of natural resource bonanzas, resolution of both the separatist question and native land claims, and an enhanced relationship with Canada's nearest and dearest neighbor may be ready to come together with the beginning of a new century to produce something of a golden age in Canada. Incredibly, no Canadian can admit to such a possibility in spite of United Nations pronouncements, foreign investor confidence and the opinions of friends around the world.

Deep spending cuts through the nineteen nineties mean that after the year 2000 every Canadian province and the federal government are now expected to be operating with a balanced budget. Cultural programs, social services, education and health care systems will all remain intact through restructuring, downsizing, "user-pay" provisions and programs that are no longer totally comprehensive, but still among the best in the world. Private sector lifestyle enhancements and new technologies will then actually lead to an increased standard of living, including new activity in sectors previously restricted to the government domain.

Long years of careful work on native land claims by federal, provincial and native leaders are expected to lead to settlements which appear expensive but which should unleash unprecedented economic activity in remote parts of the country. The advent of Nunavut to territorial status in 1999 is uplifting to the nation as a whole.

Should Quebec leave Confederation, it is becoming increasingly clear that the province would take little or nothing more out of Canada than it brought in. The original Quebec land mass was something over two hundred thousand square miles or six percent of Canada. Over ninety-nine percent of the somewhat disaffected French population still lives within that area. Canadians would be wistful to see Quebec depart, but even the prospect of continuing referenda on Quebec's future has become less likely due to changing economic and ethnic factors in that province as a whole.

The Native Cree in the northern two-thirds of Quebec are not prepared to leave Canada, and the Anglophones and Allophones, who make up half the city of Montreal, are less and less acquiescent. Even southern Natives, along the American border, intend to keep their lands in Canada, in the event of Quebec separation. The Mohawk Chief, Billy Two Rivers, of the Kahnawake Band puts it bluntly: " I do not think separation will happen, but if it did, it would be totally unacceptable and it wouldn't include our territory. We will expect Canada to defend our relationship."34

In the face of all this, and with over forty percent of the francophone population also solidly committed to Canada in some form, the tide of outright separatism appeared to peak at the end of the old century. Some confusing and expensive face-saving developments are still to be worked out in the wake of this development, but the issue is becoming permanently innocuous, much like the notion that the Southern States in America may yet "rise again" to become a separate nation.

Certainly Canadians are unlikely to resort to violence over this, except possibly in isolated incidents. The Canadian approach is for the government to appoint expensive royal commissions to tour the country and eventually report to what ever new government has been elected in the intervening years. It is a great expense but nothing like the costs of war in whatever other countries are experiencing tension. There is something essentially Canadian about royal commission reports which make excellent paper airplanes, suitable for throwing in place of real missiles.

In fact, although nothing has ever come of it, every province except Ontario has elected a "separatist" government sometime since 1867, on a platform to withdraw from (or stay out of) the Canadian confederation. The most famous separatist leaders, after Rene Levesque in Quebec, would be Joseph Howe in Nova Scotia and Louis Riel in his Saskatchewan years. The other prairie provinces had United Farmers Party governments that flirted with separatism and British Columbia entered confederation on conditions that were not met at first, leading to legislated deadlines and threats of secession.

In the east, only the Fenian raids kept New Brunswick in confederation. Immediately after the Charlottetown Conference of 1864 in Prince Edward

Island, establishing the terms of Confederation, PEI itself elected a government dedicated to keeping the host colony out of Canada. In the 1940's Newfoundland held three votes on becoming a province of Canada and the proposition was defeated in the first two.

Ontario is a special case, with interests that mirror the national interests because of a "National Policy" pushed through by Canada's first Prime Minister, Sir John A. Macdonald. Under this arrangement, the other provinces would provide raw resources for Ontario's manufacturing industries and buy back the finished products in a closed market protected by tariffs. For this reason Ontario has been very happy with Canada as it was, and has had considerably more initial difficulty than other provinces in adapting to free trade under NAFTA, which opened the Canadian borders for American and Mexican competition to Ontario's products.

However, to its own surprise, after a period of adjustment, Ontario has discovered that it can compete and expand in the new economic climate. This is possible because of the skilled labor force, natural resources available near at hand, new access to larger markets and Canadian competence in high tech fields. The recent relocation of Motorola's corporate headquarters to Mississagua, Ontario, is a case in point.

In the new integrated North American economy, Ontario is the colossus among the northern states and provinces in much the same way that Texas is in the south, California in the west, and New York in the east. These four mega states (one of them a province) with populations near or above twelve million each, are the only ones with diverse-integrated economies of their own. Ontarians have never thought of themselves in such select company but it is so without a doubt. Indeed, not even Texas, California or New York have the same combination of forests, mines, agriculture, fresh water, energy sources, manufacturing base, high-tech industries and clean cities that remain relatively free of crime.

The usual Canadian modesty notwithstanding, the other provinces will also play well in the NAFTA league and what comes "afta" too. Most of them are situated along the US border in such a configuration that they adjoin states smaller than themselves in both population and resources. Those states will also benefit from the stimulation of the new economic environment, but the usual Canadian fears about domination by the United States are entirely unfounded when considered province by province.

On the west coast, British Columbia will be to the state of Washington what California is to Oregon, providing leadership in culture as well as economics. Indeed, Vancouver is twice the size of San Francisco and will take its place as the second most important city on the Pacific.

With vast resources and two cities of over a million each, Alberta will certainly not be dominated by Montana. Saskatchewan will be in a similar position with the Dakotas. Winnipeg, Manitoba, is larger than Minneapolis or Saint

Paul in Minnesota, and may become a cultural center for the whole mid-west.

Because of its uniqueness, Quebec will have a vibrant future whatever destiny it ultimately chooses. Its resource base guarantees a strong economic future, symbolized by the new wollastone (wollastonite) mine 150 miles north of Quebec City. There are only four other sources in the world for this amazing mineral, which will be used in the twenty-first century to strengthen ceramics and plastics and replace fiber-glass. The Quebec wollastone deposit is the largest and best on earth which gave another boost to the auto industry when it first appeared in bumpers and side panels of the 1996 Chevrolet Lumina.

Either independent or under the Canadian umbrella, Quebec has long since passed the threshold of cultural viability and is not about to become a quaint "Louisiana North." Because it is so much of the essence of Canada, and because it fits so well into the emerging greater North American neighborhood, efforts must continue between federalists, inside Quebec and out, and French Canadian nationalists to find a way to recognize Quebec's uniqueness as a society. This is the heart of the issue, more than politics or economics.

The one suggestion not yet mooted is for Quebec to become a republic among the provinces within Canada, much as America contains 43 states, the Commonwealths of Massachusetts, Kentucky and Pennsylvania, the Dominion of Virginia and the old Republics of Vermont, Texas and Hawaii. Instead of a president, Quebec would elect a governor, much like Americans states. Quebec's only indirect connection with the monarchy would be at the federal level. For internal matters, Quebec would function in a constitutional manner similar to other republics within the British Commonwealth.

Such a position would isolate hard line separatists seeking total independence on one extreme, from the few unbending "status quo" federalists in Quebec on the other. It would suit the political platform of the *Action Democratique*, a moderate movement midway between the separatist *Parti Quebecois* and the federalist *Parti Liberal*, and please a majority of Quebec voters immensely.

It is in English Canada that such a proposal would founder. On the eve of every Quebec referendum on independence, everybody in the country appears ready to make what ever accommodation is necessary to prevent the break-up of Canada. Only days later, the rest of Canada lapses back into concern that even a constitutional phrase giving Quebec "special status" might mean higher status. The latest attempt to bridge the gap by simply describing Quebec as a "distinct society" within Canada has every redneck in the country upset. Acceptance of Quebec as a republic, with status that is truly "separate but equal" to that available to any province may only come about after a severe constitutional crisis. Meanwhile Federal Justice Minister, Allan Rock, and Quebec Premier, Lucien Bouchard, while eying each other warily, are both working to establish a legal framework for negotiating a typical Canadian compromise following the next crisis. Each in turn argues that negotiations would be inevitable, and weary as they are of this issue, most Canadians would still prefer another few rounds of Royal Commissions to conflict.

In the Atlantic region, or "down east", as other Canadians say, the three maritime provinces make a pleasant extension of the New England economy and culture. Nova Scotia, Prince Edward Island and New Brunswick are the same in size and population as Maine, New Hampshire and Vermont. These states and provinces have always been comfortable with each other and gravitate in orbit around Boston. Tourism is growing fast in this part of Canada, "the playground of the Atlantic."

The youngest province, Newfoundland, is still somewhat like a northern territory in certain respects. After some years of struggle with declining fish industries, the province is poised to enter an unprecedented era of resource development which began with the mammoth Hibernia offshore oil discovery and continued through Voisey's Bay and other spectacular Labrador area mineral finds in the 1990s. In the Cinderella story of Confederation, the poorest province in Canada may be poised to become the wealthiest *per capita*.

Elsewhere in the north, the Yukon, Nunavut and the Northwest Territories have, like Alaska, potential for life in the twenty-first century unlike anything yet known in those regions.

However, Canada's new lease on life in the twenty-first century will also depend in part on articulation and acceptance of its role as a full and worthy partner of America. Individual Canadians like Galbraith and McLuhan have previously been America's tutors. As a group in Hollywood and cyberspace, Canadians have been an essential part of the infrastructure of these communications industries so vital to the Information Era. This is now of the essence of North American life in an era without borders.

In the twenty-first century, Canadians will build on the Greenpeace precedent and the country's successful tripartite (government, business and consumer) green entrepreneurial experiences, to help lead America through the green revolution that is also so essential to the future.

The United States may have had the most powerful military force in the world in the twentieth century, and America still needs to keep some such capacity on standby for the future. However, it is a totally new era, as represented by nothing more striking than the entirely new military situation. The previous fifty years were lived out under a nuclear cloud that was said to have disoriented two generations of children, not to mention its impact on national budgets, tax expenditures and deficits. The world has changed.

While not every United Nations venture has been successful, Canadians are the world authorities on the techniques of peacekeeping and peacemaking, which may be an essential aspect of the new military era. The fact that peacekeeping did not work well in Bosnia until buttressed by American firepower should not overshadow the fact that scores of such situations around the world have been safely ignored by CNN, for example, precisely because UN peacekeeping under Canadian leadership has worked very well indeed.

These tactics require entirely different skills than military operations which "kick butt", as Americans realized too late in their recent ill-fated attempts to join UN peacekeeping endeavours in Somalia and Haiti. Canadians have fought well when needed, but could still take lessons from Americans in fire fights. However, if the world of the twenty-first century is as different as many hope, Americans may need to benefit from the different Canadian experience in the twentieth.

This may even be the case inside the United States itself regarding domestic terrorism, where American federal marshals have been increasingly adopting the long established techniques of the Royal Canadian Mounted Police. The story of Sitting Bull entering Canada with all his warriors and being taken into custody by a lone, unarmed, Mountie is part of the Canadian ethos which needs to become part of the modern North American communal psyche.

In the new century, Canadians will also work together with Americans on race related issues and on the larger questions of spiritual life and consensus ethics appropriate to this society. America does not need advice from anyone, but Canadians are the only ones close enough to the heart of America or objective enough in the North American context to play such a role in any event. Canadians are not frequently assertive enough to assume such a role and this will not happen according to some plan or government program. Such a development is merely a natural extension of the direction in which these two nations have been moving for a couple of hundred years.

To complete its destiny, America may need a reunion with Canada, an informal revival of the old United Empire. Canadians need America just as much in order to learn to believe in themselves and to appreciate what they have. It is time at last for Canada to mature as a nation and for Canadians to realize that they are Americans of a certain type already, in all important particulars, and always have been.

Canadian Racism
(Thought by some to be rare, it is subtle but real)

34.

THE NORTH AMERICAN DOLLAR

In the twenty-first century, the world economy will approximate that balance of free enterprise and government regulation advocated by John Kenneth Galbraith. The wars and other struggles of the twentieth century effectively sifted out the extremes.

Overall government ownership has proved totally ineffective in societies of the far left, which have collapsed in inefficiency. Laissez-faire capitalism and business backed "command-economies" have also destroyed societies on the extreme right through lack of social responsibility. Nowhere will the balance be better struck than in North America where the social responsibility of Canadian center-left systems is combining with American right-center efficiencies to offer the best of all worlds.

America already has plans to adopt the metric system which is used in Canada and most of the rest of world. Such harmonization facilitates trade, especially in raw materials. It also enables importers and exporters to conform to the regulations of other countries without expensive repackaging. In this regard, the US switch in "weights and measures" (kilograms and centimeters replacing pounds and inches) is more important than "temperature" (degrees of Celsius replacing Fahrenheit) which, for some arcane reason, the US government has decided to proceed with first.

Likewise, Canada may find it necessary to adjust its dollar value to parity with the US dollar, not a difficult undertaking even without the growing rapprochement in economies and cultures. The values were at par at various times during the twentieth century. At other times the US dollar exchange has fluctuated between a low of 70 cents Canadian and a high of $1.20 Canadian. This was frequently an unstable factor in business, favoring exporters and harming consumers, or *vice versa* in both countries, depending on which currency was up. "Pegging the dollar" is no longer in vogue among economists, but they are capable of devising other ways to establish what is in essence a common currency, as is being done in other parts of the world.

The European Community has moved toward a single currency, the Eurodollar. For symbolic reasons, much like the maintenance of the US-Canada border on maps, and the continuation of separate political institutions, the US and Canadian currencies will remain distinct in appearance, though separate valuations are becoming increasingly awkward.

This alignment might be carefully maintained in the new era so that the two dollars can be used interchangeably in both countries in a system more like the traditional relationship between the Bank of England and the Bank of Scotland whose pound notes were totally interchangeable in either jurisdiction throughout the twentieth century. Indeed, this is the model currently proposed to solve the embroglio between the Euro-dollar and the British pound, since Britain is finding it politically difficult to accept such total integration with Europe as is represented by the single currency.

The greatest single change in the North American dollar is in who controls it. In this, the two countries are already performing as one economy. The governments do not control this economy, as was attempted in more extreme cases by communist or socialist systems. Nor is the dollar controlled by private, wealthy interests, as it was in the Industrial Era of North America, and more recently in now bankrupt right wing dictatorships.

Both the government and private capital are powerful influences, but billions of dollars in mutual funds held by millions of North American small investors, and vast pools of capital held by company, union and professional pension funds are managed by a new elite of professional economists. They now control the dollar and they represent a broader constituency by far than the few wealthy families. They are also more genuinely responsive to economic realities than are most elected politicians. In this respect the Canadian and American economies are identical. Both the investments and the pensions that back them, for example, are fully portable.

As North American integration proceeds, there will be other obvious areas of rationalization. The most obvious is postage. Courier services, as the new kid on the block, have already completed this rationalization by charging the same price for service in either country, except that the dollar difference in currency exchange must be factored in.

The postal rates are already practically identical in the two countries, or within pennies, even without taking currency exchange rates into account. For this reason, the use of each others' stamps and a complete harmonization of rates is within easy reach. It would also be a tremendous boost in business convenience and serve as a model of how a rationalized currency could be honored routinely in both countries.

Surely the time has arrived for the adoption of some such powerful symbolism of the close relationship between Canada and the United States. America may feel more whole if she can somehow find the inclination to acknowledge this dynamic partnership within her own neighborhood. Canada needs some such symbolism in order to mature in self-estimation in the new century. Neither has anything to fear from the other.

BANK OF SCOTLAND ONE POUND NOTE

35.

THE VANISHING BORDER

Thirsty America has a growing need for fresh water, especially on the west coast where the shortage has become critical. There are important environmental concerns that must be addressed prior to any major diversions from the raging fresh water river systems of the Rocky Mountains of British Columbia. This matter was hardly addressed by the NAFTA agreement, since Canadians were still wary of any proposals that smacked of a loss of sovereignty over natural resources.

In the meanwhile, fresh water resources have emerged as something of a "whip hand" for Canada in the poker game of free-trade implementation. Without a few such aces, the Canadian junior partners in this high-stakes new economy can easily feel stonewalled in any negotiations with their giant neighbor.

Major diversions of fresh water are still a decade or more away, and the most stringent environmental safeguards will be required. There will also be tremendous economic benefits accruing to Canada but the matter of sovereignty is still not resolved. Canadians will certainly not allow America to suffer, but Americans are unlikely to invest billions of dollars in a project equal in magnitude to the Alaska Highway or the St. Lawrence Seaway without some measure of control or guarantee.

The solution is obvious, given the track record of the International Joint Commission. However, to prepare for that development over the next few years, American negotiators at NAFTA trade dispute tribunals could develop a somewhat more respectful attitude toward the rule of law and Canadian sensitivities with respect to the soft-wood lumber trade, grain marketing, hog production, shared coastal fisheries and other matters.

In the first decade of NAFTA the Canadian experience has been victory in practically every single dispute, but only after stalling tactics and every other imaginable device in the courts, the political realm, in threats of economic retaliation and pressure through US public opinion, on the part of "hard-nosed" Yankee traders and their representatives. Canadians have learned to play hard ball in this new league, but if Americans wish to go further in such sensitive areas of fresh water resources, the time has come to regard this neighbor's interests as identical to America's own interests across a wide spectrum of sectors.

At the same time, Canada is finding that it must concede more ground in the area of cultural industries. This is due as much to the demands of the Canadian consumer as pressure from the American media. To their surprise, however, Canadian media have discovered that many of then can survive very well indeed in a continental market. Fifty thousand Canadians now work south of the border producing cultural products in every medium for American consumption, but also for export back to Canada.

Canadian media giants along the US border clamor constantly for access to the American market. The result of all these trends is for Canadian politicians to mute their earlier misgivings about the seemingly uneven playing field, and to enact measures that can simply enhance the survival prospects of Canadian cultural industries that now appear more able to play in the big leagues than anyone expected.

The free-trade open skies agreement has served well as a model across the transportation sector, though long distance trucking has remained a sore point in spite of the fact the mighty Teamsters Union has operated on both sides of the border as the largest labor union in North America for most of one hundred years. Could there be any truth to a rumor that Jimmy Hoffa is alive and well, living underground in Moose Jaw, Saskatchewan?

The Canadian National Railway system was a conglomeration of a dozen Canadian privately owned railroads that came under government ownership of necessity between 1918 and 1923. At the close of the twentieth century it has been privatized as part of the worldwide movement away from government ownership. The shares in the CNR have been bought up partially by owners of its rival, the great Canadian Pacific Railway, which, with the CNR, is now the largest railway system in the world. The CPR-CNR system has more track in the United States than any of the five hundred American railway companies.

In much the same fashion, American air transport systems are expanding into Canada, through the alliances of Continental with Air Canada and American Airlines with Canadian. The open skies policies that came with free trade have encouraged all these free flowing expansions, giving both travellers and shippers greater efficiency as well as lower prices.

Proposals have reached the floor of the US Congress to eliminate border inspections at the US-Canada border. Under free-trade, the total amount of duty collected does not even pay for the two expensive customs departments and the hundreds of border crossing stations. Since, as of the year 2000, Americans and Canadians have "nothing to declare" when they enter each other's country, this time-consuming and expensive irritant will soon disappear. The "longest undefended border in the world" will then become the world's most invisible border.

The only items worth smuggling now are contraband from outside both countries. The laws about drug and most other illegal imports have already been harmonized, so that if an importer can get something into the one country legally, it is legal in the other country anyway. The same presumption is the case with respect to other illegal imports.

By the same token, immigration requirements are already virtually identical in both countries. Anyone who can enter Canada legally should soon have the same privilege in the US, and *vice versa*, as is already the case in Europe and virtually true between the new South Africa and its neighbors and also in Oceania between various Pacific Islands and New Zealand.

This is a worldwide trend among neighbors who trust each other. Within North America there is no need to maintain any customs or other border procedures, and there are compelling reasons to get rid of them. That long undefended border which is vanishing for all practical purposes is just part of a pattern in which other US-Canada boundaries are also becoming invisible.

In the late twentieth century approximately one million Canadians went to the States each year and a million Americans came north to Canada. Canadian travel to the United States may not increase dramatically, since that figure already represents over half of all Canadian international travel. Conversely, the US figure represents only one eighth of American travel abroad.

The likelihood is that, in the new era, twice as many Americans will discover Canada as a backyard playground, clean and secure, as well as increasingly important as a place to do business. The impact of a rise in American traffic from one million to two million per year will have significant consequences for Canada, and perhaps for the visitors as they find themselves again, in certain respects.

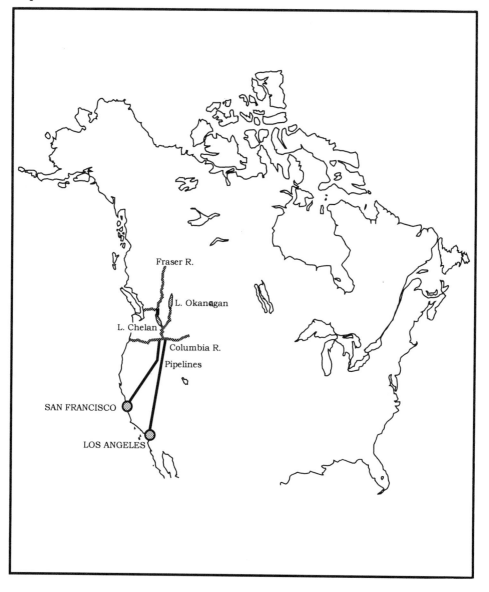

Fresh Water Source Map
(A mega project as huge as the Canadian Pacific Railway, The Alaska Highway or the St. Lawrence Seaway.)

36.

VINLAND

In the year 986 AD, an expedition set out from Iceland to colonize the south west side of Greenland under the leadership of Eric the Red. Near the end of the summer, Bjarni Herjolfsson, a trader attempting to join them with fresh supplies, was blown far off-course and became the first European in recorded history to reach North America and make a report. In one of the more exciting fields of geographic research to emerge in recent years, maps at Yale University in New Haven, Connecticut indicate that Herjolfsson landed in Newfoundland and explored the forested coast of Labrador.

First published in 1965 in the book <u>The Vinland Map and the Tartar Relation</u>, the main map (a copy) and an attached commentary dated 1440 are widely acclaimed as documentary evidence of European activity in Canada before the era of Columbus. Challenges to the authenticity of the material have been addressed by Yale in cooperation with the cartography department of the British Museum and the book was released again in 1996 with authenticating data.[35]

At around the turn of the century, the beginning of another earlier millennium, possibly in the exact year 1000 AD, Eric the Red's eldest son, Leif Ericsson, determined to exploit the discovery. Over his father's objections, he was also eager to extend a Christian influence among the Natives of which he had heard. This was the more gentle Christianity of Northern Europe, as compared with that brought later by Columbus, and it was not presented with force, despite the reputation of pre-Christian Vikings.

Ericsson followed Bjarni's map to a natural harbour and spent the winter while his crew took on board a full cargo of vines and timber. The vines would be sold as fasteners in the shipbuilding industry and they gave rise to the name Vinland, to describe this first brief European settlement in North America. Historians had located Vinland in various locations from Hudson Bay to Florida prior to the discovery of the maps now on display at Yale University and featured in this landmark book.

Very precise location of these early landings and other Nordic first settlements is now established through the excavations which have been undertaken in Newfoundland and Labrador over the last forty years. Colony sites for as many as 160 persons who arrived in four ships with domestic animals, including cattle between the years 1004 and 1006 have been unearthed and some of these are now open to the public.

These attempts at colonization were ultimately unsuccessful as permanent settlements, partly due to resistance by Inuit and Indian bands that was largely respected. However, forestry and other gathering expeditions continued for a hundred years, while the climate appeared to be getting steadily less hospitable in one of the first documented climatic changes on the planet.

Recent research has focussed on the growing evidence that, except for periods of economic recession, Nordic commerce with North America never ceased in the years between 1000 A.D. and 1492, when Christopher Columbus arrived in America with three ships. At most, Columbus may be described as the European discoverer of South America. Irish documentary evidence has certainly established that the knowledge of North America's existence continued in Europe.

Other evidence indicates that this awareness was likely shared with fishing expeditions from Normandy and Portugal. These may have been semi-regular in the thirteenth century and served as a source of information for Columbus in planning his voyage.
As the twenty-first century opens, one of the more significant shifts in North American self-awareness is the move away from the myth of "discovery" by Columbus, to a field of knowledge certain to increase dramatically as satellite scanners identify more and more of the early sites of European activity, and as these sites are excavated.

"Vinland", or Newfoundland, no longer produces vines and "Markland", or Labrador, no longer exports timber, but as the millennium began one thousand years ago, so it is ending with a climate change of some consequence. The recent global warming trend has brought about a slight rise in the average temperature in Canada that is not yet as noticeable in the United States. However, the erratic nature of weather patterns during this change has certainly been noticed in the United States as well as in Canada, and meteorologists of both countries are aware of possible harmful consequences in the long term, should there be significant melting of the polar ice cap.

The positive effects of the warming trend have been in the amelioration of a harsh edge in the Canadian climate. The tree line above the Arctic Circle has moved some fifteen miles northward in a unified pattern over the last half century. This all could make life a bit more pleasant in Canada, though the erratic nature of the transitional era is disrupting.

The warming trend has already had an effect on North American agriculture. Its erratic element has been harmful to citrus production in the Southern States and to tobacco crops on both sides of the border. One hundred years ago rapeseed grains were introduced to Canada but were not popular because of frequent frost damage. They were tried again in the middle of the last century and slowly increased in popularity as the climate changed. Now one of Canada's most valuable crops, "Canola", as it is called, is one of North America's healthiest and most plentiful supplies of vegetable cooking oil.

A similar surprising development has taken place in the Canadian wine industry. Newfoundland may not be growing grapes or any kind of vines now or in the foreseeable future, but Ontario certainly is. Before free trade there was a fledgling wine industry in the Okanagan Valley of British Columbia and somewhat larger vineyards in Ontario's Niagara region, which are at the same latitude as some vineyards in Northern California.

The Canadian industry, protected against competition from imports by high tariffs, was expected to collapse with the advent of free trade. With the help of a government research station in a town actually called "Vineland," Ontario, the industry made some significant improvements in its grape varieties, but the rise of half a degree in the "mean annual temperature" was a totally unexpected bonus that worked wonders for Canadian vintners in the nineteen nineties. That, and a few lucky discoveries of ways in which the fertile Canadian soil might react to the new grape stocks in the altered climate, produced a minor miracle in the dramatic growth of the Canadian wine industry.

The most lucrative element in this expansion has come from a distinctive new ice wine, created by certain grapes fermenting on the vine after being touched by an erratic early frost. High-priced Canadian ice wines are now popular all over the world, and at least a small part of the country was converted to the view that creative solutions to the challenges of free trade can be found. The coincidental nudge from the warming trend also helped one part of Canada to regain the title of "Vinland", a thousand years later.

Changes in climate have played a defining role in the history of ancient Egyptian, Indian and Chinese civilizations. They also account for noticeable military power shifts and economic changes elsewhere over the centuries. The climatic changes in North America can only be seen over a thousand year cycle, but the changes in the new millennium are already being noticed. This is an era of change in many aspects of North American life. Business interests appear able to adapt, but the challenge remains for other sectors of North American society in the twenty-first century.

Most Americans think of Canada as "up north" but the southern tip of Canada, at Middle Island in Lake Erie is at 41 degrees of latitude. This is so far south that a majority of States (27) lie wholly or partially to the north. From there, Canadians have to go "up north" to get to any part of Maine, New Hampshire, Vermont, Wisconsin, Minnesota, North Dakota, South Dakota, Montana, Idaho, Oregon, Washington and Alaska. These Canadians even go "up north" to reach parts of Massachusetts, Rhode Island, Connecticut, New York, Pennsylvania, Ohio, Indiana, Illinois, Michigan, Iowa, Nebraska, Wyoming, Utah, Nevada and California!

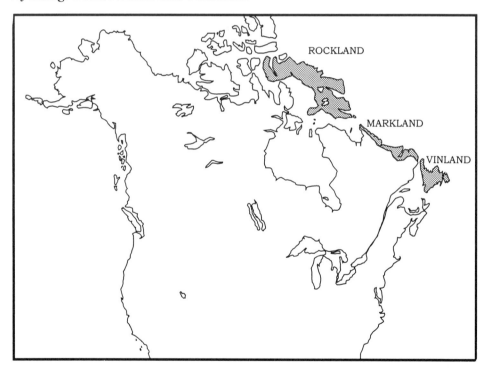

<u>Vinland</u>
("Discovered in 986 and first settled by Europeans in 1000 A.D.)

37.

XANADU

In Xanadu did Kubla Khan
A stately pleasure dome decree:
Where Alph, the sacred river, ran
Through caverns measureless to man
Down to a sunless sea.[36]

The poet, Samuel Taylor Coleridge, could not possibly have imagined Alaska, The Yukon, The Northwest Territories and Nunavut as the most likely settings for domed cities with comfortable lifestyles in a controlled environment. The river at the ends of the earth may turn out to be the fabled Northwest Passage, the caverns are the mines of the north and the Arctic is certainly a sunless sea much of the year.

The mineral strikes around Voisey's Bay are about to turn nearby Labrador from the region with the lowest per capita income in Canada into the highest in the country. In Nunavut, the tiny population of 25,000 people has negotiated control of natural resources over an area twice the size of Alaska. This means that one strike as valuable as Voisey's Bay will provide an instant payoff of more than one million dollars per household, a virtual Kuwait North!

Life in domed cities has been considered for years as the only practical way of colonizing Mars or Venus, both of which may happen before the end of the twenty-first century. Meanwhile, this Star Trek lifestyle is more likely to take place first in the northern reaches of Canada and the United States.

Even at present, each of the twenty-eight settlements that include virtually 100% of the population of Nunavut could fit inside a domed structure the size of the Skydome sports complex in Toronto. With a fully retractable dome for summertime airing out, or for psychological reasons important to humans, life in the long winters could be most pleasurable.

Living and working environments could be the best in the would, rather than among the worst. Conditioned air would replace cooped up winter atmospheres. There could be full spectrum lighting instead of months of darkness. People could have year round gardens and country club amenities like "tennis courts and swimming pools" or what ever the Inuit and their neighbors choose.

The pollution from the diamond, gold, nickel, copper and silver mines and the oil wells that will support these communities can be dealt with more cleanly than was the case in the twentieth century. In any event, the residue would be expelled from the living space domes and even the concentrated work space areas would get special treatment.

Science fiction has long presented either space or the bottom of the ocean as the last frontier. Who knows where successful northern experiences could lead by the twenty second century. Jules Verne's depictions of everyday airplane travel in *Around the World in Eighty Days*, submarine explorations in *Twenty Thousand Leagues Under The Sea*, and even a space voyage, *From The Earth to The Moon*, were all greeted with incredulous glee one hundred years ago. Each of them materialized in the twentieth century with uncanny accuracy. The riches of the north and creative applications of existing technology should almost make this vision of domed cities a reality sometime in the first half of the twenty-first century for the Inuit, Indian, and Eskimo natives and their employees from the south.

The shadow of the dome of pleasure
Floated midway on the waves;
Where was heard the mingled measure
From the fountain and the caves.
It was a miracle of rare device,
A sunny pleasure dome with caves of ice![37]

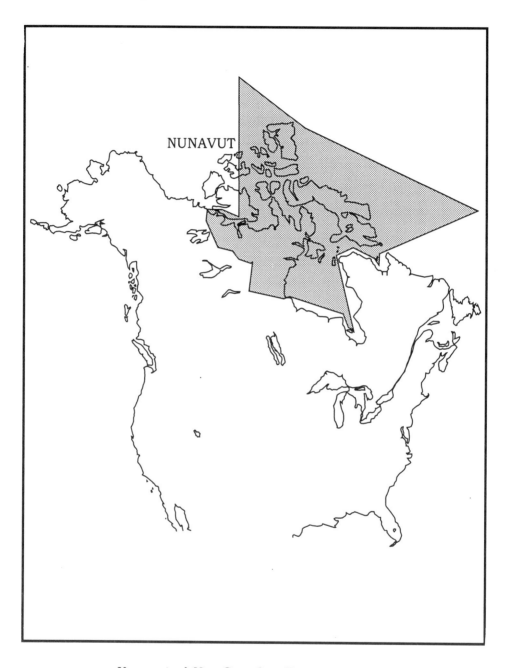

NUNAVUT

Nunavut - A New Canadian Territory in 1999
(Known as Rockland by the Norse, Nunavut is believed to be an unequalled
storehouse of minerals.)

216

38.

PHYSICIAN, HEAL YOURSELF

In the nineteenth century medical science was focused exclusively on germ based diseases like cholera, smallpox and typhoid. By the middle of the twentieth century most of these were eliminated, and by the end of the century medical science was practically devoted to the treatment of lifestyle diseases. Heart diseases related to stress or the consumption of cholesterol, and cancers often associated with smoking or the depletion of the ozone layer in the environment are examples of diseases best cured by education and changes in lifestyles.

In the twenty-first century one great advance in medical science will be in genetics. Genetic engineering in biology is already producing more and better foods so that starvation is no longer a specter on the earth, except when produced by war or corruption.

The two percent of the population currently engaged in agriculture now produces ten times the food on the same amount of land that the fifty percent of the population engaged in agriculture farmed a hundred years ago. That kind of impact on plants and animals is about to be felt in the human species with the advent of genetic therapies.

After a decade of promising but false starts, the ultimate frontier of genetic engineering came closer with the successful cloning of sheep in 1995. At an experimental farm near Edinburgh, Scotland, this modern miracle produced the first of many identical lambs with superior characteristics ready for mass production like seedless grapes. The ethical pendulum swings from tampering with nature in animals to the possibility of human cloning of "superior" persons. Human cloning will be greeted by some as a most exciting advance, but the reaction of many others will be fear and distress. "Old fashioned" families will then be those with children conceived in sexual activity and carried in the womb.

This debate will almost relegate the choice between birth control and abortion to the status of some "dark age" controversy. The transition from little or no birth control in the Agricultural Era, through active, but limited and controversial, birth control and abortion in the Industrial Era, has reached an ultimate stage in the Information Era, which will force the development of ethics to a new and higher plane. This challenge can be faced with some degree of unity since even those most strongly committed to a woman's right to an abortion would rejoice in social and other changes that might reduce the number of abortions in North America by one million per year.

Meanwhile, more disquieting developments have appeared. The development of an artificial womb in Japan has been successful in gestating a goat embryo to full term and the little kid has grown to become a normal adult goat. As the century turns, the development of an artificial womb for human reproduction will eliminate the need for surrogate mothers.

"Only slightly more speculative is a nightmarish but technically feasible procedure to extract eggs from aborted fetuses and fertilize them with sperm from a cadaver - to create children of the dead and the never-alive. Not possible yet, but likely soon to be, is the choice of "designer" offspring created by selectively implanting genes for desirable attributes like intelligence or size."[38] Such a possibility will no doubt be exploited by someone who wants very special children, but it gives a whole new meaning to the phrase "pro-choice."

"When you think of the implications of what we're going to be able to do," reflects Roger Rittmaster, an endocrinologist on the faculty of Dalhousie University in Halifax and a former president of the Canadian Fertility and Andrology Society, "it really is pretty interesting and scary."[39] Perhaps the question in all this is, where is love? The answer may even be that the scarier the options, the more likely the human spirit will seek out spiritual values. The century ahead could be the most interesting in history and the spiritual aspect

218

of the human experience may have never been so cherished.

On a more positive note, The Human Genome Project, possibly the most ambitious scientific project in history, eclipses even nuclear technology and space programs in both costs and benefits to humanity. Centered in North America but spread around the world, it began with the discovery of DNA in 1954 and will conclude in 2010 with a map or inventory of the 100,000 genes that make up each unique human being.

Through gene therapy, prediction and treatment of genetic based cancers like those of the breast or colon are a certainty. Huntington's disease, cystic fibrosis and muscular dystrophy are treatable at last, and soon will be avoidable altogether. Genetic influences in diabetes, mental illness and even alcoholism are being explored hopefully.

Major new ethical dilemmas are also on the horizon in this area also, and they too illustrate the absolute necessity to advance the old debates beyond the collapse of liberal industrial ethics and the temporary reversion to conservative agricultural ethics. The very questions are brand new and must be answered in a consensus not possible under the old polarities. The twenty-first century will be either devoid of ethics or, potentially, the most ethically conscious era in human history.

For example, if gender selection and pharmaceutical advances rocked the abortion debate, what will happen when prenatal genetic tests can tell parents their potential offspring's intelligence, musical gifts, sporting prowess, life expectancy and health problems? If young adults all learn which "adult onset" diseases they will almost certainly contract, and at what age, what will this do to marriage vows of faithfulness "in sickness and in health?" Either nobody will make such vows or they will be made with open eyes in a new ethical environment. Careers, investments and retirement plans are other areas affected by such new knowledge.

The twentieth century had no ethical framework for even thinking about these questions. Will each "family" or each person make up individual codes of ethics? Will traditional faith communities have a meaningful opportunity to work through the new context to develop commitment, integrity and compassion? Will "big brother" governments have new responsibilities to place upon school teachers? Who defends workers' interests? By picking and choosing its clients according to risk-free criteria, will the insurance industry render itself obsolete? Will everyone's genetic profile be as accessible as their resume or credit rating?

In the scientific community, the official "Ethical Component" of the Human Genome Project has called for governments to prepare legislation to protect privacy and deal with discrimination. Legislators may be totally unprepared, but in the ethical arena, the rabbis, mullahs, priests and ministers too have barely progressed beyond the proverbial counting of angels dancing on the head of a pin. Are ethical standards to be determined by situation comedies and media talk shows as they were in the late twentieth century?

Most urgent of all is the ultimate and perennial question - how do people love their neighbors when all the rules are changing? That question is urgent, though ironically, the most important questions may still have the simple answers that earlier generations learned in Sunday School, if they were paying attention.

The spiritual dimension is unlikely to disappear in the twenty-first century. To the contrary, it assumes a new urgency as people appear more concerned than ever to find a transcendent meaning in life. In the nineteenth century, faith healing, for instance, was restricted to primitive tribes. In the twentieth century it was limited to quacks and fanatics. In the new century, nobody but a fool has any doubt that both germs and lifestyle diseases are powerfully affected by the spiritual health of the patient.

Some might even assert that the spiritual dimension may be the only significant factor to override a genetic predisposition. Scientific research on the effectiveness of prayer has been undertaken at some of North America's most highly respected universities and medical teaching hospitals. Frequently supervised closely by cynical researchers anxious to disprove spurious claims, the research has been subject to all the usual safeguards of blind testing (patients not knowing which of them were prayed for) and even double blind testing (comparisons with a third group unaware that anyone was being prayed for).

The positive nature of these indications and the respected level of sophisticated research has been almost as notable a breakthrough as gene therapy itself, except that as yet the scientific community has less rational understanding of prayer. The work of Dr. Deepak Chopra, linking Eastern Indian and Oriental traditional medicines to the American experience, and the work of Dr. Herbert Benson of the Harvard School of Medicine have won an unprecedented level of both popular and academic support. Does anyone now laugh at acupuncture that works when all else fails? Is there anyone who does not appreciate a Godly physician as contrasted with the occasional hot-shot "know-it-all" who has no time or ability to talk?

In spite of the increasing sophistication of medical science, along with prayer and "alternative" therapies has come another trend. Since about the time of "Dr. Granny" on the "Beverly Hillbillies" situation comedy, everybody has become a doctor. At 100 years of age, comedian George Burns revealed that when he decided to go for longevity, he gave up physicians because they were "always finding something wrong" with him. Medical science is still valuable, perhaps increasingly so, but so is personal responsibility for one's own health. Exercise, better diets and information all contribute to the decline of lifestyle diseases. Since germs too have been largely overcome, medicine is free to move forward into new areas.

Beginning with gene-splicing treatments for colon cancer in Montreal and

Boston, gene therapies first became widely available to the public in North America shortly before the year 2000. Other such cures, far more effective than transplants, but much less dramatic, were slowly becoming available before the turn of the century, with an avalanche to follow. In the twenty-first century, health care will include the medical practitioner, the spiritual advisor and the patient herself in a routine three-pronged approach.

But all this is poised to happen with no sign of an ethical consensus in sight. This, in spite of a new openness to the importance of the spiritual component that is now also recognized in medical treatment, especially among younger physicians. The unresolved ethical issues of the twentieth century reflect on both the spiritual and the physical health of North America.

An unmarried, drug-addicted, Native teenaged girl on the streets of Winnipeg gets pregnant and the whole country is anxious about the plight of her unborn child. Because of her substance abuse habits, the public health and social welfare officials want the girl taken into custody until after the birth. The courts will not permit this abuse of her rights for fear of where such a precedent would lead. The media is full of opinions. No one gives a damn about her except to wish she would stop causing problems, and no one will give a damn about the baby after it is born except to lament its cost to the public.

A Black American recalls a set of behavior patterns he adopted years ago. When walking on the street, to soothe the terrors of white passersby, he dresses neatly, hums a classical tune, avoids eye contact and leaves a respectful amount of space. All this is to reassure Whites that he is not one of "those people" whom they imagine as poised to knife them, rob them, and rape their women. Today his strapping sixteen year old son strolled into the wrong district by mistake, and as the father looks at the blood-soaked body of his boy stretched out on the hospital gurney, he wonders if he will bother humming any more.

This kind of unfinished business from previous eras remains unresolved. Is it inevitable that the ethical dilemmas of the past, so capable of solution, will be projected into the future like a virus in the body politic that prevents society from ever fulfilling its potential? Or is it within the realm of human possibility that the optimism associated with entering a new era can energize the community and its members for the task of cleaning up old sores and healing the festering wounds of the past?

Meanwhile medical science is bringing new ethical and spiritual questions into focus in the twenty-first century on a whole different level. The search for loving spirituality and an ethic for the Information Era is a mega project as urgent as The Human Genome Project itself. Neither scientists nor clergy are yet able to propose answers adequate to promote a new public consensus. The first step will be to move beyond debating the questions of a previous era and to trust the possibility and the desire of the people to use the beginning of a new era to move on.

For example, assisted suicides pioneered, by Dr. Jack Kevorkian in North America, are now covered under legislation in increasing numbers of countries. This procedure usually involves a self-administered "super dose" of pain-killing drugs, prepared by a physician for a mentally competent person in extreme pain who cannot recover, and only after familial consent and a designated waiting period. This issue has become inescapable in an era of ever extending prolongations of life, at ever decreasing viability in some cases.

In the Conservative Agricultural Era "natural death" was the norm, no matter how gruesome or painful. In the Liberal Industrial Era the issue became one of "pulling the plug" in a few cases when life support systems could sustain but never revive the corpse. In the Information Age the ethical issue of "pushing the plunger" is even more complex. A starting point might be to limit any consideration to parties who have surpassed the Biblical "three score years and ten" (seventy years), and restricting advice, input and assistance to those who have also reached that age. The cartoon below points to questions that remain.

Jack Ohman, THE OREGONIAN

The collapse of liberal Industrial Era ethics may have sent many people scurrying back to conservative Agricultural Era ethics temporarily, in medical ethics as well as other areas of life. Establishment of new ethics for the Information Era will require the passion of religious conservatives, who believe that death is not the end, and the dispassionate objectivity of secular science.

39.

CYBER-CITIZENSHIP

A Black president of the United States, a Republic of Quebec, dual citizenship for Natives and a public discourse that takes responsible elements of the religious right more seriously may all be desirable developments in the early years of the new century. However, the science of cybernetics looms large over all of these.

From the Greek word, *cybernao*, "to guide" (which became *guberno*, "to govern" in Latin), the concept embraces the "search engines" that guide every schoolgirl that now "browses the net" and also the governing principles over arching the new era. Citizens of the twenty-first century will function in the context of a cyber-culture, whether they participate actively or just let this reality become a universe they inhabit, but refuse to understand or acknowledge.

In spite of the fears of some who are uneasy about racist revisions of history, and the anxieties of others over access to sexually explicit material on the Internet, the Information Era has become a fact of life. The big story is how voluntary self-regulation by net users has quickly developed into a mature culture of accepted protocols and even good manners. Those who abuse the system or foul it up with garbage are jammed up by a flood of negative reaction which overwhelms them and forces them out of the system. Rarely has there been a better example of how "community standards" have made government censorship unnecessary in a free and reasonably mature society.

From the beginning, as a system that was initially impossible to regulate, the Internet developed as an open system of resource sharing. People who were eager to promote their resources and ideas found it difficult to charge a fee on such an inexpensive medium for information sharing. Later the competition and variety became so great that profit incentives were transferred to another level of the system, such as direct sales and follow up products. The net has continued as a surprisingly inexpensive tool for the communication of ideas.

Young children communicating daily, free of charge, to "pen pals" on the other side of the globe, or from Ontario to grandparents in Florida, represent a home style of activity that has even greater implications for business. Both private and corporate users operate in a free manner that anthropologists associate with "cultures of abundance."40

The medium is itself a message of user-friendliness and direct relationships in a relaxed mode. People are more gentle with each other in this neighborhood of the electronic Global Village than they are on someone else's turf in a car-clogged city.

The economy of traditional western civilization was based on systems of hoarding what is owned and selling or sharing on the basis of a presumed scarcity or a limit to resources. By contrast, on the Internet incredible amounts of information are offered freely to anyone who wants them. Many are hopeful that this is a harbinger of other attitude and lifestyle changes in the twenty-first century.

As an example of the adjustments to be made, however, a particular religious group had worked hard to make a whole new niche for itself in society by storing genealogical data and making it available to the public in its libraries, as a gesture of goodwill. Suddenly that niche was gone as archival records from all over the world were put on-line by individuals and even governments.

Or again, patent laws, once the preserve of lawyers, can now be accessed by someone typing "patents" into the blank search space on the World Wide Web Crawler. Anyone can read the regulations over, choose the required legal form, even request advice from knowledgeable persons "out there," and E-mail a patent application to the government at a cost of ten dollars.

These benefits do not come without costs in terms of adjustments and some of the first questions are ethical. All this information is available in a universal envelope or package which comes largely unsorted. Naked genitals cavorting in the most bizarre acrobatic fantasies share space with grandmother's genealogy. The person who assists surfers with patent registration forms may also have touched-up graphics to prove that the Turkish genocide against Armenians never happened, or arguments "proving" that Parsee immigrants are a national security threat because they are part of a conspiracy to take over the banking systems of the world.

Hate propaganda which was banned in liberal industrial society, and sexually explicit material forbidden in conservative agricultural society, are both presented to children on the Internet via hundreds of free web site sources. A major ethical challenge in the Information Era is to find the personal maturity, the family context or the spiritual community to function in an era completely free from censorship. The parallels with attempts at prohibition of alcohol and drugs and the banning of abortion are obvious. If the human community is to function well in the new millennium, it will do so on a higher ethical plane.

The V Chip, which makes it possible to censor television programs in the home, is the last vestige of a primitive world which imagined that restricting access as long as possible was the way to contain evil influences. As was the case with booze, and is now the situation with drugs, restrictions merely raise both interest and profit margins. From abortion to censorship, the Information Era is so unrestricted that, at last, people are required to face the demons openly, explain them to their children, and to create lifestyles in family and community where healthy relationships replace restrictions as the context for mature development.

The ethical stakes are higher than ever, but as the risks grow so does the potential payoff for a society that works problems through and deals with them, as opposed to "keeping the lid on" in some fashion. The challenges facing families, churches, schools, businesses and communities can no longer be contained or squelched by coercive religious or governmental power.

Back in the mid-twentieth century, for example, when the negative forces propping up miserable marriages, such as economic dependence, the shame of divorce, legal constraints and religious prohibitions, were removed, it appeared briefly that the institution of marriage might disappear. It is still far from perfect but the marriages that have stabilized and survived have done so on the basis of positive factors that people have consciously chosen to cultivate. The rate of marital breakdown is now only marginally greater than long term averages, but the marriages that survive are healthier than ever. The same may be said regarding the negative forces of censorship in earlier times and the positive opportunity to move on, perforce, to new levels of maturity in a future in which there is no other option.

These are hopeful parallels to a spectrum of ethical issues in the freedom of the Information Era, in which positive opportunities replace negative prohibitions as the basis of decisions and choices. However, there is an ethical shift of tectonic proportions ahead for the new millennium. With it comes an incredible challenge for individuals, families, spiritual associations and even governments.

This earthquake at the start of a new millennium changes everything about education, the way business is done and the way people relate. People on the Internet help each other on the basis of shared interests alone. They take what they need and diminish nobody's hoard in doing so, because they always leave more than they take.

This culture of givers rather than takers harkens back to an earlier pioneer period in the North American past. Friendships, good manners and reputations are among the most valuable commodities on the Internet. In it there is a village of many millions where news and ideas travel fast. Everyone on earth is involved in some way, even if each neighborhood must find its own way to cope.

The fulfillment of this potential will involve community efforts which involve people across ethnic and religious lines in particular. Of course, on the net nobody knows if the person one is dealing with is Asian or white, lesbian or straight; all that matters is honesty and integrity. Privacy and anonymity are also aspects of the new era that have both positive and negative ethical connotations.

Until now, opinions and relationships have usually involved responsibilities. Will it be possible to add spirit and even love to this cyber mix?

Early indications, based on accepted "protocols" of net behavior, do indicate that these most cherished values of ages past have not disappeared into some black hole in space by any means. The technical challenges are great but the potential payoffs in expansion of the human spirit are also enormous. Meanwhile the option of continuing to fight a rearguard resistance based on either conservative-agricultural or liberal-industrial ethics is rapidly diminishing. Life in the Information Era is not for the faint of heart.

The question of censorship is not the only ethical issue raised by the Internet, but it is one that humans can get their minds around at least. Larger questions still are raised by the prospect of artificial intelligence, or "AI" as it is called, on the part of computers that can think for themselves. It can now be conceded that computers can indeed think, forcing humans to move beyond self-definition according to Cartesian limitations.

The time has arrived to advance from "I think, therefore I am" to "I love, therefore I am human."

Mind-boggling as the concept may be, computers networking together on their own via the Internet is almost too much to comprehend. The universe may be fairly buzzing with intelligent thought later in the twenty-first century and the mother of all questions now is whether this reduces the role of human beings own via the Internet is almost too much to comprehend. The universe may be fairly buzzing with intellegent thought later in the twenty-first century and the mother of all questions now is whether this reduces the role of human beings or raises it beyond any responsibility the race has yet borne.

The answer is hopefully a vast increase in human responsibility, unless it is concluded that humans were mere primitive machines themselves all along, in a deterministic universe which somehow has evolved beyond this formerly "most intelligent" species.

If mortals have a role in a new era, in which they are not necessarily the most intelligent, their higher plane will be in the area of ethics and the spiritual life. The human race seems so unready, but the realization that such has been its purpose all along may serve to focus its energies in those more lofty directions.

Because it is so intensely personal, the spirituality of North Americans has always been more important than academics and the popular media have acknowledged. For example, in the nineteen nineties, Americans contributed $56 billion dollars per year to their religious affiliations. That is fourteen times more than the $4 billion spent on professional baseball, football and basketball combined.[41]

According to the Gallup Poll[42], attendances at religious functions total over 5 billion annually in the nineties, compared to just 103 million tickets sold annually for professional football, baseball and basketball. Worship services and religious events out draw sports by a ratio of 55 to1 but this is not apparent by comparing the weekly "church page" with space given daily to sports pages in the paper.

Figures for Canada would be comparable, where the public media have likewise remained uncertain how to deal with spirituality or ignorant of its place in North American society. Those who are personally "out of the loop" in this regard perpetually see religion as a phenomenon of the past. That is likely to change in the twenty-first century as ethical demands and spiritual resources are pushed more to the fore.

The political border between the United States and Canada does not exist geographically and does not have even an artificial trace in the cyberspace of the Internet. That image of a vanishing border was presented as a parable at the beginning of this book, introducing the theme of walls that divide in society, and the need to break them down in order for everybody to have an opportunity to flourish to full potential. This is an attainable goal in North America at least, in the twenty-first century. The Internet is a final parable to make the same point in graphic imagery suitable to the Information Era.

Both the border as citizens have known it, and the net as it looms over everyone, are real enough in themselves, and people will have to deal with them. They also illustrate both the limits and the potential of existence in the human community. The fulfillment of that potential is, in the final analysis, a

Some examples of ethics suited to the twenty-first century may be summarized in terms of the twentieth century bugaboos "sex, politics and religion":

1. The energy that used to go into anti-abortion campaigns should be directed into the kind of truly "pro-life" consensus that supports new family structures and guarantees a level field of opportunity for every child, even those whose parents may be judged as "illegitimate."

2. The efforts formerly devoted to censorship should now be channelled into a heartfelt discussion of ideas with young people and sincere communication with neighbors on all subjects of interest to anyone.

3. The resources expended on futile attempts at prohibition of alcohol or the war on drugs might be rechannelled into a new spiritual consensus that puts a greater premium on community service (love of neighbors) and artistic esthetics (reflecting the glory of God), at least partly filling the void which used to lead to substance abuse.

Finally, perhaps the toughest ethical dilemma in the Information Era relates to the questions of privacy and electronic access to information about individual citizens. As children, most people have contemplated how scary it would be if other people could read their minds. Everyone would have to think pure thoughts or at least take responsibility for things that most people would rather not face.

Life in the twenty-first century might be something like that. Already it is not possible to fool the loans officer at the bank. In filling out a mortgage application, it is impossible to borrow extra on the basis of "forgetting" to mention certain other debts. On her computer screen she has data from the Better Business Bureau on those extravagant purchases the applicant made at Sears only half an hour earlier.

The first reaction of those reared in the twentieth century is to seek ways to block the truth from getting out, lest it "get into the wrong hands." Some safeguards may be possible, but the new reality of cyber-citizenship is that truth will out, more often than not, and that may not be a bad thing in many cases.

Adjustments will have to be made, and energy must be invested in ensuring accuracy, as well as the right to personal verification. But the adage, "You shall know the truth, and the truth shall make you free" has never been laden with such power. The challenge is to advance this verity beyond facts and figures to the spiritual dimension of the human quest.

In spite of these technological advances that up the ante, it may still be the twentieth century which is remembered as the Century of Technology. Indeed, it is precisely because the stakes are higher that the twenty-first century may become the Century of the Spirit.

40.

THE SPIRIT OF THE TIMES

Until now religion has been a very close second to ethnicity in the causes of pain and anguish in the human community. Along with creative and successful efforts to overcome the negative aspects of ethnic divisions (racial and national), citizens of the twenty-first century will need to create societies where there is greater understanding and respect between faith traditions in order to eliminate the scourge of religiously motivated strife.

According to Ruth Stafford Peale, daughter of a United Church of Canada minister and best known as the insightful wife and irrepressible colleague of America's beloved preacher, Norman Vincent Peale, "The answer for America is not to lose faith but to find a new spirit."[43] The vision of a twenty-first century society free of ethnic strife and religious bigotry, where technology is a blessing to the earth and not a curse, may be optimistic but its fulfillment is possible.

Positive thinking, or faith, is also a human trait that can be nurtured to become a force for positive changes. It is not a mere matter of economics or historical trends because, to some extent, societies invent their own futures. For this to happen, vision, decision and action are all required. The optimistic vision outlined here will materialize if people share it, determine to make it happen and act accordingly.

Such a fundamental change in public consensus is not only possible, but to be expected in the euphoria associated with the beginning of a new wave of civilization, the Information Era, which happens to coincide with the beginning of a new century and a new millennium.

Regardless of the needs and sensibilities of individuals or groups with respect to organized religion, another great challenge in the North America of the twenty- first century is to find a genuine public expression of spirit to which all citizens of goodwill can honestly subscribe. This public spirit is the essence of any Manifest Destiny or other forms of unity in the United Empire of North America beyond the year 2000.

In that connection it may be said that the soul of American society in the twenty-first century may not be as "religious" as it once was, but may very well be increasingly "spiritual". Religion as a straight jacket of the spirit is going through its final throes in the political machinations of the "religious right" in America, and intolerant but less influential elements in Canadian society. The liberal left in religious circles has long since lost any significant clout in both countries.

The right-wing phenomenon is an echo of the rise of fundamentalism everywhere in the world among religious souls who fear that their version of the truth may not compete well, unless it operates from a position of power. In America there are increasing signs that such extremism may be finally dissipated in the drive toward a workable spiritual consensus at the civic level at least.

The religious right has signalled that it is capable of responding to the challenge of dialogue without power, and much of the liberal religious mainstream has already made this adjustment in belief and in practice. A society where most of the Christian majority learns to see Christ in everything good would have at last rightly interpreted the teachings of Jesus.

Christians deserve special attention here, only because, through their numbers and influence, they alone have the power to unite or to divide American society. Their record of sometimes bitter division among themselves may not be a hopeful sign, but this may be more typical of the century that is passing away than of the one emerging.

Jesus said, "I am the Way, the Truth and the Life; no one comes to the Father (God) except through me."[44] The problem is that some Christians from Columbus to certain modern evangelists appear to interpret this as meaning that everyone must accept Jesus of Nazareth as they know him, as their "Personal Saviour" (a phrase not even found in their Bible). All others are damned, no matter how much they believe in God or love their neighbors. There is an urgent need for Christians to escape this exclusive position without diminishing their essential belief in the divinity of Christ.

For increasing numbers of Christians, it is the Bible itself that dynamites this ridiculous spiritual logjam. A mini Bible study lesson may be helpful here for those seeking the way to unity, not only among Christians but with other neighbors of goodwill who are increasingly numerous in North America.

In the Bible, the Gospel of John opens by identifying Jesus with the eternal, creative Word of God, the pre-existent Christ, who was part of God and functioned as the divine agent in the creation of everything good. This Cosmic Christ is identified with Jesus, but he himself insists it is not an identification limited to him as the carpenter of Nazareth.

In the eighth chapter of John's gospel, some critics confront Jesus regarding the claim that he is the exclusive route to salvation. They ask if this means that Abraham (the Jewish and Moslem patriarch) is not in heaven, since he died two thousand years before Jesus was born. Jesus replies that Abraham indeed reached heaven through him. They scoff, "you are not yet fifty years old, and you have seen Abraham?" Jesus opens the way for every person of faith by saying, "Very truly, I tell you, before Abraham was, I am."[45]

Modern Christians should welcome and promote the understanding that if Abraham is "saved," in their view, through an intuitive relationship with the Cosmic Christ, two thousand years before Jesus of Nazareth was born, then why not Leonard Cohen, two thousand years after? And if Leonard Cohen, for example, why not Mahatma Gandhi and the honest Moslem next door?

After the Chinese Communists killed one million Tibetans in the mid - twentieth century the Dalai Lama of Tibet taught no hatred for the Chinese; rather, the development of respect and a compassion for them from which Christians could learn much.

He said, "It would be much more constructive if people tried to understand their supposed enemies. Learning to forgive is much more useful than merely picking up a stone and throwing it at the object of one's anger, the more so when the provocation is extreme. For it is under the greatest adversity that there exists the greatest potential for doing good, both for oneself and others."[46]

Christians might see in this a theology of the cross and redemption through a suffering servant. Those who fail to see the spirit of Christ in the Dalai Lama might recognize a prophet at least! All of this is from a Christian universalist point of view, of course. But the Christians are the ones who have the problem, especially in North America. They so often cause problems for others in their exclusive claim to ownership of divinity in a way that would be objectionable to Jesus. Their aggressiveness is an affront to the modern spirit.

Mahatma Gandhi, the holy man of India, advised Christians well on their desire to share their faith: "Don't talk about it. The rose doesn't have to propagate its perfume. It just gives it forth and people are drawn to it. Don't talk about it. Live it. People will come to see the source of your power."[47]

The United Church of Canada has pointed toward the twenty-first century in its discussion paper, "Toward a Renewed Understanding of Ecumenism."[48] Dubbed the "TRUE" document, it proposes a broadening of spiritual coalitions. In such a context, Christians would seek to find Christ already present in the midst of those they would have formerly evangelized, and each others' faith could also present or identify its own spiritual treasures without compromise.

Few among the spiritual leaders and religious people in the world have a problem with Jesus Christ. He is universally admired and could even be widely accepted as a full manifestation of divinity were it not that the Columbus model of discipleship is more common among modern Christians than the Ericsson model. It is the aggressive arrogance of Christians that drives people from Christ, but that too may be about to change in the twenty-first century.

As they will have done in ethical areas as diverse as genome therapies and the power of prayer, the religious right, as represented by the Christian Coalition, can play a dynamic and positive role in community building in the North America of the new century. When they get over their panic reaction to the bankruptcy of liberal industrial ethics, and realize that a retreat to conservative agricultural ethics is not the only option, they will be able to contribute positively across the spectrum of community issues instead of fighting rearguard campaigns and sometimes appearing to hate their neighbors.

A sign of this move toward constructive engagement took place in the 1996 Republican presidential primary race. The Christian Coalition threw its influential political support to the more moderate Bob Dole, when its critics expected endorsement of the more extreme Pat Buchanan.

This open spirit, involving no compromise of cherished beliefs, is echoed in the establishment of Call to Renewal among mainstream Christians. A broader coalition to establish consensus ethics for the next century is on the religious horizon at least. These North American Christians are beginning to see their role in a more positive light, not to forbid but to enable.

These are hopeful signs for a future in which the spiritual gifts of each person and group are cherished. New Age Spirituality brings a fresh impetus to the quest for peace and harmony as reflected, for example, in the best seller by Teri McLuhan, Cathedrals of the Spirit, which purports to find evidences of God's presence in the shrines and sacred places of many traditions. Her book is offered not in opposition to her famous father's Christian orthodoxy, but to support and extend it in the positive context of the wider quest in this new age.

The Jewish faith offers the spiritual roots of western civilization. Muslims demonstrate commitment, and Eastern Mysticisms are profound inward journeys. Native Spirituality provides respect for the environment and the spiritual contributions of still others are of value in the North America of the twenty-first century. In this context, Christ too, understood as the cosmic spirit of creative and redemptive love, becomes a fragrance of blessing rather than a stench of bigotry in a pluralistic society.

The continental neighborhood of North America may be but a twenty first century way station en route to a world culture of the twenty second century. The practical elimination of nationalism, racial hatreds and religious bigotry in this neighborhood will serve as a major contribution to humanity. The goal is lofty but neither impossible nor impractical. It is an aspiration worthy of personal and public commitment. To refuse to move forward together may be worse than turning back.

In a commencement address at Harvard University late in the twentieth century, Aleksandr Solzhenitsyn put it this way, "The world has reached a major watershed in its history equal in importance to the turn from the Middle Ages to the Renaissance. It will demand from us a spiritual blaze; we shall have to rise to a new height of vision, to a new level of life where our physical nature will not be cursed, as in the Middle Ages, but even more importantly, our spiritual nature will not be trampled upon, as in the Modern Era. This ascension is similar to climbing onto the next anthropological stage. No one on earth has any other way left but - upward."[49]

Were God to come down from heaven in person, and choose scriptures for the future from any of the world's religions, the first might be an invitation to love God, the Divine Essence of the universe. Then with respect to human relationships, even God could do no better than to quote a Hebrew Scripture from a similar time of change in the desert era, more than three thousand years ago. Simply put, in this connection, for the twenty-first century, with respect to "your neighbor as yourself", the first and final word is "Love."[50]

ST. GEORGE'S ANGLICAN

DIVISION STREET UNITED

FOURTH AVENUE EAST

(FORMERLY DIVISION STREET)

(FORMERLY MURDOCH STREET)

TENTH STREET

CHURCH OF THE NAZARENE

FIRST BAPTIST CHURCH

Four Churches on Salvation Corners
(The spectrum of Christian traditions)

END NOTES

NOTES FOR PART ONE: WINDOWS ON THE PAST

1. Henry Wadsworth Longfellow, <u>Evangeline</u>, p. 30.

2. John Robert Colombo (ed.), <u>Colombo's Canadian Quotations</u>, p. 291.

3. Stewart H. Bull, <u>The Queen's York Rangers</u>, p.196.

4. Melvin Simpson, <u>The North American Black Historical Museum Guide</u>, p. 1.

5. Pierre Berton, <u>The Last Spike</u>, p. 205.

6. Brian A. Brown, <u>The Burning Bush</u>, p. 131.

7. Robert Service, <u>The Spell of the Yukon and Other Verses</u>, p. 26.

8. <u>Ibid</u>. p. 83.

9. <u>Ibid</u>. p. 34.

10. Reay Tannahill, <u>Sex in History</u>, p. 361.

11. <u>Ibid</u>. p. 357.

12. James H. Gray, <u>Red Lights on the Prairies</u>, p. 77.

13. <u>Encyclopaedia Britannica</u>, Eleventh Edition, pp.462 and 463.

14. Reay Tannahill, <u>op</u>. <u>cit</u>. p. 366.

15. James H. Gray, <u>op cit</u>. p. 77.

16. <u>Ibid</u>. p. 72.

NOTES FOR PART TWO: WINDOWS ON THE PRESENT

17. Traditional Maritime folk song of the prohibition era.

18. John Robert Colombo, <u>op</u>. <u>cit</u>. p. 96.

19. Bob Johnston (CBC radio), <u>This Day in History</u>, February 14, 1996.

20. John Robert Colombo, <u>op</u>. <u>cit</u>. p. 372.

21. Garth Vaughan, <u>The Puck Stops Here</u>.

NOTES FOR PART THREE: WINDOWS ON THE APOCALYPSE

22. Bruno Lacombe, "Quebec Exchange Participant Has Change of Heart 17 Years Later," The Meaford Express, August 30, 1995.

23. English translation of traditional text in public domain.

24. Chief Seattle *et al.*, attributions uncertain.

25. Bible, Genesis 2:7.

26. Dr. Jane Hurst, The History of Abortion in the Catholic Church, p. 8.

27. Ibid. p. 12.

28. Dr. D. R. Amies, Canadian Medical Association Journal, Vol. 129, Aug. 1, 1983, p. 261.

29. Deborah Jones, "Abortion Today - What Both Sides Fear Most" Chatelaine, May 1996, p. 107.

30. Ibid.

31. "World," United Church Observer, p. 26, column 3.

NOTES FOR PART FOUR: WINDOWS ON THE FUTURE

32. Gordon Sinclair, "The Americans - A Canadian's Opinion."

33. "Associated Press Report," August 3, 1996.

34. Financial Post, August 10, 1996, p. 3.

35. Montreal Gazette, "Viking Map is Looking More Like the Real Thing," February 14, 1996, p. B1.

36. Samuel Taylor Coleridge, "Xanadu," College Survey of English Literature, p. 746.

37. Ibid.

38. Chris Wood, Maclean's, "Beyond Abortion," August 19, 1996, p. 14.

39. Ibid.

40. Ken Dickson, <u>Albertalks</u>, Winter 1995, Vol. 22, no. 2, p.3.

41. George Cornell, "Associated Press Report," October 30, 1992.

42. <u>Chicago Tribune</u>, "Gallup Poll," November 2, 1995.

43. Ruth Stafford Peale, conversation with the author, Pawling, New York, May 4, 1995.

44. Bible, St. John 14:6.

45. <u>Ibid</u>. St. John 8:58.

46. Dalai Lama, <u>Freedom In Exile</u>. p. 261.

47. E. Stanley Jones, <u>Gandhi</u>, p. 62.

48. <u>Toward a Renewed Understanding of Ecumenism</u>.

49. Alexandr Solzhenitsyn, <u>World Split Apart</u>. p. 61.

50. Bible, Leviticus 19:18.

PART FIVE

APPENDICES

APPENDICES

Summary

Appendix I, by Rev. Dr. Martin Luther King Jr., is a classic which deserves to be better known. It should be read by everyone who admired his famous "I Have A Dream" but wondered where to find the ethical underpinnings or the source of the moral fibre that could empower such a vision.

Appendix II, by Premier Rene Levesque, will be of interest primarily to Americans who wish to better understand the phenomenon of French Canadian nationalism which has been to the fore of Canadian political life for several decades.

Appendix III, by Her Excellency, the Hon. Mary Simons, *et. al.* should be read by all Canadians, who, as yet, have only a vague picture of those most exciting developments in their north through the creation of the new territory of Nunavut.

Appendix IIII, by Dr. Ralph Reed, Executive Director of the Christian Coalition, is an appeal for understanding and dialogue which should be read by everyone who is distressed at the appearance of extremism in the political agenda of American religious conservatives.

APPENDICES

APPENDIX I

(The American Friends Service Committee first published this essay by Rev. Dr. Martin Luther King Jr. as an uncopyrighted pamphlet with this brief introduction.)

<u>Letter from Birmingham City Jail</u>   written: April 16 1963:
    Dr. Martin Luther King, Jr. wrote this famous essay (written in the form of an open letter) on April 16, 1963 while in jail. He was serving a sentence for participating in civil rights demonstrations in Birmingham, Alabama. He rarely took time to defend himself against his opponents. But eight prominent "liberal" Alabama clergymen, all white, had published an open letter earlier in January that called on King to allow the battle for integration to continue in the local and federal courts, and warned that King's nonviolent resistance would have the effect of inviting civil disturbances. Dr. King wanted Christian ministers to see that the meaning of Christian discipleship was at the heart of the African American struggle for freedom, justice and equality.

MY DEAR FELLOW CLERGYMEN:
While confined here in the Birmingham city jail, I came across your recent statement calling my present activities "unwise and untimely." Seldom do I pause to answer criticism of my work and ideas. If I sought to answer all the criticisms that cross my desk, my secretaries would have little time for anything other than such correspondence in the course of the day, and I would have no time for constructive work. But since I feel that you are men of genuine good will and that your criticisms are sincerely set forth, I want to try to answer your statements in what I hope will be patient and reasonable terms.

I think I should indicate why I am here In Birmingham, since you have been influenced by the view which argues against "outsiders coming in." I have the honor of serving as president of the Southern Christian Leadership Conference, an organization operating in every southern state, with headquarters in Atlanta, Georgia. We have some eighty-five affiliated organizations across the South, and one of them is the Alabama Christian Movement for Human Rights. Frequently we share staff, educational and financial resources with our affiliates. Several months ago the affiliate here in Birmingham asked us to be on call to engage in a nonviolent direct-action program if such were deemed necessary. We readily consented, and when the hour came we lived up to our promise. So I, along with several members of my staff, am here because I was invited here. I am here because I have organizational ties here.

But more basically, I am in Birmingham because injustice is here. Just as the prophets of the eighth century B.C. left their villages and carried their "thus saith the Lord" far beyond the boundaries of their home towns, and just as the Apostle Paul left his village of Tarsus and carried the gospel of Jesus Christ to the far corners of the Graeco-Roman world, so am I compelled to carry the gospel of freedom beyond my own home town. Like Paul, I must constantly respond to the Macedonian call for aid.

Moreover, I am cognizant of the interrelatedness of all communities and states. I cannot sit idly by in Atlanta and not be concerned about what happens in Birmingham. Injustice anywhere is a threat to justice everywhere. We are caught in an inescapable network of mutuality, tied in a single garment of destiny. Whatever affects one directly, affects all indirectly. Never again can we afford to live with the narrow, provincial "outside agitator" idea. Anyone who lives inside the United States can never be considered an outsider anywhere within its bounds.

You deplore the demonstrations taking place in Birmingham. But your statement, I am sorry to say, fails to express a similar concern for the conditions that brought about the demonstrations. I am sure that none of you would want to rest content with the superficial kind of social analysis that deals merely with effects and does not grapple with underlying causes. It is unfortunate that demonstrations are taking place in Birmingham, but it is even more unfortunate that the city's white power structure left the Negro community with no alternative.

In any nonviolent campaign there are four basic steps: collection of the facts to determine whether injustices exist; negotiation; self-purification; and direct action. We have gone through all these steps in Birmingham. There can be no gainsaying the fact that racial injustice engulfs this community. Birmingham is probably the most thoroughly segregated city in the United States. Its ugly record of brutality is widely known. Negroes have experienced grossly unjust treatment in the courts. There have been more unsolved bombings of Negro homes and churches in Birmingham than in any other city in the nation. These are the hard, brutal facts of the case. On the basis of these conditions, Negro leaders sought to negotiate with the city fathers. But the latter consistently refused to engage in good-faith negotiation.

Then, last September, came the opportunity to talk with leaders of Birmingham's economic community. In the course of the negotiations, certain promises were made by the merchants --- for example, to remove humiliating racial signs from the stores. On the basis of these promises, the Reverend Fred Shuttlesworth and the leaders of the Alabama Christian Movement for Human Rights agreed to a moratorium on all demonstrations. As the weeks and months went by, we realized that we were the victims of a broken promise. A few signs, briefly removed, returned; the others remained.

As in so many past experiences, our hopes had been blasted, and the shadow of deep disappointment settled upon us. We had no alternative except to prepare for direct action, whereby we would present our very bodies as a means of laying our case before the conscience of the local and the national community. Mindful of the difficulties involved, we decided to undertake a process of self-purification. We began a series of workshops on nonviolence, and we repeatedly asked ourselves : "Are you able to accept blows without retaliating?" "Are you able to endure the ordeal of jail?" We decided to schedule our direct-action program for the Easter season, realizing that except for Christmas, this is the main shopping period of the year. Knowing that a strong economic withdrawal program would be the by-product of direct action, we felt that this would be the best time to bring pressure to bear on the merchants for the needed change.

Then it occurred to us that Birmingham's mayoralty election was coming up in March, and we speedily decided to postpone action until after election day. When we discovered that the Commissioner of Public Safety, Eugene "Bull" Connor, had piled up enough votes to be in the run-off we decided again to postpone action until the day after the run-off so that the demonstrations could not be used to cloud the issues. Like many others, we waited to see Mr. Connor defeated, and to this end we endured postponement after postponement. Having aided in this community need, we felt that our direct action program could be delayed no longer.

You may well ask: "Why direct action? Why sit-ins, marches and so forth? Isn't negotiation a better path?" You are quite right in calling for negotiation. Indeed, this is the very purpose of direct action. Nonviolent direct action seeks to create such a crisis and foster such a tension that a community which has constantly refused to negotiate is forced to confront the issue. It seeks so to dramatize the issue that it can no longer be ignored.

My citing the creation of tension as part of the work of the nonviolent-resister may sound rather shocking. But I must confess that I am not afraid of the word "tension." I have earnestly opposed violent tension, but there is a type of constructive, nonviolent tension which is necessary for growth. Just as Socrates felt that it was necessary to create a tension in the mind so that individuals could rise from the bondage of myths and half-truths to the unfettered realm of creative analysis and objective appraisal, we see the need for nonviolent gadflies to create the kind of tension in society that will help men rise from the dark depths of prejudice and racism to the majestic heights of understanding and brotherhood.

The purpose of our direct-action program is to create a situation so crisis-packed that it will inevitably open the door to negotiation. I therefore concur with you in your call for negotiation. Too long has our beloved Southland been bogged down in a tragic effort to live in monologue rather than dialogue.

One of the basic points in your statement is that the action that I and my associates have taken in Birmingham is untimely. Some have asked: "Why didn't you give the new city administration time to act?" The only answer that I can give to this query is that the new Birmingham administration must be prodded about as much as the outgoing one, before it will act. We are sadly mistaken if we feel that the election of Albert Boutwell as mayor will bring the millennium to Birmingham. While Mr. Boutwell is a much more gentle person than Mr. Connor, they are both segregationists, dedicated to maintenance of the status quo. I have hope that Mr. Boutwell will be reasonable enough to see the futility of massive resistance to desegregation. But he will not see this without pressure from devotees of civil rights.

My friends, I must say to you that we have not made a single gain in civil rights without determined legal and nonviolent pressure. Lamentably, it is an historical fact that privileged groups seldom give up their privileges voluntarily. Individuals may see the moral light and voluntarily give up their unjust posture; but, as Reinhold Niebuhr has reminded us, groups tend to be more immoral than individuals.

We know through painful experience that freedom is never voluntarily given by the oppressor; it must be demanded by the oppressed. Frankly, I have yet to engage in a direct-action campaign that was "well timed" in the view of those who have not suffered unduly from the disease of segregation. For years now I have heard the word "Wait!" It rings in the ear of every Negro with piercing familiarity. This "Wait" has almost always meant 'Never." We must come to see, with one of our distinguished jurists, that "justice too long delayed is justice denied."

We have waited for more than 340 years for our constitutional and God-given rights. The nations of Asia and Africa are moving with jetlike speed toward gaining political independence, but we still creep at horse-and-buggy pace toward gaining a cup of coffee at a lunch counter. Perhaps it is easy for those who have never felt the stinging dart of segregation to say, "Wait."

But when you have seen vicious mobs lynch your mothers and fathers at will, and drown your sisters and brothers at whim; when you have seen hate-filled policemen curse, kick and even kill your black brothers and sisters; when you see the vast majority of your twenty million Negro brothers smothering in an airtight cage of poverty in the midst of an affluent society; when you suddenly find your tongue twisted and your speech stammering as you seek to explain to your six-year-old daughter why she can't go to the public amusement park that has just been advertised on television, and see tears welling up in her eyes when she is told that Funtown is closed to colored children, and see ominous clouds of inferiority beginning to form in her little mental sky, and see her beginning to distort her personality by developing an unconscious bitterness toward white people; when you have to concoct an answer for a five-year-old son who is asking: "Daddy, why do white people treat colored people so mean?"; when you take a cross-county drive and find it necessary to sleep night after night in the uncomfortable corners of your automobile because no motel will accept you; when you are humiliated day in and day out by nagging signs reading "white" and "colored"; when your first name becomes "nigger," your middle name becomes "boy" (however old you are) and your last name becomes "John," and your wife and mother are never given the respected title "Mrs."; when you are harried by day and haunted by night by the fact that you are a Negro, living constantly at tiptoe stance, never quite knowing what to expect next, and are plagued with inner fears and outer resentments; when you are forever fighting a degenerating sense of "nobodiness" then you will understand why we find it difficult to wait.

There comes a time when the cup of endurance runs over, and men are no longer willing to be plunged into the abyss of despair. I hope, sirs, you can understand our legitimate and unavoidable impatience.

You express a great deal of anxiety over our willingness to break laws. This is certainly a legitimate concern. Since we so diligently urge people to obey the Supreme Court's decision of 1954 outlawing segregation in the public schools, at first glance it may seem rather paradoxical for us consciously to break laws. One may well ask: "How can you advocate breaking some laws and obeying others?" The answer lies in the fact that there are two types of laws: just and unjust. I would be the first to advocate obeying just laws. One has not only a legal but a moral responsibility to obey just laws. Conversely, one has a moral responsibility to disobey unjust laws. I would agree with St. Augustine that "an unjust law is no law at all"

Now, what is the difference between the two? How does one determine whether a law is just or unjust? A just law is a man-made code that squares with the moral law or the law of God. An unjust law is a code that is out of harmony with the moral law. To put it in the terms of St. Thomas Aquinas: An unjust law is a human law that is not rooted in eternal law and natural law. Any law that uplifts human personality is just. Any law that degrades human

245

personality is unjust. All segregation statutes are unjust because segregation distorts the soul and damages the personality. It gives the segregator a false sense of superiority and the segregated a false sense of inferiority.

Segregation, to use the terminology of the Jewish philosopher Martin Buber, substitutes an "I-it" relationship for an "I-thou" relationship and ends up relegating persons to the status of things. Hence, segregation is not only politically, economically and sociologically unsound, it is morally wrong and awful. Paul Tillich said that sin is separation. Is not segregation an existential expression of man's tragic separation, his awful estrangement, his terrible sinfulness? Thus it is that I can urge men to obey the 1954 decision of the Supreme Court, for it is morally right; and I can urge them to disobey segregation ordinances, for they are morally wrong.

Let us consider a more concrete example of just and unjust laws. An unjust law is a code that a numerical or powerful majority group compels a minority group to obey but does not make binding on itself. This is difference made legal. By the same token, a just law is a code that a majority compels a minority to follow and that it is willing to follow itself. This is sameness made legal.

Let me give another explanation. A law is unjust if it is inflicted on a minority that, as a result of being denied the right to vote, had no part in enacting or devising the law. Who can say that the legislature of Alabama which set up that state's segregation laws was democratically elected? Throughout Alabama all sorts of devious methods are used to prevent Negroes from becoming registered voters, and there are some counties in which, even though Negroes constitute a majority of the population, not a single Negro is registered. Can any law enacted under such circumstances be considered democratically structured?

Sometimes a law is just on its face and unjust in its application. For instance, I have been arrested on a charge of parading without a permit. Now, there is nothing wrong in having an ordinance which requires a permit for a parade. But such an ordinance becomes unjust when it is used to maintain segregation and to deny citizens the First Amendment privilege of peaceful assembly and protest.

I hope you are able to trace the distinction I am trying to point out. In no sense do I advocate evading or defying the law, as would the rabid segregationist. That would lead to anarchy. On who breaks an unjust law must do so openly, lovingly, and with a willingness to accept the penalty. I submit that an individual who breaks a law that conscience tells him is unjust and who willingly accepts the penalty of imprisonment in order to arouse the conscience of the community over its injustice, is in reality expressing the highest respect for law.

Of course, there is nothing new about this kind of civil disobedience. It was evidenced sublimely in the refusal of Shadrach, Meshach and Abednego to obey

246

the laws of Nebuchadnezzar, on the ground that a higher moral law was at stake. It was practiced superbly by the early Christians, who were willing to face hungry lions and the excruciating pain of chopping blocks rather than submit to certain unjust laws of the Roman Empire. To a degree, academic freedom is a reality today because Socrates practiced civil disobedience. In our own nation, the Boston Tea Party represented a massive act of civil disobedience.

We should never forget that everything Adolf Hitler did in Germany was "legal" and everything the Hungarian freedom fighters did in Hungary was "illegal." It was "illegal" to aid and comfort a Jew in Hitler's Germany. Even so, I am sure that, had I lived in Germany at the time, I would have aided and comforted my Jewish brothers. If today I lived in a Communist country where certain principles dear to the Christian faith are suppressed, I would openly advocate disobeying that country's anti-religious laws.

I must make two honest confessions to you, my Christian and Jewish brothers. First, I must confess that over the past few years I have been gravely disappointed with the white moderate. I have almost reached the regrettable conclusion that the Negro's great stumbling block in his stride toward freedom is not the White Citizen's Councilor or the Ku Klux Klanner, but the white moderate, who is more devoted to "order" than to justice; who prefers a negative peace which is the absence of tension to a positive peace which is the presence of justice; who constantly says: "I agree with you in the goal you seek, but I cannot agree with your methods of direct action"; who paternalistically believes he can set the timetable for another man's freedom; who lives by a mythical concept of time and who constantly advises the Negro to wait for a "more convenient season." Shallow understanding from people of good will is more frustrating than absolute misunderstanding from people of ill will. Lukewarm acceptance is much more bewildering than outright rejection.

I had hoped that the white moderate would understand that law and order exist for the purpose of establishing justice and that when they fail in this purpose they become the dangerously structured dams that block the flow of social progress. I had hoped that the white moderate would understand that the present tension in the South is a necessary phase of the transition from an obnoxious negative peace, in which the Negro passively accepted his unjust plight, to a substantive and positive peace, in which all men will respect the dignity and worth of human personality.

Actually, we who engage in nonviolent direct action are not the creators of tension. We merely bring to the surface the hidden tension that is already alive. We bring it out in the open, where it can be seen and dealt with. Like a boil that can never be cured so long as it is covered up but must be opened with all its ugliness to the natural medicines of air and light, injustice must be exposed, with all the tension its exposure creates, to the light of human conscience and the air of national opinion before it can be cured.

In your statement you assert that our actions, even though peaceful, must be condemned because they precipitate violence. But is this a logical assertion? Isn't this like condemning a robbed man because his possession of money precipitated the evil act of robbery? Isn't this like condemning Socrates because his unswerving commitment to truth and his philosophical inquiries precipitated the act by the misguided populace in which they made him drink hemlock? Isn't this like condemning Jesus because his unique God-consciousness and never-ceasing devotion to God's will precipitated the evil act of crucifixion? We must come to see that, as the federal courts have consistently affirmed, it is wrong to urge an individual to cease his efforts to gain his basic constitutional rights because the quest may precipitate violence. Society must protect the robbed and punish the robber.

I had also hoped that the white moderate would reject the myth concerning time in relation to the struggle for freedom. I have just received a letter from a white brother in Texas. He writes: "All Christians know that the colored people will receive equal rights eventually, but it is possible that you are in too great a religious hurry. It has taken Christianity almost two thousand years to accomplish what it has. The teachings of Christ take time to come to earth." Such an attitude stems from a tragic misconception of time, from the strangely rational notion that there is something in the very flow of time that will inevitably cure all ills.

Actually, time itself is neutral; it can be used either destructively or constructively. More and more I feel that the people of ill will have used time much more effectively than have the people of good will. We will have to repent in this generation not merely for the hateful words and actions of the bad people but for the appalling silence of the good people. Human progress never rolls in on wheels of inevitability; it comes through the tireless efforts of men willing to be co-workers with God, and without this hard work, time itself becomes an ally of the forces of social stagnation.

We must use time creatively, in the knowledge that the time is always ripe to do right. Now is the time to make real the promise of democracy and transform our pending national elegy into a creative psalm of brotherhood. Now is the time to lift our national policy from the quicksand of racial injustice to the solid rock of human dignity.

You speak of our activity in Birmingham as extreme. At first I was rather disappointed that fellow clergymen would see my nonviolent efforts as those of an extremist. I began thinking about the fact that I stand in the middle of two opposing forces in the Negro community.

One is a force of complacency, made up in part of Negroes who, as a result of long years of oppression, are so drained of self-respect and a sense of "somebodiness" that they have adjusted to segregation; and in part of a few middle class Negroes who, because of a degree of academic and economic security and because in some ways they profit by segregation, have become insensitive to the problems of the masses.

The other force is one of bitterness and hatred, and it comes perilously close to advocating violence. It is expressed in the various black nationalist groups that are springing up across the nation, the largest and best-known being Elijah Muhammad's Muslim movement. Nourished by the Negro's frustration over the continued existence of racial discrimination, this movement is made up of people who have lost faith in America, who have absolutely repudiated Christianity, and who have concluded that the white man is an incorrigible "devil."

I have tried to stand between these two forces, saying that we need emulate neither the "do-nothingism" of the complacent nor the hatred and despair of the black nationalist.   For there is the more excellent way of love and nonviolent protest. I am grateful to God that, through the influence of the Negro church, the way of nonviolence became an integral part of our struggle.

If this philosophy had not emerged, by now many streets of the South would, I am convinced, be flowing with blood. And I am further convinced that if our white brothers dismiss as "rabble-rousers" and "outside agitators" those of us who employ nonviolent direct action, and if they refuse to support our nonviolent efforts, millions of Negroes will, out of frustration and despair, seek solace and security in black-nationalist ideologies, a development that would inevitably lead to a frightening racial nightmare.

Oppressed people cannot remain oppressed forever. The yearning for freedom eventually manifests itself, and that is what has happened to the American Negro. Something within has reminded him of his birthright of freedom, and something without has reminded him that it can be gained. Consciously or unconsciously, he has been caught up by the Zeitgeist, and with his black brothers of Africa and his brown and yellow brothers of Asia, South America and the Caribbean, the United States Negro is moving with a sense of great urgency toward the promised land of racial justice. If one recognizes this vital urge that has engulfed the Negro community, one should readily understand why public demonstrations are taking place.

The Negro has many pent-up resentments and latent frustrations, and he must release them. So let him march; let him make prayer pilgrimages to the city hall; let him go on freedom rides and try to understand why he must do so. If his repressed emotions are not released in nonviolent ways, they will seek expression through violence; this is not a threat but a fact of history. So I have not said to my people: "Get rid of your discontent." Rather, I have tried to say that this normal and healthy discontent can be channeled into the creative outlet of nonviolent direct action. And now this approach is being termed extremist.

But though I was initially disappointed at being categorized as an extremist, as I continued to think about the matter I gradually gained a measure of satisfaction from the label. Was not Jesus an extremist for love: "Love your enemies, bless them that curse you, do good to them that hate you, and pray for them which despitefully use you, and persecute you." Was not Amos an extremist for justice: "Let justice roll down like waters and righteousness like an ever-flowing stream." Was not Paul an extremist for the Christian gospel: "I bear in my body the marks of the Lord Jesus."

Was not Martin Luther an extremist: "Here I stand; I cannot do otherwise, so help me God." And John Bunyan: "I will stay in jail to the end of my days before I make a butchery of my conscience." And Abraham Lincoln: "This nation cannot survive half slave and half free." And Thomas Jefferson: "We hold these truths to be self-evident, that all men are created equal ...." So the question is not whether we will be extremists, but what kind of extremists we will be. Will we be extremists for hate or for love? Will we be extremist for the preservation of injustice or for the extension of justice?

In that dramatic scene on Calvary's hill three men were crucified. We must never forget that all three were crucified for the same crime---the crime of extremism. Two were extremists for immorality, and thus fell below their environment. The other, Jesus Christ, was an extremist for love, truth and goodness, and thereby rose above his environment. Perhaps the South, the nation and the world are in dire need of creative extremists.

I had hoped that the white moderate would see this need. Perhaps I was too optimistic; perhaps I expected too much. I suppose I should have realized that few members of the oppressor race can understand the deep groans and passionate yearnings of the oppressed race, and still fewer have the vision to see that injustice must be rooted out by strong, persistent and determined action.

I am thankful, however, that some of our white brothers in the South have grasped the meaning of this social revolution and committed themselves to it. They are still too few in quantity, but they are big in quality. Some, such as Ralph McGill, Lillian Smith, Harry Golden, James McBride Dabbs, Ann Braden and Sarah Patton Boyle, have written about our struggle in eloquent and prophetic terms.

Others have marched with us down nameless streets of the South. They have languished in filthy, roach-infested jails, suffering the abuse and brutality of policemen who view them as "dirty nigger lovers." Unlike so many of their moderate brothers and sisters, they have recognized the urgency of the moment and sensed the need for powerful "action" antidotes to combat the disease of segregation.

Let me take note of my other major disappointment. I have been so greatly disappointed with the white church and its leadership. Of course, there are some notable exceptions. I am not unmindful of the fact that each of you has taken some significant stands on this issue. I commend you, Reverend Stallings, for your Christian stand on this past Sunday, in welcoming Negroes to your worship service on a non-segregated basis. I commend the Catholic leaders of this state for integrating Spring Hill College several years ago.

But despite these notable exceptions, I must honestly reiterate that I have been disappointed with the church. I do not say this as one of those negative critics who can always find something wrong with the church. I say this as a minister of the gospel, who loves the church; who was nurtured in its bosom; who has been sustained by its spiritual blessings and who will remain true to it as long as the cord of Rio shall lengthen.

When I was suddenly catapulted into the leadership of the bus protest in Montgomery, Alabama, a few years ago, I felt we would be supported by the white church. I felt that the white ministers, priests and rabbis of the South would be among our strongest allies. Instead, some have been outright opponents, refusing to understand the freedom movement and misrepresenting its leadership; and too many others have been more cautious than courageous and have remained silent behind the anesthetizing security of stained-glass windows.

In spite of my shattered dreams, I came to Birmingham with the hope that the white religious leadership of this community would see the justice of our cause and, with deep moral concern, would serve as the channel through which our just grievances could reach the power structure. I had hoped that each of you would understand. But again I have been disappointed.

I have heard numerous southern religious leaders admonish their worshippers to comply with a desegregation decision because it is the law, but I have longed to hear white ministers declare: "Follow this decree because integration is morally right and because the Negro is your brother." In the midst of blatant injustices inflicted upon the Negro, I have watched white churchmen stand on the sideline and mouth pious. irrelevancies and sanctimonious trivialities. In the midst of a mighty struggle to rid our nation of racial and economic injustice, I have heard many ministers say: "Those are social issues, with which the gospel has no real concern." And I have watched many churches commit themselves to a completely other worldly religion which makes a strange, unbiblical distinction between body and soul, between the sacred and the secular.

I have traveled the length and breadth of Alabama, Mississippi and all the other southern states. On sweltering summer days and crisp autumn mornings I have looked at the South's beautiful churches with their lofty spires pointing heavenward. I have beheld the impressive outlines of her massive religious-education buildings. Over and over I have found myself asking: "What kind of people worship here? Who is their God? Where were their voices when the lips of Governor Barnett dripped with words of interposition and nullification? Where were they when Governor Wallace gave a clarion call for defiance and hatred? Where were their voices of support when bruised and weary Negro men and women decided to rise from the dark dungeons of complacency to the bright hills of creative protest?"

Yes, these questions are still in my mind. In deep disappointment I have wept over the laxity of the church. But be assured that my tears have been tears of love. There can be no deep disappointment where there is not deep love. Yes, I love the church. How could I do otherwise? I am in the rather unique position of being the son, the grandson and the great-grandson of preachers. Yes, I see the church as the body of Christ. But, oh! How we have blemished and scarred that body through social neglect and through fear of being nonconformists.

There was a time when the church was very powerful, in the time when the early Christians rejoiced at being deemed worthy to suffer for what they believed. In those days the church was not merely a thermometer that recorded the ideas and principles of popular opinion; it was a thermostat that transformed the mores of society. Whenever the early Christians entered a town, the people in power became disturbed and immediately sought to convict the Christians for being "disturbers of the peace" and "outside agitators."

But the Christians pressed on, in the conviction that they were "a colony of heaven," called to obey God rather than man. Small in number, they were big in commitment. They were too God-intoxicated to be "astronomically intimidated." By their effort and example they brought an end to such ancient evils as infanticide. and gladiatorial contests.

Things are different now. So often the contemporary church is a weak, ineffectual voice with an uncertain sound. So often it is an archdefender of the status quo. Far from being disturbed by the presence of the church, the power structure of the average community is consoled by the church's silent and often even vocal sanction of things as they are.

But the judgment of God is upon the church as never before. If today's church does not recapture the sacrificial spirit of the early church, it will lose its authenticity, forfeit the loyalty of millions, and be dismissed as an irrelevant social club with no meaning for the twentieth century. Every day I meet young people whose disappointment with the church has turned into outright disgust.

Perhaps I have once again been too optimistic. Is organized religion too inextricably bound to the status quo to save our nation and the world? Perhaps I must turn my faith to the inner spiritual church, the church within the church, as the true "ecclesia" and the hope of the world.

But again I am thankful to God that some noble souls from the ranks of organized religion have broken loose from the paralyzing chains of conformity and joined us as active partners in the struggle for freedom. They have left their secure congregations and walked the streets of Albany, Georgia, with us. They have gone down the highways of the South on tortuous rides for freedom. Yes, they have gone to jail with us. Some have been dismissed from their churches, have lost the support of their bishops and fellow ministers. But they have acted in the faith that right defeated is stronger than evil triumphant. Their witness has been the spiritual salt that has preserved the true meaning of the gospel in these troubled times. They have carved a tunnel of hope through the dark mountain of disappointment.

I hope the church as a whole will meet the challenge of this decisive hour. But even if the church does not come to the aid of justice, I have no despair about the future. I have no fear about the outcome of our struggle in Birmingham, even if our motives are at present misunderstood. We will reach the goal of freedom in Birmingham, and all over the nation, because the goal of America is freedom. Abused and scorned though we may be, our destiny is tied up with America's destiny.

Before those pilgrims landed at Plymouth, we were here. Before freedom's tool, the pen of Jefferson, etched the majestic words of the Declaration of Independence across the pages of history, we were here. For more than two centuries our forebears labored in this country without wages; they made cotton king; they built the homes of their masters while suffering gross injustice and shameful humiliation-and yet out of a bottomless vitality they continued to thrive and develop. If the inexpressible cruelties of slavery could not stop us, the opposition we now face will surely fail. We will win our freedom because the sacred heritage of our nation and the eternal will of God are embodied in our echoing demands.

Before closing I feel impelled to mention one other point in your statement that has troubled me profoundly. You warmly commended the Birmingham police force for keeping "order" and "preventing violence." I doubt that you would have so warmly commended the police force if you had seen its dogs sinking their teeth into unarmed, nonviolent Negroes. I doubt that you would so quickly commend the policemen if you were to observe their ugly and inhumane treatment of Negroes here in the city jail; if you were to watch them push and curse old Negro women and young Negro girls; if you were to see them slap and kick old Negro men and young boys; if you were to observe them, as they did on two occasions, refuse to give us food because we wanted to sing our grace together. I cannot join you in your praise of the Birmingham police department.

It is true that the police have exercised a degree of discipline in handling the demonstrators. In this sense they have conducted themselves rather "nonviolently" in public. But for what purpose? To preserve the evil system of segregation. Over the past few years I have consistently preached that nonviolence demands that the means we use must be as pure as the ends we seek. I have tried to make clear that it is wrong to use immoral means to attain moral ends. But now I must affirm that it is just as wrong, or perhaps even more so, to use moral means to preserve immoral ends. Perhaps Mr. Connor and his policemen have been rather nonviolent in public, as was Chief Pritchett in Albany, Georgia but they have used the moral means of nonviolence to maintain the immoral end of racial injustice. As T. S. Eliot has said: "The last temptation is the greatest treason: To do the right deed for the wrong reason."

I wish you had commended the Negro sit-inners and demonstrators of Birmingham for their sublime courage, their willingness to suffer and their amazing discipline in the midst of great provocation. One day the South will recognize its real heroes.

They will be the James Merediths, with the noble sense of purpose that enables them to face jeering, and hostile mobs, and with the agonizing loneliness that characterizes the life of the pioneer. They will be old, oppressed, battered Negro women, symbolized in a seventy-two-year-old woman in Montgomery, Alabama, who rose up with a sense of dignity and with her people decided not to ride segregated buses, and who responded with ungrammatical profundity to one who inquired about her weariness: "My feets is tired, but my soul is at rest." They will be the young high school and college students, the young ministers of the gospel and a host of their elders, courageously and nonviolently sitting in at lunch counters and willingly going to jail for conscience' sake.

One day the South will know that when these disinherited children of God sat down at lunch counters, they were in reality standing up for what is best in the American dream and for the most sacred values in our Judaeo-Christian heritage, thereby bringing our nation back to those great wells of democracy which were dug deep by the founding fathers in their formulation of the Constitution and the Declaration of Independence.

Never before have I written so long a letter. I'm afraid it is much too long to take your precious time. I can assure you that it would have been much shorter if I had been writing from a comfortable desk, but what else can one do when he is alone in a narrow jail cell, other than write long letters, think long thoughts and pray long prayers?

If I have said anything in this letter that overstates the truth and indicates an unreasonable impatience, I beg you to forgive me. If I have said anything that understates the truth and indicates my having a patience that allows me to settle for anything less than brotherhood, I beg God to forgive me.

I hope this letter finds you strong in the faith. I also hope that circumstances will soon make it possible for me to meet each of you, not as an integrationist or a civil rights leader but as a fellow clergyman and a Christian brother. Let us all hope that the dark clouds of racial prejudice will soon pass away and the deep fog of misunderstanding will be lifted from our fear-drenched communities, and in some not too distant tomorrow the radiant stars of love and brotherhood will shine over our great nation with all their scintillating beauty.

Yours for the cause of Peace and Brotherhood,
Martin Luther King, Jr.

APPENDICES

(Note from the author: This response to a published statement by eight fellow clergymen from Alabama (Bishop C. C. J. Carpenter, Bishop Joseph A. Durick, Rabbi Hilton L. Grafman, Bishop Paul Hardin, Bishop Holan B. Harmon, the Reverend George M. Murray, the Reverend Edward V. Ramage and the Reverend Earl Stallings) was composed under somewhat constricting circumstance. Begun on the margins of the newspaper in which the statement appeared while I was in jail, the letter was continued on scraps of writing paper supplied by a friendly Negro trusty, and concluded on a pad my attorneys were eventually permitted to leave me. Although the text remains in substance unaltered, I have indulged in the author's prerogative of polishing it for publication.)

APPENDICES

APPENDIX II

(This essay, "What Does Quebec Want?", was offered by Rene Levesque, the newly elected Premier of Quebec, as a foreword to <u>Separatism</u> by Brian A. Brown, in 1976. Much of the same material has appeared in abbreviated form in various other publications; it is copyrighted by Brian A. Brown.)

i.

What does Quebec want? The question now has an echo: what does the West want? There could be others like "what does the Atlantic region want?" except that until now nobody has been listening. Brian Brown has correctly identified the movement for Quebec independence as the catalyst for a new and better Canada. There are special reasons for Quebec's quest and so we have been the first to articulate the issues. Dr. Brown has kindly offered me this opportunity to delineate the Quebec perspective as a prelude to his own vision for the rest of the country.

What does Quebec want? The question is an old cliche in Canadian political folklore. Again and again during the more than 30 years since the end of World War II, it's been raised whenever Quebec's attitudes made it the odd man out in the permanent pull and tug of our federal-provincial relations. In fact, it's a question which could go back to the British conquest of an obscure French colony some 15 years before American Independence, and then run right through the stubborn survival of those 70,000 settlers and their descendants during the following two centuries.

By now there are some six million of them in Canada, not counting the progeny of the many thousands who were forced by poverty, especially around the turn of the century, to migrate to the United States, and now constitute substantial "Franco" communities in practically all the New England states.

But Quebec remains the homeland. All along the valley of the St. Lawrence, from the Ottawa River down to the Gaspe peninsula and the great Gulf, in the ancient settlements which grew into the big cities of Montreal and Quebec, in hundreds of smaller towns and villages from the American border to the mining centers and power projects in the north, there are now some 4.8 million "Quebecois." That's 81 per cent of the population of the largest and second most populous of Canada's ten provinces.

What does this French Quebec want? Sometime during the next few years the question may be answered. And there are growing possibilities that the answer could very well be - independence.

Launched in 1967-68, the Parti Quebcois, whose platform is based on political sovereignty, now fills the role of Her Majesty's Government in the National Assembly - as we nostalgically designate our provincial legislature. In its first electoral test in 1970, it already had 24 per cent of the votes. Then in 1973, a second general election saw it jump to 30 per cent, and, although getting only six out of 110 seats, become what our British-type parliamentary system calls the Official Opposition, i.e., the government's main interlocutor and challenger.

The victory of the Parti Quebecois in the present election is part of an irreversible trend. The former provincial government, a branch of that same Liberal Party which also holds power at the federal level under Pierre Elliott Trudeau, has failed both Quebec and Canada. It was in power for six years and ever since its second and Pyrrhic victory in 1973 (102 seats) it has been leading both the province and the country steadily downhill.

The scandal-ridden atmosphere surrounding the Olympic construction sites, and the incredible billion-dollar deficit which is now a reality, are just the most visible aspects of a rather complete political and administrative disaster. A host of social and economic troubles, some imported but many more of its own making, surround the same governing party in Ottawa. They too continue the attempt to scare voters into supporting federalism at the expense of common sense.

Within Quebec the French voter is now leaning quite clearly toward a new political future. As for the Anglophone minority of over a million people, whose natural attachment to the status quo normally makes them the staunchest supporters of the reigning federalist party, they are confused as never before. Composed of a dwindling proportion of Anglo-Saxon descendants of eighteenth-century Irish immigrants, and a steadily growing "ethnic" mosaic (Jewish, Italian, Greek, etc.), in the crunch most of this minority will probably end up, as usual, supporting the Liberals. But not with the traditional unanimity. Caught between the Charybdis of dissatisfaction and the Scylla of secessionism, many are looking for some kind of "third force." Others, especially among younger people, are ready to go along with the Parti Quebecois, whose own minority position in Canada will soon find support in other regions.

Within Quebec what we have done is phenomenal with future ramifications for Canada which deserve thoughtful consideration. At first sight, this looks like a dramatically rapid development, this burgeoning and flowering over a very few years of a political emancipation movement in a population which, until recently, was commonly referred to as quiet old Quebec. But in fact, its success would mean, very simply, the normal healthy end result of a long and laborious national evolution.

ii.

There was the definite outline of a nation in that small French colony which was taken over, in 1763, by the British Empire at its apogee. For over a century and a half, beginning just before the Pilgrim Fathers landed in the Boston area, that curious mixture of peasants and adventurers had been writing a proud history all over the continent. From Hudson Bay to the Gulf of Mexico, and from Labrador to the Rockies, they had been the discoverers, the fur-traders, the fort-builders. Out of this far-ranging saga, historically brief though it was, and the tenacious roots which at the same time were being sunk into the St. Lawrence Lowlands, there slowly developed an identity quite different from the original stock as well as from France of the ancient regime; just as different, in its way, as the American identity had become from its own British seeds. Thus, when the traumatic shock of the conquest happened, it had enough staying power to survive, tightly knit around its Catholic clergy and its country landowners.

Throughout the next hundred years, while English Canada was being built, slowly but surely, out of the leftovers of the American Revolution and as a rampart against America's recurrent attacks of Manifest Destiny, French Quebec managed to hang on - mostly because of its "revenge of the cradles." It was desperately poor, cut off from the decision-making centers both at home and in Great Britain, and deprived of any cultural nourishment from its former mother country. But its rural, frugal society remained incredibly prolific. So it grew impressively, at least in numbers. And it held on obstinately, according to its lights and as much as its humble means made it possible, to those two major ingredients of national identity - land and language.

The hold on land was at best tenuous and, as in any colonial context, confined to the multitude of small farm holdings. Everything else - from the growth of major cities to the setting-up of manufacturing industries and then the rush of resource development - was the exclusive and undisputed field of action of "les Anglais," the growing minority of Anglo-Saxon and then assimilated immigrant groups who ran most of Quebec under the compact leadership of Montreal-based entrepreneurs, financiers and merchant kings.

As for the French elite, it remained mostly made up of doctors, lawyers, and priests - "essential services" for the bodies and souls of cheap labour, whose miraculous birthrate kept the supply continuously overabundant. And naturally, there were politicians, practically all of that typical colonial breed which is tolerated as long as it keeps natives happily excited about accessories and divided on essentials.

Needless to say, the educational system was made both to reflect this type of society and to keep it going nicely and quietly. There was a modest collection of church-run seminaries, where the main accent was on recruiting for the priesthood, and which, for over a century, led to just one underdeveloped university. For nine-tenths of the children there was nothing but grammar school, if that. Read and write barely enough to sign your name, and then, without any time for "getting ideas," graduate to obedient respectful employment by any boss generous enough to offer a steady modest job.

Such was the culturally starved and economically inferior, but well-insulated and thus highly resistant, French Quebec which, 109 years ago, was led into the final mutation of British North America and its supreme defense against American expansionism: Confederation, of four eastern colonies as a beginning, but soon to run north of the border "from sea to sea". Into that impressive Dominion, originally as one of four and eventually one of ten provinces, Quebec was incorporated without trouble and generally without enthusiasm. From now on, it was to be a minority forever, and, with the help of a dynamic federal immigration policy, a readily diminishing one. In due time, it would probably merge and disappear into the mainstream, or at the most remain as a relatively insignificant and yet convenient ghetto: La difference.

As the building of Canada accelerated during the late nineteenth and early twentieth centuries, a tradition was established that Quebec was to get its measured share of the work, anytime there was enough to go around - and the same for rewards. And so, in a nutshell, it went until fairly recently. All told, it hasn't been such a bad deal, this status of "inner colony" in a country owned and managed by another national entity. Undoubtedly, French Quebec was (as it remains to this day) the least ill-treated of all colonies in the world. Under a highly centralized federal system, which is much closer to a unitary regime than American federalism, it was allowed its full panoply of provincial institutions: cabinet, legislature, courts, along with the quasi-permanent fun of great squabbles, usually leading to exciting election campaigns, about the defense or extension of its "state rights"!

On three occasions during the last 80 years, one of "its own" has even been called upon - at times when there was felt a particular need to keep the natives quiet - to fill the most flattering of all offices, that of federal Prime Minister. Last but not least of the three, Mr. Trudeau, did as splendidly as was humanly possible for most of the last ten years in this big-chief-of-Quebec dimension, but the inevitable way of all (including political) flesh, has been catching up with so-called French Power in Ottawa. No replacement seems to be in sight.

iii.

But this is getting ahead of our story. To understand the rise of Quebec's own new nationalism and its unprecedented drive toward self-government, we must go back at least as far as World War II. Not that the dream had completely vanished during the two long centuries of survival which have just been described - from an admittedly partisan, but, I honestly believe, not unfair view-point. In the 1830's, for instance, there even was an ill-advised and disastrous armed rebellion by a few hundred "Patriots," leading to bloody repression and lasting memories about what not to do. And it is rather significant, by the way, that it took until just now before the poor heroic victims of that abortive rebellion became truly rehabilitated in popular opinion.

Small and impotent though it was, and in spite of feeling that this condition would possibly last forever, French Quebec never quite forgot the potential nation it had once been, never quite gave up dreaming about some miracle which might bring back its chance in the future; in some distant, indescribable future. Now and then, there were stirrings: a writer, a small political coterie there; a great upsurge of nationalist emotions, in the 1880's around the Riel affair - the hanging by "les Anglais" of the French-speaking leader of the Prairie Metis; then in 1917, on the conscription issue, a bitter and frequently violent confrontation between the Empire-minded English and the "isolationist" French; faint stirrings again in the Twenties; stronger ones in the Thirties.

Then World War II, with a repeat, in 1944, of the total disagreement on conscription. But mostly, here as elsewhere, this most terrible of all wars was also a mid-wife for revolutionary change. Thankfully, in less disruptive a manner than in other parts of the world, it did start a revolution in Quebec. Wartime service, both overseas and on the industrial home-front, dealt a mortal blow to the old order, gave an irresistible impetus to urbanization and started the break-up of the traditional rural-parish ideal, yanked women by the thousands into war-plant industry and put as many men into battle-dress, leading both to discovery of the great wide world. For a small couped-up society, this was a more traumatic experience than for most others. And then when the post-war years brought the Roaring Fifties, unprecedented mobility, and television along with a consumer society, the revolution had to become permanent.

The beginning of the 1960's saw it baptized officially: The Quiet Revolution, with the adjective implying that "quaint old Quebec" couldn't have changed all that much. But it had. Its old set of values literally shattered, it was feeling collectively naked, like a lobster during its shedding season, looking frantically about for a new armour with which to face the modern world.

The first and most obvious move was toward education. After so prolonged and scandalous a neglect of this most basic instrument of development, it was quickly realized that here was the first urgent bootstrap operation that had to be launched. It was done with a vengeance: From one of the lowest in the Western world, Quebec per capita investment in education rapidly became, and remains, one of the very highest. Not always well spent (but who is to throw the first stone?), with many mistakes along the way, and the job still far from complete, which it never will be anyway; but the essential results are there, and multiplying. Human resources are, at long last, getting required development, along with a somewhat equal chance for all and a normal furious rise in general expectations.

The same, naturally, is happening also in other fields, quite particularly in that of economics, the very first were such rising expectations were bound to strike against the wall of an entrenched colonial setup, with its now intolerable second-class status for the French majority, and the stifling remote control of nearly all major decisions either in Ottawa or in alien corporate offices.

Inevitably, there had to be a spillover into politics. More than half of our public revenue and most of the decisions that count were and are in outside hands, in a federal establishment which was basically instituted not by us or for us, but by others and, always first and foremost, for their own purposes. With the highly centralized financial system that this establishment constitutionally lords over, this means, for example, that about 80 per cent of Quebec savings and potential investment capital ends up in banks and insurance companies whose operations are none of our business. It also means, just for example once again, that immigration is also practically none of our business; and this could have, murderous effects on a minority people with a birth rate, changed like everything else in less than a generation, down from its former prodigious level to close to zero population growth.

Through the 1960's, these and other problems were interminably argued about and batted back and forth between federal politicians and bureaucrats ("What we have we hold, until we get more") and a succession of insistent but orthodox, no more than rock-the-boat, nationalists in Quebec. But while this dialogue of the deaf was going on and on, the idea of political independence reappeared as it had to. Not as a dream this time, but as a project, and very quickly as a serious one. This developed by leaps and bounds from easily ridiculed marginal groups to small semi-organized political factions, and finally to a full fledged national party in 1967-68. These were the same two years during which, by pure coincidence, Mr. Trudeau was just as rapidly being elevated to the heights as a new federalist champion from Quebec.

But in spite of his best efforts and those of his party's branch-plant in provincial government, and through an increasing barrage of money, vilification and rather repugnant fear-inducing propaganda, the voters have democratically brought the Parti-Quebecois to power. Which brings us right back to our starting-point....

What was long considered unthinkable has now happened. Where do we go from here?

iv.

The way we see it, it would have to go somewhat like this. There is a new Quebec government which is totally dedicated to political independence. But this same Quebec, for the time being, is still very much a component of federal Canada, with its quite legitimate body of elected representatives in Ottawa. This calls, first of all, for at least a try at negotiation. But fruitful talk between two equally legitimate and diametrically opposed levels of government, without any further pressure from the population - that would be a real first in Canadian political history!

Obviously, there would have to be the referendum which the Parti Quebecois proposes in order to get the decisive yes-or-no answer to the tired question: What does Quebec want? (This was precisely the procedure by which the only new province to join Confederation during our recent democratic past, Newfoundland, was consulted in 1948-49 about whether or not to opt in. So why not about out?). If the answer is "yes", out, then the pressure is on Ottawa, along with a rather dramatic surge of outside attention, and we all get a privileged opportunity to study the recently inked Helsinki Declaration and other noble documents about self-determination for all peoples.

Fully confident of the basic integrity of Canadian democracy, and just as conscious that any silliness would be very costly for both sides, we firmly believe that the matter would then be brought to a negotiated settlement. Especially since the Parti Quebecois, far from aiming at any kind of mutual hostility or absurd Berlin Wall, will then repeat its standing offer of a new kind of association with the rest of Canada. Our aim is simply full equality by the only means through which a smaller nation can reasonably expect to achieve self-government. But we are definitely not unaware of the shock waves that such a break, after so long an illusion of eternity, is bound to send through the Canadian political fabric.

We do not accept the simplistic domino theory, where Quebec's departure is presented as the beginning of fatal dislocation, with "secession" spreading in all directions like a galloping disease until the Balkanized bits and pieces are swallowed up by the huge maw next door. In spite of the somewhat unsure character of its national identity and its excessive satellization by the American economic and cultural empire, Canada-without-Quebec has enough "difference" left, sufficient traditions and institutional originality, to withstand the extraction of its "foreign body" and find a way to go on from there. It might even turn out to be a heaven-sent opportunity to revamp the overcentralized and ridiculously bureaucratized federal system, that century-old sacred cow which, for the moment, nobody dares to touch seriously for fear of encouraging Quebec's subversive leanings!

Be that as it may, we know there would be a traumatic moment and a delicate transition during which things might go wrong between us for quite a while, or else, one would hope, start going right as never before. With this strange new-colored Quebec on the map between Ontario and the Maritime provinces, Canada must be kept from feeling incurably "Pakistanized", so we must address ourselves without delay to the problem of keeping a land bridge open with as much free flow of people and goods as is humanly possible; as much and more as there is, I would imagine, between Alaska and the main body of the United States over the western land bridge.

Such a scenario would call, as a decisive first step, for a customs union, as full-fledged as all Canadians consider to be mutually advantageous. We have, in fact, been proposing that ever since the Parti Quebecois was founded, and naturally meeting with the most resonant silence in all orthodox federalist circles. But in the midst of that silence, not a single responsible politician, nor for that matter a single important businessman, has been heard to declare that it wouldn't happen if and when the time comes.

For indisputably such a partnership, carefully negotiated on the basis of equality, is bound to be in the cards. Nothing prevents one envisaging it, for instance, going immediately, or at least very quickly, as far as the kind of monetary union which the European Common Market, with its original six and now nine members, has been fitfully aiming at for so many years. And building on this foundation, it would lead this new "northern tier" to a future immeasurably richer and more stimulating than the 109 year-old bind in which two nations more often than not feel and act like Churchill's two scorpions in the same bottle.

v.

What of Quebec's own national future, both internal and international, in this context of sovereignty-cum-interdependence?

The answers here, for reasons that are evident, have to be brief, even sketchy and essentially tentative. The perspective of independence for people who haven't been there yet, is bound to be an uncertain horizon. The more so in a period of history like ours, when so much is changing so fast you get the feeling that maybe change itself is becoming the only law to be counted on. Who can pretend to know exactly what or where his country will be twenty-five or even just ten years from now?

One thing for sure, is that Quebec will not end up, either soon or in any forseeable future, as the anarchic caricature of a revolutionary banana republic which adverse propaganda has been having great sinister fun depicting in advance. Either Ottawa is very simply inspired by prejudice or the origin of this nonsense is mostly to be found in the tragic month of October 1970 and the great "crisis" which our political establishments, under the astutely calculating Mr. Trudeau, managed to make out of a couple of dozen young terrorists, whose ideology was a hopeless hodgepodge of anarchonationalism and kindergarten Marxism, which had no chance of having any kind of serious impact. What they did accomplish was two kidnappings and, most cynically welcome of all, one murder - highly unfortunate but then also particularly par for the course in the international climate at the time.

What was not par at all, however, was the incredible abuse of power for which those events, relatively minor per se, were used as a pretext: The careful buildup of public hysteria, army trucks rolling in during the night, and then, for months on end, the application in Quebec, and solely in Quebec, of a federal War Measures Act for which no peacetime precedent exists in any democratic country. A great spectacle produced in order to terrorize the Quebecois forever back into unquestioning submissiveness, and outside, to feed the mill of scary propaganda about how dangerous this tame animal could nevertheless be!

In actual fact, French Quebec, with its normal share of troubles, disquiet and, now, the same kind of social turmoil and search for new values that are rampant all over the Western world remains at bottom a very solid, well-knit and non-violent society. Events new and demanding nationalism has about itself something less strident and essentially more self-confident than its current pan-Canadian counterpart. For Quebec has an assurance of identity, along with a relative lack of aggressiveness, which are the result of that one major factor of national durability lacking in the rest of Canada: A different language and the cultural fabric that goes with it.

Now how does the Parti Quebecois see this independent society begin to find its way? What is the general outline of the political, social and economic structure we hope to bring forth? Serious observers have been calling our program basically social-democratic, rather comparable to the Scandinavian models although certainly not a carbon copy since all people, through their own experiences, have to invent their own "mix".

The way we have been trying to rough it out democratically through half a dozen national party conventions, ours would call for a presidential regime, as much of an equal-opportunity social system as we could afford, and a decent measure, as quickly as possible but as carefully as indicated, of economic "repatriation." This last would begin to happen immediately, and normally without any great perturbation, through the very fact of sovereignty: With the gathering in of all of our public revenues and the full legislative control which any self-respecting national state has to implement over its main financial institutions, banks, insurance companies and the like.

In the latter case, this would allow us to break the stranglehold in which the old British-inspired banking system of just a handful of "majors" has always kept the people's money and financial initiative. The dominant position in our repatriated financial circuit would be handed over to Quebec's cooperative institutions, which happen to be particularly well developed in that very field, and, being strongly organized on a regional basis, would afford our population a decent chance for better-balanced, responsible, democratic development. And that, by the way, is just one fundamental aspect of the kind of evolution toward a new economic democracy, from the lowest rung in the marketplace up to board-room levels, which all advanced societies that are not already doing so had better start thinking about in the very near future.

As to non-resident enterprise, apart from the universal minimums concerning incorporations and due respect for Quebec taxes, language and other classic national requirements, what we have been fashioning over the last few years is an outline of a policy which we think is both logical and promising. It would take the form of an "investment code," giving a clean-cut picture, by sectors, of what parts of our economic life (e.g., culturally oriented activities, basic steel and forest resources) we would insist on keeping under home ownership, what other parts we would like to see under mixed control (a very few selected but strategic cases) and, finally, the multitude of fields (tied to markets, and to technological and-or capital necessities) where foreign interests would be allowed to stay or to enter provided they do not tend to own us along with their businesses.

In brief, Quebec's most privileged links and most essential relationships will be with its Canadian partners. Next in importance is the United States whose own independence developed much like our own though earlier. Then Quebec would look to other Francophone countries as cultural respondents, and to France herself. Such are the peaceful and, we confidently hope, fruitfully progressive changes which may very well appear on the map of North America in the next decade. A positive response to this opportunity for English Canada is the subject of this book.

APPENDICES

APPENDIX III

(This report was produced by Her Excellency, The Hon. Mary Simons and others in 1995 for the Nunavut Implementation Commission as its first release following the vote to establish this new territory. This and subsequent reports in the public domain are readily available on the Nunavut Internet Web Site.)

'Footprints in New Snow'
Nunavut: The Historical, Jurisdictional and Political Contexts

(a) The Historical Context:
April 1, 1999 will be an exciting day in the history of Canada. On that day, the Nunavut Act will come fully into force, and the new Nunavut Territory and Nunavut Government will come into existence. The internal boundaries of Canada will change for the first time since the entry of Newfoundland and Labrador into Canada in 1949.

APPENDICES

A new member of Confederation will be born in the Arctic. Equipping the people of Nunavut with a territorial government of their own will reinforce Canada's sense of being "true North, strong and free."

For many Canadians, "Nunavut" is as novel as it is intriguing. Yet, "Nunavut" is an old idea, as well as a contemporary one. "Nunavut" is a link to the past, as well as a claim to the future. "Nunavut" is an established reality, as well as an emerging one. These contradictions result from "Nunavut" carrying a number of meanings.

In the language of the Inuit majority in the eastern and central portions of the existing Northwest Territories (NWT) - "Nunavut" means "our land." Inuit are the aboriginal people of the Canadian Arctic and of other parts of the circumpolar Arctic (Greenland, Alaska, the eastern tip of Siberia). The ancestors of today's Inuit have lived in the Canadian Arctic for at least a millennium, and possibly a lot longer. In living "off the land," that is to say, in living off the rich mammal, fish and bird life of Arctic lands and seas, Inuit have developed and sustained a unique way of life.

This way of life has adapted to the changes introduced into the North by European peoples, but it has not been submerged by those changes. Viewed in the context of cultural originality and continuity, "Nunavut" is not a new concept at all. Rather, "Nunavut" is a term that has been part of the accepted vocabulary for uncounted generations of Inuit who have lived out their lives in their ancestral homeland.

In more recent times, "Nunavut" has come to take on new meanings. The political re-awakening of aboriginal peoples throughout Canada touched Inuit no less than others. Older Inuit, who had been born into a world largely free of control from outside, saw the need to channel cross-cultural forces into more constructive forms. Younger Inuit, who had acquired an in-depth knowledge of the law and politics of "the South" in church-administered residential schools, organized around the legal opportunities opened up by the Supreme Court of Canada in its 1973 decision in the Calder case. "Land claims" organizations were formed, and "land claims" negotiations begun.

For many Inuit, "Nunavut" became shorthand for the basket of political and proprietary demands brought to the land claims table by Inuit representatives, a basket that included a range of items extending from fee simple ownership of surface and mineral lands, to hunting, fishing and trapping rights, to joint Inuit/government management boards that could plan and regulate the use of Nunavut lands, waters and resources in a way that would emphasize public involvement and confidence.

Included in the basket of Inuit political and proprietary demands assembled by Inuit land claims organizations was an item that exceeded the bounds that had been set under the land claims policy of the Government of Canada: the creation of a new territory, with its own territorial government, in the eastern and central portions of the NWT, to be called "Nunavut."

From the outset, Inuit land claims organizations emphasized that the government of this new territory should be a "public" one, that is, a government which would be answerable to a legislative assembly elected by all citizens meeting residence and age qualifications and whose activities would be subject to Constitutional and statutory guarantees against discrimination. Despite such assurances, the federal government for many years resisted agreement to any formula which would link the conclusion of a Nunavut land claims agreement with a commitment to create a new Nunavut Territory and Government through the division of the NWT.

Only in the period following the conclusion of a comprehensive land claims agreement-in-principle in April 1990, was a compromise found which was mutually acceptable to Inuit land claims organizations and the Government of Canada. Under this approach, the commitment to create the Nunavut Territory and Government was to be recited in the text of the Nunavut final land claims agreement, but the commitment was given life through the detailed provisions of stand-alone legislation.

As a consequence, two pieces of legislation were proposed to Parliament in the summer of 1993, and proceeded in lock-step through the various stages of Parliamentary scrutiny and approval: the Nunavut Land Claims Agreement Act, which ratified the Nunavut Agreement, and, the Nunavut Act, which created a Nunavut Territory and Government and provides an institutional footing as to how its laws would be made, executed, and interpreted.

For outside observers, who have learned about "Nunavut" through periodic announcements of good news - e.g., the success of various plebiscites, the Inuit ratification of the Nunavut Agreement, the signature ceremony in Iqaluit in May 1993, the enactment of legislation - it would be easy to overlook the many years of sustained research, negotiating and communications efforts culminating in the enactment of the Nunavut Land Claims Agreement Act and the Nunavut Act. Lives were invested, and risks were run. The briefest of summaries of the complex events that unfolded in the period leading up to the summer of 1993 is set out in this Appendix.

Finally, in placing "Nunavut" in historical context, it is important to acknowledge that the meaning of "Nunavut" is not and cannot be fixed. "Nunavut" is a means, not an end in itself.

The dynamic and evolutionary aspect of Nunavut will be obvious over the next few years. The period leading up to 1999 will be filled with the events surrounding the design, organizing and setting up of the legislative, administrative and judicial branches of the new Nunavut Government.

For its part, the Nunavut Implementation Commission (NIC) has been given a mandate to advise the Government of Canada, the Government of the Northwest Territories (GNWT), and Nunavut Tunngavik Incorporated (NTI) on a variety of topics central to the smooth inauguration of the new Nunavut Government. The NIC is conscious of the great amount of work that will be involved in fulfilling its mandate.

The NIC is equally conscious of the even greater amount of work that will be associated with the conversion of advice into action. Elected leaders and officials of the Government of Canada and the GNWT will be busy carrying out a long list of tasks in the period leading up to April 1, 1999, ranging from the development of Cabinet submissions, to the management of large infrastructure projects, to the identification and dividing up of territorial governments assets and liabilities, to the timely recruitment of new staff.

However challenging, the years leading up to April 1, 1999, are just a beginning. All those organizations and individuals taking part in the ambitious work of setting up the new Nunavut Government are helping to begin something important, not to complete it. In the final analysis, the most compelling meanings of "Nunavut" will be the ones defined, and constantly re-defined, by the people of Nunavut for themselves over the generations to come.

(b) The Jurisdictional Context
There are a number of jurisdictional aspects of the Nunavut Territory and Government that are worth noting.

The Nunavut Territory will be precisely that, a territory. Carving the Nunavut Territory out of the existing NWT will change Canada from a federation made up of ten provinces and two territories to one made up of ten provinces and three territories. Of the provinces and territories, Nunavut will be both the biggest and the smallest: the biggest in terms of its geographic size (approximately 20% of Canada); and, the smallest in terms of its population (although if the population of Nunavut is approaching 30,000 by 1999, there may be more people living in Nunavut than Yukon).

A review of the provisions of the Nunavut Act suggests that Nunavut will be a territory similar to the others. The provisions of the Nunavut Act, although cast in more modern language and better reflecting the emergence of responsible government in the North (for example, in the concentration of executive authority in the hands of a Cabinet responsible to the legislature), are not out of keeping with the provisions of the older Yukon Act and Northwest Territories Act.

The three federal statutes dealing with the organization of northern territories share comparable text in relation to such things as the office of a federally appointed Commissioner, the law making powers of the territorial legislative assembly, and the preservation of a federal power to disallow territorial legislation. None of the three statutes constituting territories establishes "a Crown in right of the territory."

While allowing for the transfer of the beneficial use and enjoyment of certain lands to territorial governments, none of the three statutes provide for a general vesting of natural resources in a territory; the transfer of substantial authority over "Crown lands" requires the completion of collateral inter-governmental agreements, such as energy and minerals accords, and their implementing legislation.

Two other features of the Nunavut Act serve to reinforce the similarities between Nunavut and the two existing territories. The first feature is the "grandfathering" through of all the laws of the NWT into Nunavut. Under this approach, the statute books of the NWT and Nunavut will be virtually identical on April 1, 1999; substantive divergences will only arise as the legislatures of the two territories exercise their law making powers to different ends. The second feature is the coming fully into force of all the jurisdictional powers and duties of the Nunavut Legislative Assembly and Government on April 1, 1999.

While the Nunavut Act neither requires nor prevents a staged build-up in the administrative capacity of the Nunavut Government in the post-1999 period, the Nunavut Act provides for the complete assumption of legislative and executive responsibilities by the Nunavut Legislative Assembly and Government on April 1, 1999. On that day, the Nunavut Legislative Assembly and Government will be as fully seized with the burdens and discretions of office as their sister institutions in Yukon and the Mackenzie Valley.

The jurisdictional similarities between Nunavut and other territories will no doubt colour both how the Government of Nunavut is perceived by the Government of Canada and how the Government of Nunavut perceives there to be concerns common to all northern territories. Such perceptions will have obvious implications in relation to such things as how the federal government organizes itself to assign front-line responsibility for managing relations with the Nunavut Government, the policy rationale behind determining federal financial support for the operation of the Nunavut Government, and the role played by the Nunavut Government in inter-governmental processes involving federal, provincial and territorial governments.

The commonalities characteristic of territories and their governments will be an important reference point in how Nunavut is governed. At the same time, it will also be important to remember a number of things that will distinguish Nunavut from other territories.

One of the matters commonly recited in the past to distinguish between provinces and territories has been the lack of Constitutional security for territories. With the transfer of the Hudson's Bay lands to Canada in the nineteenth century, the Parliament of Canada asserted unqualified law making control over much of the north-western quadrant of North America.

This control was exercised to create the provinces of Manitoba, Saskatchewan and Alberta. It was exercised to expand the provinces of Manitoba, Ontario and Quebec. It was exercised to create the Yukon Territory. By 1912, Parliament's authority had been used so as to reduce the Northwest Territories to the boundaries that will pertain until 1999, when the creation of Nunavut will once again shrink the area subject to the Northwest Territories Act.

While it might be suggested that political conventions, co-incident with the attainment of responsible government, have developed which would argue against any amendments being made to the Yukon Act or the Northwest Territories Act without the concurrence of the relevant territorial legislature, there are no legal obstacles to the amendment of those statutes by Parliament. This is not the case with respect to Nunavut.

Unlike Yukon and the Northwest Territories, the creation of the Nunavut Territory and Government has been brought about by almost two decades of effort by the aboriginal people of the Nunavut area. This effort, amply evidenced in the documentary history of the region, culminated in the inclusion of Article 4 within the Nunavut Agreement.

It describes the Nunavut Agreement as a "land claims agreement" for the purpose of section 35 of the Constitution Act, 1982, and its various provisions have Constitutional status and protection. While the precise legal consequences attending the wording of the commitment to create the Nunavut Territory and Government are open to interpretation, it would appear that Nunavut has a Constitutional dimension not shared with other territories.

In addition to the legal implications of Nunavut's Constitutional dimension, it is important to note the strong moral weight of the Nunavut Political Accord. This Accord was entered into on October 30, 1992 (shortly before the Inuit vote on the ratification of the Nunavut Land Claims Agreement) by the Government of Canada, the GNWT and the Tungavik Federation of Nunavut (TFN).

The Accord, whose terms are in effect until July 1, 1999, contains many important assurances to the people of Nunavut and other parts of the existing NWT concerning how the new Nunavut Government will be accomplished and operate. Of primary importance in this regard are provisions of the Accord dealing with finances, particularly the following:

8.1 Prior to the coming into force and effect of the provisions of the Nunavut Act creating the Nunavut Territory, Canada, following consultation with other parties hereto, shall establish the financial arrangements for the Government of Nunavut. Recognizing the desirability of formula based financing, such financial arrangements may be analogous to those which currently exist for the GNWT with such modifications as may be necessary.

8.3 Prior to the coming into force and effect of the provisions of the Nunavut Act creating the Nunavut Territory a process shall be established by the parties to consult on the matters referred to in 8.1 and 8.2 herein and to clarify, as necessary, the financial arrangements referred to in 8.1 and 8.2.

8.4 In establishing the financial arrangements referred to in 8.1, and following consultation with other parties hereto, Canada shall determine and fund reasonable incremental costs arising from the creation and operation of the Government of Canada.

8.5 The financial arrangements referred to in 8.1 and 8.2 shall support the need for financial stability for the territories and provide both territorial governments the opportunity to continue to provide public services for residents, recognizing the existing scope and quality of such services.

Another important set of provisions in the Accord is that set dealing with training and human resources planning. The Accord recognizes the "central importance" of training, and stipulates that planning efforts should "consider all aspects of training activities including skills surveys, pre-employment education, skills upgrading, co-operative education and on-the-job training opportunities." The heavy emphasis placed on employment, training, and related education issues in the Nunavut Political Accord is consistent with a similar emphasis placed on such issues in the Nunavut Agreement. A specific article of the Agreement (Article 23) is devoted to Inuit employment within government. The objective of that Article is stated to be:

23.2.1 The objective of this Article is to increase Inuit participation in government employment in the Nunavut Settlement Area to a representative level. It is recognized that achievement of this objective will require initiatives by Inuit and by Government.

The article defines "a representative level" as "a level of Inuit employment within Government reflecting the ratio of Inuit to the total population of the Nunavut Settlement Area." The definition of "representative level" is stated to apply to "all occupational groupings and grade levels" within government employment in Nunavut.

Articles 4 and 24 of the Nunavut Agreement, accompanied by the Nunavut Political Accord, have profound consequences for how the Nunavut Government will operate, and on the planning process leading to its coming into operation. While Parliament and the federal government have traditionally had wide flexibility in how to legislate in relation to territories and to conduct relations with their governments, Nunavut will stand on a significantly different footing. The legal, political and moral commitments made to Inuit and other residents in Nunavut, especially in relation to government finances and employment, must serve as the bedrock on which all other undertakings are built.

There are two other jurisdictional aspects to Nunavut that should be noted.

The first is in relation to the offshore. The Nunavut Territory will encompass a greater expanse of offshore than any other province or territory in Canada. Under the terms of the Nunavut Act, Nunavut will include all the marine areas that knit together the Canadian Arctic archipelago, as well as all the marine areas of Hudson Bay and Hudson Strait that are north of the sixtieth parallel north latitude (and the islands in Hudson Bay and James Bay south of the sixtieth parallel).

From the point of view of both effective management of marine areas, which are covered with ice for most of the year, as well as from the point of view of reinforcing Canadian sovereignty, Nunavut's extensive offshore jurisdiction is entirely sensible. One practical implication of this extensive offshore jurisdiction, however, is that the Nunavut Government must have adequate administrative capacity to fulfil its jurisdictional responsibilities in the offshore. It should be noted that administration of a portion of the Nunavut offshore may be affected in a significant way by offshore land claims negotiations now taking place between northern Quebec Inuit, represented by Makivik Corporation, the Government of Canada and the GNWT.

The final jurisdictional aspect of Nunavut that should be noted is the lack of explicit reference to Nunavut in relevant parts of the Constitution Acts, 1867 to 1982 dealing with representation in the Senate and application of the Canadian Charter of Rights and Freedoms. In terms of what is most desirable, there can be little dispute: it is desirable that Nunavut be guaranteed a Senate seat in the same fashion as other territories; it is desirable that the Charter apply fully to the Nunavut Government; and, it is desirable that the appropriate Constitutional texts be amended so as to make what is desirable explicit.

While it is difficult to imagine how any organized body of opinion in Canada would be opposed to such Constitutional amendments, experience has taught that the term "simple Constitutional amendment" is a contradiction in terms in Canada. Accordingly, while the matters of Senate representation and Charter coverage are ones which are not urgent, and can be dealt with further in the period leading up to 1999, it is important that they not be lost to sight.

(c) The Political Context
An assessment of the political context surrounding the setting up of the Nunavut Government might usefully begin with a couple of questions. Why is Nunavut so important to Inuit? Why should it be important to all Canadians? Mary Simon, an NIC Commissioner who has since gone on to become Canada's Ambassador for Circumpolar Affairs, spoke to these questions in an address prepared for the convocation of Queen's University in October 1994:

Inuit constitute some 80 to 85 per cent of the population of Nunavut, and an even higher percentage of those people who are committed to living there permanently. The impact of the outside world on Inuit in the nineteenth and twentieth centuries took away much of our self-reliance and some of our self-respect. We were colonized. Unlike aboriginal peoples in almost every other part of North America, however, we were not demographically overwhelmed. For obvious reasons of climate and ecology, the Arctic was not "homesteaded."

While northern non-renewable resource development opportunities have attracted, and will continue to attract, the interest of outside investors, there is no combination of resource mega-projects on the horizon that will reverse the numerical predominance of Inuit in the population of Nunavut. Indeed, given the dynamics of a young and growing Inuit population in the North, a key priority for the Nunavut Government will be creating enough economic activity in Nunavut to persuade young, talented Inuit to stay in the North.

The creation of the Nunavut Territory and Government will equip Inuit and other residents of Nunavut with a set of political institutions having two important characteristics: they will command a significant degree of legislative, administrative, and fiscal control over matters that affect the day to day existence of Nunavut households and communities; and, they will be answerable to the people of Nunavut.

No one expects that the acquisition of these institutional controls will, in and of itself, solve the problems facing the people of Nunavut - and these problems are formidable, ranging from the setbacks to the traditional subsistence economy from the anti-fur lobby, to the debilitating levels of suicide and family violence, to the heavy dependence on intergovernmental financial transfers from Ottawa. But the creation of the Nunavut Territory and Government will represent an important - and necessary - first step in allowing Inuit and other residents to take control of their own lives and futures, to generate their own opportunities, calculate their own trade-offs, and make their own choices.

This process of regaining control is not confined to the Nunavut part of the Arctic. Throughout much of the circumpolar world, from the Greenland Home Rule Government, through the regional governments emerging in northern Quebec and the Beaufort Sea region, and to the North Slope Borough of Alaska, a network of sub-national, autonomous regional governments has begun to take shape. It is to be hoped that new and strengthened links among the peoples of the circumpolar North will help to replace the old Cold War tensions with a new era of international co-operation.

The very scale of the Nunavut undertaking means it cannot be overlooked. Nunavut will constitute some 20 percent of the land mass of Canada. Its boundaries will extend over a larger marine area than the boundaries of any Canadian province. For the first time in Canadian history, with the partial exception of the creation of Manitoba, in 1870, a member of the pan-Canadian federal-provincial-territorial club is being admitted for the precise purpose of supplying a specific aboriginal people with an enhanced opportunity for self-determination.

This is ground breaking stuff. It is no accident that the news conference in 1991 that announced the break through commitments to the creation of Nunavut as part of an overall settlement of Inuit land rights was covered in many countries by cable network news, and that Nunavut continues to be of interest to media from around the world.

Nunavut is of importance to the Inuit and other residents of Nunavut, and to Canadians outside of Nunavut as well, but the significance of Nunavut also travels well beyond Canada's boundaries.

Commitment to Nunavut is consistent with Canada's understanding of itself as an arctic nation, seeking to conduct its own affairs in the Arctic in recognition of its unique geographic, environmental, economic, and cultural characteristics and in concert with the policies of the other circumpolar nations.

Viewed from a circumpolar angle, Nunavut will, anchored in Canadian sovereignty, take is place among a group of circumpolar governments in regions such as Alaska, Greenland, Iceland, parts of Norway, Sweden and Finland, and parts of Russia. Consistent with this circumpolar jurisdictional evolution combining domestic and international elements, the creation of Nunavut will give added incentive to create strong regional governments within the Beaufort Sea and northern Quebec (Nunavik) regions of arctic Canada.

Nunavut's international significance is not confined to the circumpolar arena. At a time when the global community is increasingly conscious of the legal rights and moral claims of aboriginal peoples throughout the world, Canada's commitment to Nunavut stands as concrete expression of its willingness to share a genuine degree of legislative and administrative power with aboriginal citizens.

Nunavut stands for the proposition that, at least in some demographic circumstances, it is possible to supply additional practical political authority to aboriginal peoples without significant modifications needing to be made to the fundamental individual rights and freedoms of aboriginal and non-aboriginal residents alike.

Canada's credibility in the eyes of the international public has been a great deal enhanced by the commitment to Nunavut. This credibility must be safeguarded and amplified by making Nunavut as successful in operation as it has been in conception.

In examining the political context that will pertain to the period leading up to the coming into existence of Nunavut in 1999, great weight needs to be given to the economic circumstances of both the residents of Nunavut and of Canada in its entirety.

Ample evidence exists to underscore the point that a large proportion of the residents of Nunavut are experiencing economic distress. Statistical information cannot adequately relay hardships engendered by lack of employment, low income levels, poor educational achievement levels, and overcrowded housing conditions. Such statistics do, however, convey some sense of the magnitude of current economic problems in the Nunavut area.

The current population of Nunavut is young and growing. Putting aside for a moment the range of impacts that may be associated with the creation of the Nunavut Government, there is good reason to fear that some of the economic problems already starkly apparent in Nunavut may become even more troubling in the future.

Given this situation, it is clear that a major priority in the design, implementation and financing of the Nunavut Government must be to alleviate the regional economic problems that are now apparent and are tending to become worse.

The economic challenges facing the Nunavut areas cannot be divorced from the economic challenges facing Canada. Whatever the prospects may be for economic self-sufficiency in Nunavut in the distant future, the next several generations of Nunavut residents will continue to rely on fiscal transfers from the taxpayers of Canada in order to sustain an acceptable level of public services in Nunavut.

Notwithstanding, as all Canadians know, our public finances are greatly encumbered, and our collective room for budgetary manoeuvring drastically reduced, by the size of accumulated federal government and provincial government debts, particularly that portion owed to non-Canadians, and the annual financing costs associated with the servicing of those debts.

A number of key facts are self-evident. The Government of Canada is in a tight financial squeeze. The Government of Canada will need to manage its financial affairs very carefully in the period leading up to the coming into operation of the Nunavut Government. The Government of Canada will need to continue to manage its affairs very carefully in the initial years of operation of the Nunavut Government.

The implications of these facts are straightforward. The Nunavut Government should be designed to be set up and to function in as efficient a way as possible. To this end, maximum planning effort must be devoted to ensuring that the economic opportunities accompanying the creation of the Nunavut Government are converted into a heightened degree of economic self-reliance in Nunavut. Political self-determination and economic self-reliance are linked. In this regard, appropriate investments in educational and training programs for Nunavut, with appropriate emphasis on the promotion of the Inuit language as a working language, will be crucial.

APPENDICES

APPENDIX IIII

(These remarks were presented by Dr. Ralph E. Reed, Executive Director of the Christian Coalition to the National Press Club in Washington, D.C. on October 12, 1994. They are copyrighted by the Christian Coalition and reprinted by permission.)

The Faith Factor in American Life

Thank you for that generous introduction. Anyone who is - as I am - engaged as a participant in the rough and tumble of politics, has reflected often on the wisdom of our founders in granting special protection to freedom of the press, just as they did to the freedom of religious expression.

APPENDICES

The movement that I represent, the pro-family movement, is engaged in an ongoing dialogue with you in the media and with the American people about who we are, what we believe, and what we seek for this nation. So it is a distinct pleasure and a genuine honor to be with you today in this, one of the great citadels of our democracy.

In 27 days the American people will go to the polls in what is certain to be one of the most consequential elections of the post-World War II period. Clearly, 27 days is an eternity in American politics, and it is far too early to make predictions about the outcome of this campaign. But one thing is certain: religious conservatives are likely to have a major impact, not only in this election, but in American politics for years to come.

So it behooves us not to stereotype them, marginalize them, or attempt to demonize their leaders. It is our responsibility to understand them, what causes them to get involved with politics, and what kind of America they believe in. Who are these citizens and what has motivated them to become involved?

We know from extensive survey data that religious conservatives represent about one-fourth of the entire electorate, one of the largest voting blocks in the entire electorate - maybe the largest. The VRS exit polls in 1992 found that one out of four voters personally identified to a conversion experience and testified that they went to church four times or more a month. In a recent *Newsweek* poll, the number was as high as 31 percent. Almost one out of three voters that will darken the threshold of a voting booth 27 days from now will be a religious conservative.

Contrary to the popular stereotype, it is not a male-dominated movement. Indeed, according to the *Newsweek* poll, 62 percent are female, only 38 percent male. Half of those women work outside the home. Seventy-six percent of them are married, and 66 percent have children.

And contrary to another stereotype, they are not 'poor, uneducated and easy to command.' Sixty-six percent of them either have attended or have graduated from college. Fourteen percent have advanced professional or graduate degrees, a figure that is 3 percent higher than the general population.

In terms of party affiliation, little more than half are Republicans, between a third and 40 percent are Democrats and the rest are independents. Two-thirds are Protestant, and one-third is Roman Catholic. They are well-educated, middle-class baby boomers whose primary concern is the safety, protection and education of their children.

We believe that in a democracy any segment of the electorate so large and diverse deserves a voice in our government commensurate with its numbers. That is why the Christian Coalition has undertaken the largest nonpartisan voter education and get-out-the-vote effort in its history. In the next several

280

weeks we will distribute 33 million nonpartisan voter guides that detail where every candidate stands on a broad range of issues: taxes, spending, crime, drugs, education, term limits, abortion and health care.

These nonpartisan voter guides will be distributed in shopping centers, churches, synagogues, union halls and polling locations - wherever voters gather. They will not endorse any candidate. But they will give voters of both parties and all faiths the information they need to cast an informed ballot on Nov. 8.

Between now and Election Day we will continue to advance the issues in which we believe, always endeavoring to do so with grace, with dignity, and with respect for our opponents. But we will not measure our success on the outcome of these races. For there is at stake in America today an issue far more profound than the fortunes of any candidate or political party. It is the outcome of a debate about the role that religion should play in our public life and the role that religious people and values should have in influencing government policy.

There is an emerging consensus in the land about the need for values in both our private and public lives. Nesting baby boomers are returning to the churches and synagogues of their youth to give spiritual anchors to their children. *Newsweek* recently put Jesus on its cover. In a remarkable cover story this April, *U.S. News* found that 57 percent of the American people pray daily and 80 percent believe that the Bible is the inspired word of God. It concluded that, apart from Israel, America is the most religious nation in the world.

Winston Churchill once said, 'The American people always do the right thing, after they have exhausted every other possibility.' After the sexual revolution of the Sixties, the cultural narcissism of the Seventies and the self-indulgent acquisitiveness of the Eighties, Americans are turning inward and upward to fill what Pascal called the God-shaped vacuum that is in every person's soul.

This rediscovery of time-honored values has affected our politics. A former vice president, once ridiculed and lampooned for warning America about the dangers of illegitimacy, is heralded by the *Atlantic Monthly* with a provocative headline: "Dan Quayle was right". Where once it was shock-jock Howard Stern and Roseanne Barr at the top of the best-seller lists, today it is William Bennett and his Book of Virtues.

Jim Sasser of Tennessee, who is seeking the post of Democratic leader in the United States Senate, used the first television commercial in his re-election campaign to proclaim his commitment to voluntary prayer in school. Where once a Democratic candidate for president said, "I am tired of politicians preaching to us about family values," that same Democrat, President Bill Clinton, recently gave a speech in New Orleans in which he called for a return to morality and a renewal of faith in God.

Americans are seeking once again to build personal and private lives that are enriched by faith. And accompanying that search for spiritual meaning is a new appreciation for an old public wisdom. That wisdom was summed up more than a century and a half ago, when the great French observer Alexis de Tocqueville wrote, "Despotism may be able to do without faith, but democracy cannot." After traversing our young republic, he concluded, "America is great because America is good, and if America ever ceases to be good, it will cease to be great."

This is that quality in the American character that Czech President Vaclav Havel spoke to this past Fourth of July in an address at Independence Hall in Philadelphia, when he said, "Man can realize liberty only if he does not forget the One who endowed him with it." Religious values are not a threat to democracy; they are essential to democracy. Faith in God isn't what is wrong with America; it is what is right with America.

Yet even as the American people are yearning for a return to their spiritual roots, a strange hostility and scowling intolerance greets those who bring their religious beliefs into the public square. As Yale professor Stephen Carter recently concluded in his book, The Culture of Disbelief, 'We have created a political and legal culture that presses the religiously faithful to be other than themselves, to act publicly, and sometimes privately as well, as though their faith does not matter to them.'

The result is a discomfort and disdain for public expressions of religion that often curdles into intolerance. Consider:

In Massachusetts, a United States Senator attacked his opponent not because of his voting record, not because of where he stood on the issues, but because he was once an elder in his church. How ironic, considering who that senator was.

In South Carolina, a candidate for attorney general attacked a gubernatorial candidate who happened to be an evangelical Christian by saying that "his only qualifications for office are that he speaks fluently in tongues and handles snakes."

A columnist recently referred to politically active evangelicals and Roman Catholics as "the American equivalent of Shiite Muslims," managing in a single breath not only to offend 40 million Americans, but 100 million Muslims around the world.

Surgeon General Joycelyn Elders, the highest ranking medical officer in the Clinton administration, has become a symbol of this administration's insensitivity to religious values and religious people. She has used the bully pulpit of that office to do something that has never been done before, and that is attack someone because of their religious beliefs. She said in a speech in New York City that people of faith were "un-Christian people who are selling out our children in the name of religion."

The last time our nation confronted the so-called religion issue, John F. Kennedy addressed the Houston Ministerial Association on September 12, 1960 - exactly 34 years and one month ago today. He said, "if 40 million Americans lost their chance of being president on the day they were baptized, then it is the whole nation that will be the losers in the eyes of history, and in the eyes of our own people."

In that same address, Kennedy answered the critics of his Catholicism by asserting that the real issue in that campaign was "not what kind of church I believe in, for that should be important only to me, but what kind of America I believe in." Religious conservatives must do likewise.

We believe in a nation that is not officially Christian, Jewish, or Muslim. We believe in a separation between church and state that is complete and inviolable. We believe in a nation in which any person may run for elective office without where they attend church or synagogue ever becoming an issue. We believe that there should be no religious test, implicit or explicit, to serve in any position of public trust.

We believe this not simply because the state needs protection from the church, but even more importantly, because the church needs to be protected from the state. The God we serve is not so feeble or insecure as to require the agency of the state to win His converts or accomplish His purposes. Nor do we want to hand over the sacred tablets of our faith to the same government that has given us the Keating Five, the House Post Office scandal, and has not balanced its budget in over a quarter century.

We believe in a nation of safe neighborhoods, strong families, schools that work, a smaller government, lower taxes, and citizen legislators that rotate in and out of office and return back to the communities from whence they came, so they can live under the laws they have been passing for everyone else.

We believe in an America where all citizens are judged based on the content of their character and not on their gender, race, religious beliefs or ethnic background. Where parents can send their children to the school of their choice: public, private or parochial. Where schools teach children to read, write and master the disciplines of science, geography and history. Where parents can send their child to a playground near their home without worrying whether that child will come home alive. Where more marriages succeed than fail. Where more children are born in wedlock than outside it. Where children are counted a blessing rather than a burden by both families and government.

This is the kind of America we believe in. It is a vision of an expansive future, not an intolerant past. I am reluctant to use military metaphors when describing the pro-family movement. But I have found in the self description of another religious group the embodiment of our hope for America.

In the words of its leader, it was "a special army. With no supplies but its sincerity, no uniform but its determination, no arsenal except its faith, no weapon but its conscience. It was an army that would move but not maul. It was an army that would sing but not slay. It was an army that would flank but not falter. It was an army whose allegiance was to God and whose strategy and intelligence were the eloquently simple dictates of conscience."

This was how Martin Luther King Jr. described his movement of conscience that forever transformed this nation. We will never know the suffering and the indignity that they knew. But in our own time we reluctantly have entered the political arena based on a sense of right and wrong, motivated by conscience, animated by faith, seeking to impart dignity to a society that has grown increasingly callous and coarse.

We also understand that our vision for America cannot be attained principally through political action. It must be achieved through the way we live our lives privately and publicly.

If you want to understand our movement you must not simply cover our political activity or our political organizations. You must see these people doing the things they always have done, unheralded and unproclaimed. Working in homes for unwed mothers, in crisis pregnancy centers, in prison and in jails. Teaching the illiterate how to read in homeless shelters and in inner city schools. In hospitals, caring for the hurting and binding up the wounds of the broken hearted.

That is the work of faith. You will find it in our churches, synagogues, and homes - one act of goodness at a time. As Emerson once said, "What we are speaks louder than what we say." At times our movement has placed too much emphasis on politics. But we are learning, as some liberals painfully learned when they attempted to build a Great Society through government fiat, that politics is a poor substitute for cultural renewal. Samuel Johnson once said, "How small, of all that human hearts endure, that part which laws or kings can cure."

As I say in my new book, Politically Incorrect, when Christ entered a village, he met the needs of the people first. If they were hungry, he gave them food. If they were thirsty, he gave them drink. If they were blind, he made them to see. If they were lame, he made them walk. If they were deaf, he made them hear. He met needs first and preached later, and that made all the difference.

We must seek not to dominate, but to participate. Our goal must not be power, but protection - of our homes, our families and the liberty we all cherish.

We must seek not to rule, but to serve. The spark of our movement can be found in the belief of an essentially religious, conservative people that they can no longer afford not to be involved in politics. Why? Because for 30 years the government has waged war on social pathologies, and the social pathologies are winning.

We now live in a nation in which one out of every three children is born out of wedlock. Right now in America there are tens of millions of children who never have known a father. Who may not know anyone who has a father.

We now live in a nation in which one out of every two marriages ends in divorce. We have the lowest rate of family formation of any nation in the Western industrialized world.

We now live in a nation in which one out of every three pregnancies ends in abortion. Since 1973 there have been more than 30 million children who never will know what it means to be held, to be loved, or to be nurtured. That is an incomprehensible tragedy for all of us.

We now live in a nation in which one out of every four high school students walking across a graduation stage cannot read the diploma they were just handed. And in this city, an African-American male under the age of 35 has a higher likelihood of being killed than an American soldier did in Vietnam.

A friend of mine teaches kindergarten in Washington, D.C. This past year, six of her students were either shot or witnessed the shootings of family members. One little boy spent month after month in the hospital only to emerge to see another of his family members shot to death in front of him. She had a 5-year-old who stole everything that he could get his hands on. Frequently it was food. She learned that his crack-addicted parents did not feed him when he was younger. He grew up having to steal food.

Yet gazing out across this unchartable social chaos, there are still some who insist that the greatest threat to our democracy is if people who believe in God and moral values get involved in politics. I believe that we need more religious people in public life, not less.

One final thought. We are a growing movement, and in the long train of history, we are still in relative adolescence. We have much to learn, and we have much to communicate about who we truly are and what we believe. We do not have all the answers, nor do we lay claim to them.

It was Edmund Burke who said, "Our patience will achieve more than our force." Ours is a movement of decent, honorable, hard-working men and women who I believe are the backbone and social fabric of this great nation. But even we must acknowledge that some with faith have not always acted out of charity or love.

When doctors who perform abortions are slain at the hands of disturbed and demented men claiming to act in the name of God, not only our movement but our entire nation suffers. I agree with the U.S. Conference of Catholic Bishops that, "The violence of killing in the name of pro-life makes a mockery of the pro-life cause."

When a group of Christian leaders distributes a pamphlet that claims, "To vote for Bill Clinton is to sin against God," they are guilty of bad theology, and that manner of speech is not consistent with an ethic of democratic fairness.

When a prominent minister claimed that "God does not hear the prayers of Jews," he raised the ugly specter of anti-Semitism that has no place in our public life.

We do not identify with these statements, and we will avail ourselves of every opportunity to say so. At the risk of stating the obvious, let me observe that our movement is no different than any other. We have elements that do not speak for us, nor we for them. And these individuals are no more representative of the mainstream pro-family movement than the terrorism practiced by the Black Panthers exemplified the civil rights struggle. The fact that a few carried their rage to violent excess did not signal the moral bankruptcy of the crusade for a color-blind society.

We live in exciting and challenging times. As difficult as they may seem, they do not compare to the dark days of the Civil War, when our nation was nearly torn asunder, when the American experiment in self-government very nearly perished from the face of the Earth, when brother faced brother across a thousand bloody battlefields.

At a particularly trying time during that war, President Lincoln received a letter from a clergyman who assured him, "God is on our side." Lincoln replied as only he could. "I know that the Lord is always on the side of right," he said. "But it is my constant anxiety and prayer that I and this nation should be on the Lord's side." His concern was that he was doing God's work, not the other way around.

Lincoln's prayer must be our prayer. To be found on His side, not only in what we say, but in how we say it, not only in public but in private. Not only in our words, but in our deeds. Not only in what we stand against, but in what we stand for. Not only in who we are, but in who we strive to become.

If that is our motto and that is our prayer, then with God's help we can heal our land and restore America to greatness. Thank you, and God bless you.

BIBLIOGRAPHY

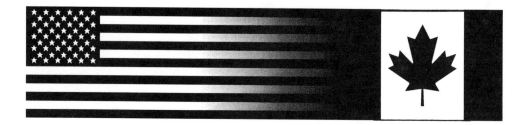

SELECT BIBLIOGRAPHY

Albert, Lionel and William Shaw. Partition: The Price of Quebec's Independence. Montreal: Thornhill, 1980.

Benson, Herbert with Marg Stark. Timeless Healing. New York: Scribner, 1996.

Bercuson, David Jay and Barry Cooper. Deconfederation: Canada Without Quebec. Toronto: Key Porter, 1991.

Berton, Pierre. The Last Spike. Toronto: McClelland and Stewart Limited, 1971.

Berton, Pierre. The National Dream : The Great Railway 1871-1881. Toronto: McClelland and Stewart Limited, 1971.

Bishop, Jerry E. and Michael Waldholz. Genome. New York: Simon and Schuster, 1990.

Brown, Brian A. The Burning Bush. Dawson Creek: Echo Publishing, 1976.*

Brown, Brian A. The Canadian Challenge. Saanichton: Hancock House Publishers Ltd., 1978.*

Brown, Brian A. Foresters: The Canadian Quest for Peace. Erin, Ont.: The Boston Mills Press, 1991.*

Brown, Brian A. The New Confederation. Saanichton: Hancock House Publishers Ltd., 1977.*

Brown, Brian A. Separatism. Dawson Creek: Echo Publishing, 1976.*

Bstan-'dzin-rgya-mtsho,Dalai Lama XIV. Freedom in Exile : The Autobiography of the Dalai Lama. Great Britain: Hodder and Stoughton Ltd., 1990.

Bull, Stewart H. The Queen's York Rangers. Erin, Ont.: Boston Mills Press, 1984.

* Available from the author at Sutacriti Park, RR#2, Kemble, Ont. N0H 1S0

BIBLIOGRAPHY

Chopra, Deepak. Ageless Body, Timeless Mind. New York: Harmony Books, 1993.

Collins, James C. and Jerry I. Porras, Built to Last. New York: Harper Business,1994.

Colombo, John Robert, ed. Colombo's Book of Canada. Edmonton: Hurtig Publishers, 1978.

Colombo, John Robert, ed. Colombo's Canadian Quotations. Edmonton: Hurtig Publishers, 1974.

Colombo, John Robert. Colombo's Canadian References. Toronto: Oxford University Press, 1976.

Covey, Stephen R. The Seven Habits of Highly Effective People: Powerful Lessons in Personal Change. New York: Simon & Schuster, 1990.

Encyclopaedia Britannica. Eleventh Edition, (1911), XIX.

Falwell, Jerry, ed. The Fundamentalist Phenomenon: The Resurgence of Conservative Christianity. Garden City, New York: Doubleday, 1981.

Galbraith, John Kenneth. The Good Society. New York: Houghton Mifflin Company, 1996.

Grant, B.J. When Rum Was King. Fredericton, N.B.: Fiddlehead Poetry Books & Goose Lane Editions, 1984.

Gray, James Henry. Booze: The Impact of Whisky on the Prairie West. Toronto: Macmillan of Canada, 1972.

Gray, James H. Red Lights on the Prairies. Toronto: Macmillan of Canada, 1971.

Hunt, C.W. Booze Boots and Billions: Smuggling Liquid Gold. Toronto: McClelland and Stewart, 1988.

Hurst, Jane. The History of Abortion In The Catholic Church. Washington: Catholics For A Free Choice, 1983.

Inter-Church Inter-Faith Committee, The United Church of Canada. Toward a Renewed Understanding of Ecumenism. Toronto: The United Church of Canada, 1994.

Jones, E. Stanley. Gandhi : Portrayal of a Friend. Nashville: Abingdon Press, 1993.

McDonald, Kenneth. Keeping Canada Together. Toronto: Ramsey Business

Systems, 1990.

Peters, Tom. Liberation Management. London: Macmillan, 1992.

Peters, Tom. Thriving on Chaos. London: Pan Books, 1989.

Ponting,J. Rick, ed. Arduous Journey: Canadian Indians and Decolonization. Toronto: McClelland and Stewart Limited, 1986.

Reid, Scott. Canada Remapped. Vancouver: Pulp Press, 1992.

Senge, Peter M. The Fifth Discipline. New York: Currency Doubleday, 1994.

Service, Robert William. The Best of Robert Service. Toronto: McGraw-Hill Ryerson, 1953.

Sinclair, Gordon. The Americans (A Canadian's Opinion...) Toronto: Conestoga Music, 1973.
Solzhenitsyn, Alexsandr I. A World Split Apart: Commencement Address Delivered at Harvard University June 8, 1978. New York: Harper & Row, 1978.

Stowe, Harriet. Uncle Tom's Cabin. New York: George Braziller Inc., 1966.

Tannahill, Reay. Sex in History. New York: Stein and Day, 1980.

Toffler, Alvin. Future Shock. New York: Random House, 1970.

Toffler, Alvin. Power Shift: Knowledge, Wealth, and Violence at the Edge of the 21st Century. New York: Bantam Books, 1990.

Toffler, Alvin. The Third Wave. New York: William Morrow and Co., Inc., 1980.

Varty, David. Who Gets Ungava? Vancouver: Varty and Company, 1991.

Vaughn, Garth. The Puck Stops Here. Halifax: Goose Lane Editions (Penguin), 1996.

Witherspoon, Alexander M., editor. The College Survey of English Literature. New York: Harcourt, Brace and Company, 1951.

Wright, Ronald. Stolen Continents. Toronto: Penguin Books Canada Ltd., 1992.

<u>INDEX</u>

INDEX

INDEX OF MOST IMPORTANT OR FREQUENT PEOPLE, PLACES AND INFORMATION

INDEX

INDEX

CROSS CULTURAL PUBLICATIONS INC.

PERMISSIONS AND COPYRIGHTS

Cross Cultural Publications, Inc.

CrossRoads Books

Notre Dame, IN 46556

Also from Cross Cultural Publications, Inc.:

The New Testament of the Inclusive Language Bible
ISBN: 0-940121-22-0   **$19.95 US**

The Gospel According to Us
ISBN: 0-940121-38-7   **$14.95 US**

Our Racist Legacy
ISBN: 0-940121-36-0   **$21.95 US**

Order from your bookseller or from

Cross Cultural Publications, Inc.
P.O. Box 506
Notre Dame, IN 46556 USA

Printed at the Presses of
EVANGEL PRESS
2000 Evangel Way
Nappanee, IN 46550-0189